Adult Education in Academia

Recruiting and Retaining Extraordinary Facilitators of Learning

Second Edition

Adult Education in Academia

Recruiting and Retaining Extraordinary Facilitators of Learning

Second Edition

Bahaudin G. Mujtaba
Robert C. Preziosi

INFORMATION AGE
PUBLISHING

Greenwich, Connecticut • www.infoagepub.com

Library of Congress Cataloging-in-Publication Data

Mujtaba, Bahaudin.
  Adult education in academia : recruiting and retaining extraordinary
facilitators of learning / Bahaudin Mujtaba, Robert C. Preziosi.
      p. cm.
  Includes bibliographical references and index.
  ISBN 1-59311-476-1 (hardcover) – ISBN 1-59311-475-3 (pbk.)
  1. Adult education. 2. Adult education–Administration. I. Preziosi,
Robert C. II. Title.
  LC5215.M82 2006
  374.1–dc22

                                                    2006002398

Copyright © 2006 Information Age Publishing Inc.

Printed in the United States of America

This book is dedicated to those who facilitate in an extraordinary manner where complex concepts are learned, retained and effectively applied to produce extraordinary results.

CONTENTS

PART I
Recruiting and Retaining Extraordinary Facilitators

PART II
Integrating Cyberspace Technology to Facilitate Learning

PART III
Appendices

FOREWORD

"When love and skill work together, expect a masterpiece."
—John Ruskin

Now, more than ever, it is critical to understand the adult learner. In the last decade, as an instructional technologist and professor, I have witnessed the changing needs of the adult learner and I have concluded that the old methods of instruction simply do not work. The workforce has changed a great deal. With outsourcing, mergers, and reorganizations being constant in today's global business environment, middle managers, directors and CEO's alike are being forced to learn new skills and acquire new knowledge. Skill-sets have changed and, to be effective, so must *we* change the way in which we deliver instruction to the adult learner. To complicate matters, learning occurs not only in traditional classroom settings, but more and more learning is being facilitated online, all with a diverse learner like we have never seen before. So how do we motivate today's adult learner? How does *our* approach have to change in order to actively engage students in facilitating learning? How do we deal with the diversity of our students? *Adult Education in Academia* has the answers.

This book was written by two exceptional educators who are both professors and leaders in their field. If you are a professor, a professional trainer or an administrator in charge of faculty development for your institution, then this book is for you. Six characteristics of extraordinary teachers are reinforced throughout the book:

1. Have great passion for your work.
2. Know what to teach, how to teach, and how to improve.

Adult Education in Academia, pages xi–xii
Copyright © 2006 by Information Age Publishing
All rights of reproduction in any form reserved.

3. Excel at creating exciting classroom environments.
4. Connect exceptionally well with students.
5. Challenge students to reach their full potential.
6. Get extraordinary results using a variety of skills.

This book helps you achieve these goals by offering a variety of practical techniques, tips and guidelines for becoming an extraordinary facilitator. From learning theories, needs assessment, effective teaching tools, online and cyberspace essentials, classroom diversity management, to mentoring and socialization, this text will be your bible for the 21st century.

This book is comprehensive, stimulating, and relevant for anyone who wishes to better understand how to motivate the adult learner, and to improve his or her own personal performance. To paraphrase Ruskin's quote, with passion and skill combined, expect a miracle. Enjoy the journey!

—Dr. Patty Castelli,
Lawrence Technological University
College of Management; Southfield, Michigan

PREFACE

Facilitation of learning is both an art and a science. Integrating the art and science of teaching leads to the fact that extraordinary facilitation is situational and requires the art of influencing others as per their level of readiness and skill. Determining a student's level of readiness through a needs assessment process is the science of effective education and extraordinary facilitation.

Extraordinary faculty members understand that "education is not the filling of a pail, but the lighting of a fire" as originally stated by William Butler Yeats. Today's global environment of education has brought enormous diversity into the classroom and, thus, it is imperative to understand the learner and facilitate objectives in an audience-centered manner. As such, extraordinary facilitators need to continuously enhance their repertoire of teaching tools in order to effectively light the fires of learning with their learners. *Adult Education in Academia* offers roadmaps and tools for responding effectively to the changing needs of learners, educators, trainers, and administrators.

The material discussed in various chapters is useful for all diverse teachers and trainers who want to effectively facilitate information to their learners while keeping them engaged in the learning process. The contents are written with a cross-cultural flavor and diversity since today's educators are able to teach global audiences. The book aims to introduce the reader to a comprehensive recruitment process for potential educators, development of faculty, retention practices of extraordinary faculty members, effective facilitation skills, adult learning, online education, peer review process, and assessment of learning to deliver a quality program to all students regardless of geographic location or teaching modality. The material is designed

Adult Education in Academia, pages xiii–xiv
Copyright © 2006 by Information Age Publishing
All rights of reproduction in any form reserved.

to be useful to employees, faculty members, associate deans, deans, and program directors both in public and private education arenas.

The book is also written for faculty development and training as well as for use by higher education administrators. Colleges and universities wishing to adopt this material for their faculty development programs may contact the authors or the publisher. Schools, trainers and educators adopting this book or any of its chapters may contact the publisher or an author for receiving the available supplementary facilitator's materials such as sample faculty training manuals, exercises, activities, and PowerPoint slides for presentation.

This book discusses that extraordinary educators know what to teach, how to teach, as well as how to continuously assess and improve. These extraordinary educators excel at creating exciting learning opportunities since they connect well with learners who learn the skills to reach their full potential. This book offers practical techniques, tips and guidelines for the creation of an extraordinary learning environment. It discusses learning theories, needs assessment, twenty first century facilitation tools, essentials of cyberspace education, diversity management, outcomes assessment, mentoring of new educators, and retention of extraordinary human resources. Ralph Waldo Emerson said that "the person who can make hard things easy is the educator," and *Adult Education in Academia* provides educators with simple to implement tools to make learning more fruitful for students while assessing and enhancing the process for documentation and accreditation. Each of these real world practical facilitation techniques offers opportunities for becoming and being an extraordinary educator.

Thank you for reading this information on extraordinary adult education with good intentions and hopefully you can pass on the relevant material to others who can use it to effectively educate our current and future leaders.

Bahaudin and Bob

PART I

RECRUITING AND RETAINING EXTRAORDINARY FACILITATORS

CHAPTER 1

ADULT LEARNING AND HIGHER EDUCATION

Facilitation of learning to adults in higher education can be seen as both an art and a science. Integrating the art and science of teaching leads to the fact that extraordinary facilitation is situational and requires the art of influencing others as per their level of readiness and skill. Determining a student's level of readiness through a formal or informal needs assessment process is the science of effective education and extraordinary facilitation. Extraordinary educators and institutions do not just talk about the need to transform higher education since that would not go far enough. They must talk about it and live it through their actions and dynamic infrastructure. In an era when higher education schools are struggling to keep pace with the twenty first century trends and the complex challenges faced by the international community, educators need to champion and pioneer the development of systematically integrated approaches to leadership that will place learners at the forefront of application and theory.

As the world of higher education continues to become more complex, advanced levels of cyberspace technology are utilized; creating an interactive market that has truly become global through the guidance of professional hybrid educators. Extraordinary education programs should stand apart from others for many reasons through the help of their human resources asset: First, as Dean Randolph Pohlman states in his message to faculty members, extraordinary programs "emphasize entrepreneurial, innovative, and creative applications taught by professors who bring to the classroom a mix of excellence in teaching, research, and business experience." Second, extraordinary higher education programs and faculty members should have flexible delivery systems in order to effectively meet the needs of the adult students who work in national and international organizations. Finally, extraordinary programs and educators make it convenient for working adult and full-time students to get their education in a manner consistent with their learning styles and availability while providing individual attention to ensure their success.

Higher education programs and faculty members must be committed to work as a high performing team in partnering with their adult students to effectively meet the needs of the international community. Extraordinary programs and high performing teams of educators should seek faculty who are committed to the needs of adult students, who are energized by the spirit of adult learning and facilitation, and who share in excitement of seeing extraordinary achievements measured on a global scope. Such extraordinary educators must join together as a high performing team to provide students with the needed and required knowledge, skills, and experience which can be used to produce incredible results for themselves and the global community.

The material discussed in the proceeding chapters is useful for teachers and trainers who want to effectively facilitate information to their audience while keeping them engaged in the learning process. The authors, in this book, introduce the reader to the recruitment of potential educators, development of faculty, retention of extraordinary faculty members, effective facilitation skills, adult learning, online education, and assessment of learning in higher education to deliver a quality program to their students regardless of geographic location or teaching modality. The material is designed to be useful to trainers, faculty members, faculty coordinators, program managers, program directors, associate deans, deans, and presidents of higher education institutions both in public and private arenas.

FOUR KINDS OF STUDENTS

In the book titled "Zen Golf," four types of cups are described to symbolize four kinds of students. In this case, instruction is symbolized by water being poured. The following are the four types of cups:

The First Cup is Upside Down. This upside down cup represents a student who is supposedly in class to learn, but pays no attention. You may have experienced something similar while reading a book: Your eyes move across the words all the way down the page, but when you get to the bottom, you realize you were day dreaming and have no idea what you read. That is what happens when a cup is turned upside down. No matter how much is poured, nothing gets in.

The Second Cup Is Right Side Up and Doesn't Have A Hole in It. With this right side up cup with no hole, you hear what is being taught, but you forget it all too soon.

The Third Cup Is Right Side Up and Doesn't Have A Hole in It, But the Inside Is Covered With Dirt. With this right side up cup that has no hole but is covered with dirt, when the clear water of instruction is poured in, the dirt makes it cloudy. This symbolizes the way we can distort what we hear, interpreting and editing it to fit into our preconceived ideas or opinions. Nothing new is actually learned. If the instruction matches how we already see things, it is taken as confirmation. Anything new that doesn't match our opinion is resisted, ignored, or disregarded.

The Fourth Cup Represents The Ideal Way To Be A Student. It Is Up Right, Receiving What Is Taught. While this is the ideal cup with right side up and very receptive, it also has no holes, retaining what is taught. It is clean, open to learning something new. To whatever extent possible, one should be like the fourth cup. It is delightful when someone who, like the fourth type of cup, comes back and describes the results of working on what was discussed in the class or a workshop, and has even begun to apply the instruction to other aspects of his or her life.

Sometimes one's past conditioning and stereotypes can get in the way of absorbing new information. As such, it might become necessary to let the old go in order to make room for the new ideas and information. For example, once upon a time, a young man had read all the books he could find about Zen. He heard about a great Zen master and requested an appointment with him to ask for teachings. When they were seated, the young man proceeded to tell the master everything he had understood from his reading, saying that Zen is about this and Zen is about that, and so on.

After some time the Zen master suggested that they have tea. He performed the traditional tea ceremony while the student sat at attention, bowing when served saying nothing. The master began to pour tea into the student's cup. He poured until it was full, kept pouring. The tea ran over the edge of the cup and onto the table. The master kept pouring as the tea ran off the table and onto the floor. Finally, the student couldn't contain himself any longer. He shouted, "Stop! Stop pouring! The cup is full—no more will go in!" The master stopped pouring and said, "Just like this cup, your mind is full of your own opinions and preconceptions. How can you learn anything unless you first empty your cup?"

EDUCATION AND QUALITY

Cyberspace education, where one can complete a degree without ever leaving home or even getting out of the bedroom, is a reality and it is not going to be disappearing anytime soon. While online education has been the buzz of the decade, it is not for everyone and it requires getting used to the technology. Adult students can and should be selective in choosing a graduate program for enrollment as today's masters of business administration (MBA) programs in a private school can cost around $15,000 to over $100,000 depending on the program and school offering the degree. The business of higher education has become very competitive as schools move far beyond their main campuses to offer programs nationally and internationally. Just in the South Florida area, students can choose from over 30 different universities and colleges to complete various degree programs.

Many of the top schools involved in higher education offer the complete MBA program through the online modality. Students need not be concerned about the modality of the distance education programs since many of the same faculty members who teach in the traditional programs at the main campuses also teach at distant sites and online programs. As such, the quality and outcomes achieved are likely to be the same for all programs when the classes are facilitated by competent and well-prepared faculty members. Research comparing student outcomes between online and onground classes demonstrate that there is learning equivalency between the two modalities.

The term distance education has become synonymous with instruction and facilitation provided through cyberspace technologies via the Internet. As a result, many of such programs are commonly referred to as online education. There are different types of Internet-based courses: *first*, there is the distance learning programs which are supplemented by use of the Internet technologies as a support mechanism as opposed to being the primary medium of delivery; *second*, there is the computer conferencing medium where Internet is the primary delivery utilizing asynchronous discussions and emails; *third*, there is the virtual course where all or most aspects of the course are delivered online. The first and third format is what the H. Wayne Huizenga School of Business and Entrepreneurship has been heavily using for its distance education and online programs where students can complete all of their course requirements online. However, online students may choose to take some or all of their courses onground. The virtual classes have a teacher/facilitator directing discussions, learning of course content, the evaluation of assignments, and they provide feedback on a weekly basis to students. As a matter of fact, experienced and skilled online educators are able to use colorful graphics, audio and video streams, and hypertext links to bring out the learning as well as to involve the various senses of learners to increase their understanding. In the online world, adult students are expected to be actively involved in the knowledge generation process while regularly interacting with the instructor and their colleagues each week about the material to be learned as guided by the faculty. Faculty members make the difference in student learning as their facilitation skills can be either exciting or boring (pretty much the same as onground courses). Online faculty members tend to involve the learner through their formal and informal facilitation since that is what leads to real learning. As such, the faculty serves as a facilitator in the learning process as is the case in the onground sessions.

Student involvement is even more important in the online environment if the material is to be learned, utilized and retained by the graduates of a course in the long-term. When choosing a graduate online program, prospective students should:

1. Assess their learning styles, their preferences and their interests.
2. Assemble a list of various programs that are likely to best meet the aforementioned needs.
3. Learn about the credentials of the faculty and their teaching philosophy to see if they match or accommodate their dominant learning style.
4. Interview the school's administrators and advisors, and determine their student services offerings and their level of technical assistance for online students.
5. Determine each program's graduation and employability rates after graduation as well as the program's overall rankings.
6. Spend more time with the programs that look the most attractive to understand the school, its culture and their overall quality.
7. Select a program that best matches their needs and learning philosophy and a school that provides helpful information to make sure students are able to finish the program in a reasonable time period.

Since students have many choices in today's competitive environment of higher education, schools must also understand their needs and offer them the appropriate tools so they can be successful using today's cyberspace technologies. Of course, the virtual course requires students and faculty members who have the latest computer hardware and updated user skills. So, if you are not technologically competent, stick with traditional classes for the time being and quickly update yourself with computers, internet surfing, and uploading and downloading files in the cyberspace because online and cyberspace education will probably be a part of your learning.

ADULT LEARNING, ASSESSMENT AND THE
EXTRAORDINARY EDUCATOR

This section provides literature on delivering content through learner participation while increasing learning using creative modalities and participants' dominant learning styles without increasing administrative cost to the school. Personal experiences of about 40 years in corporate executive and training as well as best practices gleaned from several different universities (graduate/undergraduate business programs using cutting edge technologies) are discussed and highlighted. Learner participation and interaction are critical to effective "experiential facilitation techniques" that increase learning and retention with adult participants. A major element of being or becoming effective educators involves understanding how students learn best and then integrating activities that best suit learning styles regardless of teaching modality. Compared to children and teens, adults need to be involved in the learning process.

Adult Learning and Learning Assessment

There has been a consistent pattern in the requirement for the development of a systematic approach to outcomes assessment by the accrediting agencies in the past decade. Accrediting bodies such as SACS, IACBE, and AACSB have all heavily focused on the inclusion of demonstrated literature on the achievement of learning outcomes and strategic planning to enhance student learning.

Compared to children and teens, adults need to be more involved in the learning process in order for the learning to be effective. Learner participation and interaction are critical to effective facilitation techniques that increase learning and retention with adult learners. A major element of being or becoming an effective educator involves understanding how each group of learners learn best and then integrating activities that best suit their learning styles regardless of teaching modality. Dr. W. Edwards Deming, business consultant and author, said "Learning is not compulsory. Neither is survival." Adults understand this concept and learn because they want to use the learning to achieve their personal and professional goals.

The field of adult learning was pioneered by Malcolm Knowles as he emphasized many characteristics of adult learners:

- Adults are *autonomous* and *self-directed*.
- Adults have accumulated a foundation of *life experiences* and *knowledge* that may include work-related activities, family responsibilities, and previous education.

- Adults are *goal-oriented.*
- Adults are *relevancy-oriented.*
- Adults are *practical*, focusing on the aspects of a lesson most useful to them in their work.
- As do all learners, adults need to be shown *respect.*

While considering the above characteristics, faculty members can acknowledge the wealth of experiences that adult students can integrate into the classroom. These adults should be encouraged to take initiative in their learning and they must become a part of the learning process through effective facilitation by the faculty that allows students to become a part of the learning experience. The following elements should be considered about adults in the educational environment:

1. Adults want learning experiences that assist them with specific and immediate challenges.
2. Adults are likely to engage in learning activities before, after, or even during any challenges facing them (these are all teaching moments) and they are likely to engage in learning that promises to help them cope with the transition.
3. Adults seek out a learning experience because they have a use for the knowledge or skill. They are likely to use learning as a means to an end and not necessarily an end in itself.
4. Adults are concerned about their self-esteem and ego that influence their behavior. Facilitation should respect their dignity and self-esteem concerns.
5. Adults have expectations that must be heard and progressively integrated into the learning process.
6. New learning and concepts should to be linked with previous knowledge, thus, allowing them to cross over to new territories without much fear.
7. Adults can effectively focus on a limited number of concepts at a given time. The faculty should effectively balance the presentation of new material, discussions, sharing of relevant experiences, and the time simultaneously.

Faculty members and facilitators should recognize that adults want their learning to be problem-oriented, personalized and appropriate to their need for direction and personal responsibility.

Learning Institutions' Knowledge Generation and Conditioning

Learning institutions tend to generate knowledge by empowering their employees to become continuous learners rather than being passive doers based on what they know from their certification or degree upon hiring. There are many significant changes happening in the area of business education both nationally and internationally. Such changes will have a profound impact on education, training, human resources, and in all areas of business.

Dr. W. Deming, the American father of Japanese management, said the prevailing system of Western management has destroyed people's natural learning process. People are born with intrinsic motivation, self-esteem, desire or curiosity for learning, and enjoy learning. The destruction starts with toddlers, a prize for the best Halloween costumes, gold stars by teachers for good behavior, and grades in grade school through high school and university. On the job, people, teams, and divisions are ranked to work for the ones on the top, punishment for the bottom, management by incentive, bonus plans and other systems that are unknown and untested.

Learning and Societal Conditioning

What is the first thing that comes to mind when one hears the word "learning"? Perhaps school and, more specifically, possibly primary school. For many, learning is boring and doesn't attract attention because it is associated with school. People are given the impression that school is not about learning. It is about accomplishing something in order to get someone else's approval. It is about taking in information and digesting it in such a way that you can reproduce it according to what the authority approves and when they want it.

People have a natural passion for learning. The famous anthropologist, Edward Hall, once said "The drive to learn is the most basic drive in the human species, more basic than the desire to reproduce." Human beings are designed to learn and to live as learners and to enhance the standards of living in the world. Unfortunately, most primary education programs have been about controlling and not learning. So, destruction sometimes starts with toddlers because we destroy their hunger for learning early in their lives through the so called "boring" education process as they are conditioned to obey the teacher and memorize the concepts rather than understand them. While one may hope that this "boring" process does not continue into higher education, the reality points out that many higher educators in business simply model what they had observed in their primary schooling since they have not been exposed to any other forms of "teaching how to teach" tools.

Learning is about the enhancement of one's capacity for effective action (Senge, 1992). Learning is about building knowledge. Knowledge is not just the ownership of information but rather knowledge is one's capacity for effective actions. Human beings are designed to learn by nature. Each person has the natural drive, capacity and hunger to learn. Learning has many cornerstones and a few of them, stated below, were discussed by Peter Senge (1992) at the American Society for Training Development (ASTD) Conference.

1. The learner learns what the learner really wants to learn. The learning occurs where the learner has a real need for it. The impulse to learn should precede the learning activity. This is especially true of adult learners.

2. We learn by doing. Learning is not disconnected from doing. Learning is in the body. Learning comes from action and from experiencing something. Learning occurs where people are doing the work and not at the top of the organizations.

3. Learning is a process where one moves back and forth between a world of action and a world of reflections. John Dewey said, 100 years ago, that learning is a continuous process. As such, "learning is a process to: discover, invent, produce, and reflect." This process moves continually between a world of action and a world of reflections. Learning moves between the discovery and the reflection process. In reality, in most American firms we run around in the circles of "invent" and "produce" and do as much as we can to get greater quantity, so learning does not occur. Learning has to integrate action with reflection in order for it to be effective.

4. We need to distinguish extrinsic from intrinsic motivations. We are designed to learn, so we have the intrinsic motivation to learn. When we try to extrinsically motivate learners, we usually destroy their intrinsic motivation to learn. We don't and can't motivate people for long-term learning through external motivators.

Note: Since the third cornerstone talked about learning as a process, we must clearly understand the definition of a process in the context of a service driven operation. A *process* is a specific group of activities and subordinate tasks which results in the performance of a service that is of value. The process and the learning are inseparable, which means that the process is the learning. Process delivers value through quality facilitation, involving the audience in the learning process and flexibility to make adjustments as needed. An effective process is "results driven," deriving its form from learner requirements, experiences and needs. The learners' understanding levels gauge the value and effectiveness of the process.

Designing training or a facilitation session is different from designing an organizational learning process. Training will always be needed to help people and their organizations to enhance their capacity to create knowledge that produces results. Learning happens through action and by doing. In knowledge generating institutions, the human aspect of knowledge is a necessity. There are at least two reasons why people are moving into creating learning and knowledge producing institutions.

1. Competitive necessity or as Deming puts it, "fear" that if we don't do it we will lose our jobs and be dead in the business world. We know that fear does not work well with all individuals, at least not in the long-term. Yes, people will change if you put fear in them in some cases.
2. Institutions improve in this direction because they want to and because they aspire to a new vision. Basically, effective leadership is about tapping the inspiration that exists in the organization because people want to become a learning institution, and not necessarily because they need to survive.

Learning Assessment of Stated Objectives

Effective facilitators know that they need to assess learning in terms of the course's stated objectives (exit competencies) and be able to provide evidence that demonstrates the achievement of learning outcomes to employers and other relevant stakeholders. The same principle applies in the academic world regardless of whether one is teaching traditional adult students (full-time students) or non-traditional adult students (part-time students that are working professionals).

Academicians know that taking the strategic plans for measuring and assessing student achievement, analyzing them for improvement purposes, and implementing the resulting analysis throughout the university can present many challenges for schools committed to a process improvement philosophy. Universities use a good variety of tools that support the model of planning, delivery, assessment, reflection, and continuous improvement of student learning. However, none of the tools can take the place of the faculty member's key role in effective deployment, improvement, and documentation of student learning in each session of his/her course. For example, an experienced faculty member can adjust his/her lecturing or facilitation while assessing the audience to see how much they know and how fast they are able to process the information. Continuous improvement comes from keeping one's finger on the pulse of the customer (students) to get the right data and information in a timely manner so appropriate actions can be taken after its assessment.

Assessment can be seen as the process of establishing and/or understanding the learning outcomes that meet the learners' needs, assessing students to determine whether or not they have achieved the learning outcomes through factual evidence, documenting those results, and reflecting on how to continually improve the process of teaching, learning and learner assessment. The purpose of the assessment process is to continually improve and document or credential learning. A structured review of the assessment model can enhance the assessment process by providing a framework that supports thoughtful planning, communication to relevant stakeholders before and during the learning process, deployment of valid and reliable assessment strategies, informed reflection on the results, as well as improvement of teaching, learning and assessment.

When it comes to personal reflections for improvement, faculty members tend to have three formats for facilitation of learning: one, the facilitation they plan to do; two, the facilitation they actually do; and, three, the facilitation they wish they had done. This type of reflection can certainly lead to improvement when the third format is put back into the loop thereby improving the next facilitation they plan to do. This closes the loop and improves the learning process for the students. It has been said that some universities have three undergraduate curricula: The one that appears in the catalog, the one that professors teach, and the one that students actually learn. It is the faculty member's moral imperative to find out the degree to which the curriculum asserted on paper or imagined by academic leaders accurately portray what goes on in the minds of students. Making the curricula visible so their usefulness in terms of demonstrated learning and results through students can be documented as evidence is the business of *assessment*, an activity practiced by each faculty teaching the course. The American Association of Collegiate Schools of Business (AACSB, 1996) defined assessment as "the systematic collection, review, and use of information about academic programs in order to improve student learning, development, and success." Their guidelines and suggestions for assessment include the following:

1. Assessment should be guided by the school's missions.
2. The main purpose of assessment is to improve academic programs.
3. Assessment of student learning should be a collaborative process.
4. Assessment of results should not be used for faculty or staff evaluation.
5. Assessment activities should include multiple measures. Course learning outcomes can and should be assessed both inside and

outside of the classroom through the staff, faculty and university administrators.

6. Students should be active participants in the assessment process.
7. Assessment measures should focus on the most important outcomes.
8. Assessment results should be used for decision-making to improve the learning and the institution.
9. The assessment process itself should be continuously evaluated and improved.

Huizenga School administrators encourage and empower faculty members to measure the level of learning in their courses through various direct and indirect measurements for continuous personal and institutional improvement purposes. So, it is the faculty member's responsibility to make sure students learn the stated course objectives and learning outcomes. It is also each faculty member's responsibility to assess student learning, provide timely feedback to students for improvement purposes and to be able to demonstrate or provide evidence of student learning for those who successfully complete the course. Most schools try to accommodate a certain amount of academic freedom in the facilitation of learning objectives; however, every deviation from the syllabus and its learning objective should be evaluated in terms of meeting the stated course objectives and academic performance of the students once they complete the program. All successful students are expected to achieve the stated objectives and/or exit competencies regardless of location or delivery modality. New competencies gained as a result of academic freedom cannot be substituted for those stated competencies described in the course outline/syllabus. All exit competencies and outcomes must remain the same as per the standard syllabi. So, individual faculty members should not eliminate assignments or session objectives without prior discussion with the relevant stakeholders. Of course, faculty members can always add assignments and assessment methodologies but should be cautious about reducing or completely changing assignments as that may alter the outcome.

Classroom Best Practices

Nova Southeastern University's business school, the Huizenga School, is a good example of how a school can create a value driven culture to ensure staff and faculty are focused on achieving the stated program and course learning outcomes. Their main objective at the Huizenga School is to support the mission/vision of Nova Southeastern University by providing high-quality educational business programs of distinction as well as service to the community. They do this by:

- Preparing students for lifelong learning and leadership roles in business and their selected professions;
- Offering academic programs at times convenient to students while uniting them with competent faculty in jointly acquiring and applying knowledge in professional settings; and by
- Being consistent in achieving the required curriculum/course outcomes as a result of successfully completing each course/session regardless of location, modality or faculty.

With competent faculty members, there is no doubt that actions in regard to classroom instruction will achieve the above objectives and more. The objective, on the administrative side, is to provide faculty members all the support possible so they have a successful educational experience with students. However, their overall objectives and imperatives of academic success can be summed in the following points:

- Know the "mission"; so that you can progress in the right direction.
- Know the profession/industry/subject; so that you can effectively advise, suggest, direct, and/or facilitate the learning objectives.
- Know the job; so that you can simplify the operation and how it is done.
- Know the policies; so that you can apply and enforce them.
- Know the students; so that you can meet and exceed their needs.

Knowing the mission, profession, job, policies, and students will help everyone be focused and serve them qualitatively. Students bring different learning styles and experiences with them. It is incumbent upon everyone at the institution to assess/know if the students are achieving stated educational milestones and outcomes in each session of each course and in their degree programs.

Evaluating the Outcomes

Nova Southeastern University is a learning centered institution. Its academic vision can be embodied in the answers to a few crucial questions implemented by individual faculty members. At the end of every session, faculty members are encouraged to ask themselves the following questions:

1. Have I taught students the objectives of the course?
2. Do my students understand what they should know as a result of taking the course, reading the assignments, and completing the required quality of work?

3. Have I challenged students to higher standards in their professions and in critical thinking?
4. Have I tested the students to (and can they) demonstrate their new knowledge with the quality required?
5. Has the session enhanced their ability to innovate, compete, create value, and think critically in their organizations?

If each faculty can answer yes to such questions with regard to their students, then they will fulfill the mission of the institution and may become "*extraordinary teachers*"! The following list includes some of the essential responsibilities of each faculty to assist them in becoming extraordinary faculty.

1. To become familiar with the school mission as well as its academic policies.
2. To administer the course assigned in a professional and ethical manner consistent with both school policies and procedures.
3. To teach the courses assigned according to established course content guidelines as prescribed by the course outline/syllabus and to work on curriculum related to assigned course.
4. To inform students in writing of all course requirements.
5. To maintain accurate scholastic and attendance records for one calendar year, and to make this information available to the University.
6. To provide a telephone number or e-mail address where students can contact for information or clarification about course content. Generally, be available to students both before and after the course sessions for academic assistance.
7. To begin class on time and end class as scheduled with great content for all sessions. Generally, to adhere to the prescribed contact hours.
8. To encourage students to take advantage of all the educational resources available at Nova Southeastern University's physical and electronic library.
9. To maintain professional competence in the field by remaining current through reading, writing, presenting, publishing, and/or actively participating in professional development organizations.
10. To conduct all functions related to the Huizenga School and Nova Southeastern University in a professional and ethical manner.

In today's fast-paced, rapidly changing world, individuals in business, government, and nonprofit organizations need convenient, accessible, and superior educational opportunities. Only by utilizing highly qualified faculty possessing academic and practical experience, providing personal interaction with students and effectively using leading edge technology, can schools prepare students for success. The success of each school is evaluated by the success of their students in mastering and applying knowledge to create value in their respective business, government, and nonprofit organizations. Effective leaders, as is the case in most successful schools, understand that they can only realize their vision if all faculty, staff, and administrators are dedicated to anticipating the needs of their students; and, as such, if they can constantly change courses, curricula, delivery methods, and services to students according to these (changing) needs.

Through faculty development workshops and personal sessions with faculty members, the Huizenga School aims to make sure their faculty members have all the tools needed to be extraordinary teachers. Extraordinary teachers continuously learn and pass on relevant (updated) information to their students as identified in the book *Extraordinary Teachers: The Essence of Excellent Teaching* by Dr. Frederick Stephenson, Associate Professor of Marketing and Distribution at the University of Georgia's Terry College of Business. The book is basically a compilation of about thirty six papers written by teachers that are considered to be extraordinary and have also received the Josiah Meigs Award for Excellence in Teaching (the highest teaching honor given by the University of Georgia). Throughout the book, six characteristics of extraordinary teachers are discussed. Extraordinary teachers:

1. Have great passion for their work.
2. Know what to teach, how to teach, and how to improve.
3. Excel at creating exciting classroom environments.
4. Connect exceptionally well with students.
5. Challenge students to reach their full potential.
6. Get extraordinary results using a variety of skills.

Dr. Stephenson goes on to mention the applicability of the six characteristics no matter at what level one is teaching. All faculty members should continually demonstrate these characteristics in order to deliver superior value through extraordinary teaching.

The goal for faculty members at Huizenga School is to be and keep on becoming extraordinary teachers. They want students to say that "my professor had great passion for the subject area, knows how to teach, created an exciting environment where I wanted to learn and participate, connected my experience to the learning objectives of the session/course, challenged me to stretch and learn beyond my known abilities, and assisted me in achieving extraordinary outcomes."

Extraordinary teachers are innovative in achieving the stated learning outcomes and they involve students in the learning process. Dr. Marcia Silver, assistant professor at the Farquhar College of Arts and Sciences' Division of Social and Behavior Sciences, often creates innovative and fun experiments for her students to involve them in the learning process. For example, in her Adulthood and Aging class, in an effort to help the traditional nineteen to twenty-two year old students understand some of the personal and societal difficulties that the elderly experience because of reduction in sensory perceptual abilities, in 2003, Dr. Silver asked her class to participate in a simulated sensory loss. Students were given eyeglasses smeared with Vaseline to simulate blurred vision and cataracts, earplugs to simulate loss of hearing, as well as ace bandages, walkers, and canes to experience loss of mobility. As part of the assignment, the "elderly" students are asked to walk along the corridors of the building, climb stairs, buy snacks from nearby vending machines, and sit or stand while encumbered with the various apparatuses. The final component of the experiment charged students to write an essay about the entire experience while integrating academic concepts with practical experiences. While students enjoy being involved in the simulation, the experiment often accomplishes its objective because the learners are involved in the process. Based on the completed essays, the outcomes show that the class develops empathy and a greater understanding of some of the physical and emotional challenges that face the elderly.

"Get the Star Treatment" was the title of an article published at NSU's website about a professor of public health at NSU's Health Professions Division, Dr. Cyril Blavo. According to the article, Dr. Blavo is well aware that his job is to impart information to create learning while also striving to make the process memorable and fun for students. Dr. Blavo understands that adult learners need to be involved in the process in order for them to learn best. When students enter his classes, they have the freedom to put themselves into the lesson by getting involved. He stated that:

> I don't want them just scribbling away. Regurgitation isn't learning. I always challenge my students to reach their optimum level. I must have trained more than 1,000 doctors now, and the majority tells me they still keep my notes! That's why you hardly ever see me behind a lectern. I'm usually walking up and down the aisles, interacting with my students. I get quite animated! My classes are more of a conversation, with students getting much more of the spotlight than I do. To me, it's vital I really get to know the students as well as teach them how to think. When a university feels impersonal, students feel lost. Here, everyone knows everyone and individuals are always coming through my door with new ideas. When professors invest more of themselves, students get more out of it. Knowledge for the sake of knowledge is not what today's students are looking for. As educators, we have a responsibility to prepare them to succeed in a rapidly changing world. (December, 2003)

So, extraordinary teachers (just like the aforementioned faculty members) involve their students to the extent possible based on their individual learning styles, in order for learning to be long-term and memorable for adult students. They take care of students by providing them with "star treatment." Educators and college officials can use a similar analogy to see how faculty members can best create long-term learning by seeing students as guests who are temporarily in their class and will soon leave.

COLLABORATIVE REFLECTIONS
AND LONG-TERM RETENTION

In today's business schools, affective teaching of business topics such as ethics has become a high priority due to inappropriate behaviors of some businesses or individuals associated with such names as Enron, WorldCom, Knight Trading Group, Inc., Adelphia, Martha Stewart, Goldman Sachs, and Siebel. These companies and individuals associated with the inappropriate actions have severely disgraced the U.S. business market, possibly due to top executive greed. The instructor in today's business environment must provide students with practical and valid exercises that will embrace student understanding and long-term learning towards appropriate business standards and ethics through effective Collaborative Learning Objectives. Students today have to take personal responsibility for gaining knowledge by becoming self-reliant learners and understanding their own best learning styles. The section provides a review of interactive styles of education, Bloom's Taxonomy of Learning, theories of learning, and learning for long-term retention. The assumption is that if students learn better, then there is less tendency toward cheating in the education sector, which will carry over to the work arena, thereby reducing inappropriate behaviors and corporate greed (Mujtaba and Kennedy, 2005).

Collaborative Learning and Bloom's Taxonomy

Learning, like eating and socializing, is a natural human desire and, for most people, it starts at a warp speed when they are born. The process of learning involves seeing, hearing, sometimes reflecting, as well as the storing and retrieving of information. Researchers have stated that human beings have three memory storage areas: the sensory register, short-term memory, and long-term memory. The information in the long-term memory affects how the sensory register filters the information from the surroundings. If people can improve the quality of the information in their long-term memory, their sensory register will work more accurately, providing more of the information needed. Understanding how people store and recall information is only part of the learning process. Formal theories on how individuals learn have existed since the 1800s. Over time, three main categories of learning theories have developed and they are known as the behavioral theory, the cognitive theory, and the humanistic theory. The behavioral learning theory involves learning (a result) through direct interaction with a stimulus. The cognitive learning theory involves learning through the use of learning tactics and the incorporation of a learning strategy. The humanistic learning theory involves learning through interpersonal relationships, which include a nurturing of the learner's needs and emotions. All three of the learning theories are valid and all three provide the ability to accurately store information in long-term memory. The learning theory one chooses to incorporate depends on learning style and the situation around which the learning is based.

Learning tactics include rehearsal, mnemonics, self-questioning, and note taking. Rehearsal is the technique of repeating information to keep information in short-term memory long enough for current use or one can elaborate the rehearsal process to store information in long-term memory. Mnemonic tactics include making rhymes, making acronyms, using the peg word method, using the location method, and using keywords. Self-questioning involves asking oneself specific questions pertaining to the information. Note taking is, as the name suggests, writing notes dealing with a larger set of information. The use of a learning plan helps organize the way people accomplish a learning goal. To develop and implement a learning plan, one must first have an understanding of meta-cognition. Meta-cognition is an awareness of how people think and how the thoughts affect academic progress. A learning plan includes analyzing the learning situation, planning which learning tactics will be used, implementing the plan, monitoring progress, and modifying any parts of the plan that need altering. Through the use of learning tactics and learning plans, students will be able to learn more effectively and efficiently as life-long learners. Students and teachers who are aware of these learning tactics and learning plans can collaboratively (jointly) work toward effectively achieving the learning outcomes of the course, including topics that are packed with sensitive content such as cultures, diversity and ethics.

College professors and instructors today could teach business ethics more effectively by using Collaborative Learning Objectives. Collaborative learning objectives bring forth structured open discussions on the course material and lectures with students in order to obtain effective learning in the classroom. The level of student participation in the college classroom must be increased to include the students' point of view, such as in the case analysis method. When analyzing a case in the classroom during the discussion phase of the lecture, it is paramount that the student be called upon to discern specific factors from the case, which relates to the topic of the instructor's lecture or course learning outcome. The student should be held accountable for his/her participation and remarks based on the facets of the case material covered in the classroom.

According to Sims (2004), teaching business ethics without effective two-way dialogue is a recipe for failure. The instructor must provide for open (structured) discussion on the business ethics topic. It is a proactive step that educators must perform in all college classes in order to identify business ethical issues of the time while increasing long-term retention. An open structured discussion in the classroom concerning the topic at hand provides students with encouragement and a collaborative effort on the part of the instructor and student, which fosters the affective learning of business ethics. Structured classroom discussions are necessary to prevent students from taking the discussion to a different topic or providing any unrelated or erroneous material to the discussion. Waters (1988) substantiated that many people fear this type of forum, due to its undermining affects of an authority's credibility. However, according to Sims (2004), open classroom discussion on the topic enhances higher commitment to teaching business ethics.

The basis of business in the United States is "Capitalism." According to Adam Smith's theories in his work "The Wealth of Nations people produce products or services other people want or need; thus, the business owners' strategy is to create the greatest profit for the business, referred to as the "Invisible Hand" (Wren, 1994, p. 31). Business leaders seek ways to dismantle any hindrance to the business, in which the organizational leaders seek to obtain the maximization of profit and to sustain it as long as possible which is the nature of business under Capitalism. However, according to Daly (1996), there are limits to growth based on biological, physical, and ethical factors. Daly states that a major paradigm shift is needed to bring forth a conscientious result of economic activity, because the realization to sustain perpetual business growth under capitalism is erroneous and flawed, especially when one realizes the scope of the world's natural resource constraints and world poverty levels. Businesses such as Enron, WorldCom, and others sought the benefits for the few key executives, without any moral consciousness towards their stakeholders. Thus, to envision proactive ethical morality of business leaders for the future, academia must set the right teaching standard through effective collaborative learning, which provides realistic insights for students who will be future business leaders.

Desjardins and Diedrich (2003) created case scenarios in which students conducted their own research and developed the life-cycle of the product(s) they were investigating. Thus, the student, through the active facilitation by the professor creates case scenarios that are totally encompassing, from product initiation and design through its actual resource allocation and assembly. Desjardins and Diedrich's (2003) article depicts their students' course expectations of business ethics, which are to develop and write the case study in its entirety, including visiting sites, interviewing people, and learning about the product's consequences. Desjardins & Diedrich's main aspect of the life cycle case study approach is to compel students to concentrate on specific business standards.

One of the best methods of teaching students using case analysis is use of the student's textbook. Business textbooks of today should not just provide content of the material to be covered in class, but actual cases of both positive and negative outcomes of business performance based on their particular field. When examining these cases, the instructor should develop a theme based on the objectives of what the student should accomplish in the course. For example, when discussing the Enron situation in class with students, the instructor should want students to lead a discussion to determine the factors leading to the demise of Enron. Then, the instructor provides insights to accentuate the continuing details of the case to provide a practitioner point of view. During this process the student must be able to explain in critical thinking approaches, the factors that are pivotal in this case, such as the actions by the company, the erroneous and deceiving manner of its executives and finally the consequences of the firm affecting all stakeholders. The last step is vital during the last part of the in-class discussion since remedies of determining how one can prevent this from happening again should be sought through real world approaches and the use of realistic methods by other businesses should be sought and adopted. Thus, by having students disclose their opinions, based on factual relevance of the case and real world situations, the instructor creates effective student collaborative learning in the classroom. The instructor facilitates the learning process by creating relevancy from actual cases and through his/her effective facilitation during the entire process.

The Critical Thinking Approach, according to Kubasek, Brennan and Brown (2003), and the edited version of Bloom's Taxonomy of learning enhances the business students' ethical approaches in six consistent steps. The students' overall understanding of the content is revealed in a way that purports practitioner relevancy for the students' overall implication to the business world. Thus, critical thinking addresses the ideas of reality in today's business world. Bloom's Taxonomy of learning is a hierarchy of six cognitive operations. The operation at the higher level subsumes all those at the lower levels. Critical thinking according to Bloom answers the questions in regard to each of the following areas:

- *Knowledge:* The lowest level of learning for students and it is a prerequisite for all other steps to follow. This level relies on the students' ability to recall information through memory.
- *Comprehension:* The student must seek the knowledge and show understanding though collaborative learning, through open structured classroom discussion. Students must explain their reasoning

and understanding through case citations or references by what
they have read.

- *Application:* The student applies what they have learned by using
examples and comparable analogies. During this step, the instructor must encourage effective facilitation of Collaborative Learning
(open structured discussion) in the classroom.
- *Analysis:* The student must have the ability to distinguish the parts of
knowledge applied & comprehended in the case; thus, the student
must be able to discover the underlying structure and hidden meanings and assumptions of the case.
- *Synthesis:* The student must be able to creatively combine the knowledge obtained during the analysis from several points of view, from
the instructor, other students, from the case or other citations. Thus,
the students can reassemble component parts into a "New Structure
or Thought Process" not previously apparent from the case.
- *Evaluation:* This is the highest level the student must master in order
to think critically and reach. The student must be able to critically
appraise the knowledge of the case and apply it within a similar
situational factor. Thus, the student must be able to analyze and
synthesize business related situations based off of the case method.
Students then will make final critical judgments of the case during
the Collaborative Learning class session.

The Critical Thinking Approach by Kubasek, Brennan, and Brown (2003)
and the edited version of Bloom's *Taxonomy of Learning* correspond to
the skills of knowledge, comprehension, application, analysis, and synthesis for effective student case analysis. The latter steps correspond
to the highest thinking skills for both the Critical Thinking Approach
and Bloom's Taxonomy of Learning, through the final evaluation section of both models. The instructor who is facilitating the business ethics course should encourage and pursue the highest thinking skills for
students in each case using the critical thinking approach and Bloom's
Taxonomy of Learning. Only through effective Collaborative Learning on the instructor's part will the student be successful. The Critical
Thinking Approach and Bloom's Taxonomy of Learning seek to evaluate and determine the realities of varying businesses by applying ethical
standards to specific business scenarios.

There are different levels at which people operate during the learning
process. Two people may use the same learning tactic, but get very different
results. Part of the difference in results may be because of the differences
in the level of interactivity between the learner and the learning process.
Benjamin Bloom believed in the cognitive learning theory. Bloom's Taxonomy of Educational Objectives (more commonly known as "Bloom's

Taxonomy") is the most popular method of organizing the level at which people operate during the learning process. By utilizing the Taxonomy, one can better judge the level at which s/he is working and the level at which s/he wants to work. One can refer to Table 1 (Bloom's Taxonomy of Learning Levels) to learn the Taxonomy levels, a characteristic of the level, and some action verbs associated with each level.

Bloom's Taxonomy can be an extremely valuable set of information. As one proceeds from the knowledge level to the evaluation level, the complexity of the work increases. If people utilize the Taxonomy levels when they are "doing" or learning (activities, exercises, using learning tactics), they will have an understanding of the level at which they are working. Realizing one's level of interactivity can help a person to stay focused on the task at hand. For example, when asking questions and using the self-questioning learning tactic, people don't want to limit themselves to only the lower levels (knowledge, comprehension). It is best to be in the higher levels so that one can get the most out of the experience.

Table 1.   Bloom's Taxonomy of Learning Levels

Level	Level Characteristics	Action Verbs		
Knowledge	• specific • ways and means for dealing with specifics • remembering previously learned facts	cite label name reproduce	define list recall select	identify match recognize state
Comprehension	• translation • interpretation • extrapolation • understand and grasp the meaning of information	convert describe estimate explain	extend examples illustrate interpret	paraphrase summarize translate
Application	• using abstractions • using previously learned information in new and concrete situations	apply compute construct discover	modify operate predict prepare	relate show solve use
Analysis	• breaking a whole into its parts • relationships and organization of parts to the whole	analyze associate	infer outline	point out
Synthesis	• putting the parts together in a new form • plan for operation • unique communication	combine compile compose create design develop	devise iterate modify organize plan propose	rearrange reorganize revise tell write
Evaluation	• making judgments • evidence of logical consistency • ability to make decisions	appraise assess compare	conclude contrast evaluate	judge weigh

Learning and Lifelong Learners

Getting a good education is important to survival and advancement of the human species. And how a good education process is learned and in-grained in students' minds can vary greatly according to learning styles, reading habits, and experiences. Each person has his or her own identity, which stems from his or her own habits, experiences and learning styles. While habits and learning styles become routine and somewhat dominant (difficult to change) at various stages of life, they can be enhanced and/ or replaced with different habits. People can change less effective learn-ing styles and acquire or replace them with better and enhanced learning styles. Learners need good reasons and an understanding of their dom-inant/preferred learning styles, learning habits, as well as their left and right brain activities.

In primary schools, most people were taught to read "out loud" and "sound" the words in order to understand and comprehend them better. This is especially true for those who learn a second language at an adult age. For example, non-English speakers have a tendency to read a sentence word for word because of having to learn English and not knowing many words during initial years in the United States of America. This creates a habit of reading much slower than one's potential and therefore reading can became boring and difficult. However, through research and learning about reading, it has been said that one can double and triple his or her reading speed and comprehension by altering his or her reading habits. Evelyn N. Wood, guru and founder of Speed Reading for Business Profes-sionals, says that speed-reading is not an invention but a discovery. After seven years of study and research, she discovered that speed-reading is a skill, which people can learn to enable them to read several thousand words per minute. She teaches people to avoid sounding out words in their minds and instead move their eyes across the page in a "stop-and-go" pattern. She is able to train people to read a group of words and lines instead of read-ing words. The human mind functions and comprehends much better and faster than the average human being can read. Therefore, the more words and sentences one can see at a given time the more he or she will be able to read, learn and comprehend. In order to increase learning ability, people can always attempt to read better and comprehend more of what they read because the average person forgets about 80% of what he or she hears with-in 24 hours. In long-term, most individuals have a tendency to retain:

- 10% of what they read,
- 20% of what they hear
- 30% of what they see
- 50% of what they hear and see

- 70% of what they say, and
- 90% of what they say and do.

So, as can be seen from statistics on what readers actually retain, you are likely to remember 10% of this material; therefore, some repetition of important topics is necessary. Overall, learning is a personal choice and no one can force it upon people without one's own personal desire. Therefore, one needs to take personal responsibility and accountability for his or her own learning in order to fulfill his or her goals and obligations. Furthermore, learning requires steadfastness in order to stay with the chosen course of action and mission. Nothing comes easy for people; however some people are better at finding the way of getting things done because of their experience and dedication. So, patience and perseverance are the keys to a successful learning process and getting results. Personal responsibility and perseverance can help an individual fulfill his or her dreams and obligations through life-long learning or becoming a self-reliant learner. Self-reliant learners seek active learning opportunities, are committed to life-long learning, are self-motivated, constantly seek and provide feedback as appropriate, know their preferred learning styles, and continuously learn, apply, and evaluate the learning process. Jac Fitz-enz (1995), author of the book titled *How to Measure Human Resources Management*, discussed four abilities that are required in order to be successful in today's changing environment. First is the ability to excel at one's job. Second is to learn enough about the technology of the industry to be able to earn a partnership with the customer. Third is the ability to acquire fluency in financial terminology. Fourth is the ability to extract objective data and present it in an influential manner. Since jobs, technology, terminology, and data change continuously it is necessary to be a life-long learner. Being a life-long learner requires learning visually (seeing), verbally (hearing), and vocally (voice, touch, smell, and so on) at all times.

In order to be a life-long learner (self-reliant learner), one must understand the conditions that make up the learning experience. For example, most people are great visual learners and should attempt to acquire knowledge in that fashion when possible. However, sometimes one cannot control the conditions under which one receives information. Some of the conditions might be within one's circle of influence or control and some are not. For example, there may be background noises coming from next door, airplanes, parties in the neighborhood, government military training, and other such cases that can distract a person while trying to meditate or focus. Depending on the location and circumstances, one may, or may not, be able to control those external conditions and variables. As one gains control over the variables, which contribute to (or harm) the learning process, one can improve his or her ability to make the most of the learning experience. Examples of some possible controllable learning conditions include dedication to the topic or information, input one has in the learning process, self-confidence, personal biases or paradigms (conscious or subconscious preconceived notions about something), level of motivation, the amount of preparation for the learning experience, location and time of learning, and the kind of clothes one wears.

Many times one may feel as if a condition is not controllable when it may or may not be. One's ability to control the learning conditions within his or her circle of influence is dependent upon the level of patience, endurance, commitment, and personal responsibility. Examples of some uncontrollable learning conditions that are difficult to change and fall in one's circle of concern can include the teachable moment, physiological conditions, past experiences, and predominant learning style. The teachable moment is that time at which there is learning readiness and the timing is appropriate for active learning. During the teachable moment, the entire learning process falls directly into place. People generally experience teachable moments in school when the whole class is actively involved in the discussion and everyone in the class is actively tuned in and participating. Professional sports teams also experience a type of teachable moment. Athletic sport teams exhibit this teachable moment type of experience when their own teams play together, effortlessly, and accurately. Parents experience teachable moments when they are preparing to have their first baby. They go to classes, watch other parents, ask other parents, read books, and watch educational movies and television channels to be the best parent they can be. During this time of preparation their motivation is very high, their intention is sincere, and their reasons for doing so are clear and meaningful.

Generally, the circle of concern in learning conditions is much smaller than the circle of influence because as adults people are able to control many of the variables that affect the learning process. Therefore, adults are 100% responsible for their own education and life-long learning responsibilities. As a rule of thumb, the only real learning conditions one cannot change are those that involve the past, because when the opportunity to learn is gone at a specific moment, it is gone forever at that specific moment. However, one can learn at new "learning moments" when they arise. Some people are born with certain learning disabilities that require them to learn differently. For example, those who are blind and/or deaf need special training, equipment, and resources to help them become self-reliant learners or life-long learners. Helen Keller is a prime example of a person who is a life-long or self-reliant learner and consequently has made great contributions to the various ways people learn, to literature, and to the society in general by being a great role model. When she was asked what is more hazardous than not having the ability to see, she said "having sight without a vision." So, taking responsibility and having a vision of the future are the precursors to accomplishing pre-determined goals. In order to continue learning and grow as individuals, people need strong and clear reasons in order to stay on track and persevere.

Remembering, Thinking, and Learning

In today's fast-paced business world most people do not think for themselves. Many people confuse the term remembering with thinking which is not thinking at all. While thinking develops the mind, remembering simply reinforces long-term retention. So, remembering is simply being able to recall information from the past, which can be done without thinking or learning. While remembering is a good quality to have, learners should spend more time thinking, which is about creativity and originality. Often the terms "learning" and "thinking" are used interchangeably, yet they have different implications and meanings. Learning is the process of gaining comprehension, knowledge, or mastery through experience or laborious study and contemplation. Conversely, thinking is the process of formulating, concisely understanding, reasoning, or reflecting in one's mind. Therefore, simply thinking about something does not guarantee that the information transferred into memory or that it can be recalled at a later date. Learning is the process of getting the information through thinking from the mind and storing it in the memory. Of course, repetition and reinforcement can increase retention of the learned information. There are two general ways of learning: active and passive. When one participates and interacts during learning, s/he is learning actively. When one does not participate or interact during learning s/he is learning passively.

Passive Learning

When a toddler is watching a children's television program, the toddler may dance and sing with the music. The toddler is not interacting; he or she is reacting to what is playing. The responses toddlers exhibit during a children's television show are examples of information learned passively. While watching a television show, the viewer "passively" watches the show develop. A viewer has no way of interacting with the program. One can obviously learn while being passive, but passive learning is not the best way of learning complex information. Passive learning takes more time to assimilate the information into long-term memory than active learning. Do you remember all of the information from the television shows watched last week, last month, or last year? Perhaps not as effectively or in a detailed manner; especially, given the number of hours spent and attention given to the characters and storylines while watching them.

Active Learning

Watching a television program is a form of passive learning, but the television isn't always a passive device. With the development of new technologies like digital television, one can interact with what is happening on the television screen. Digital televisions and digital programs permit the viewer to select his/her favorite television shows and choose how the show will develop. Digital televisions and digital sports programs permit one to pick one's favorite camera angle for the "big game." Because there is interaction and choice, using digital television programs can be a form of active learning. The more involvement people have during any learning experience, the better they will remember and be able to apply the knowledge. This is why on-the-job training has been so effective and the least costly. The cliché "It's like riding a bike," is accurate because most people do not forget how to ride a bike. People remember how to ride a bike because they were on it and interacted with it, not because they watched someone else ride it.

Left and Right Brain Learning

In order to improve, learners must understand their strengths and weaknesses. Furthermore, they should use their strengths often and improve on those weaknesses as much as possible. Once the weaknesses are identified, one can then start a plan for making improvements and accomplishing his or her goals. In learning, one should not compare him or herself to another person because every person on this planet is different in how he or she learns best. There is no best method of learning that fits every individual in all situations, except that one should learn in a manner that best fits his or her learning style and needs. A left brain/right brain inventory is a tool that shows a broad view of how people learn. Taking an inventory is a useful first step in learning how one learns. The purpose of such inventories is to provide one with a general understanding of the way one thinks. This understanding will help one to become a more productive learner. Refer to Table 2 to see how people normally use their left-brain and some of the characteristics of left-brain dominant people.

Similarly, Table 3 shows how people use their right-brain and some of the characteristics of right-brain dominant people. Although everyone uses characteristics from both of the lists in Tables 2 and 3 in different situations, non-dominant people usually do not have a preference. Non-dominant people use a variety of techniques daily during their interaction and learning process. While a Left Brain/Right Brain inventory can help people recognize the way they think, the Learning Style Inventory can provide an understanding of the way they learn. This information helps people become more efficient learners if they choose to use them appropriately. The past and current researchers and writers such as Carl Rogers, David G. Myers, Lou Tice, James V. McConnell, Peter Senge, Anthony Robins, Dean E. Wooldridge, Lawrence Kohlberg, J. Piaget, H. W. Magoun, Stephen R. Covey, Alexander P. Spence, Darley et al., Lindgren et al., Robert Smith, Carol Gilligan, Earl Nightingale, James William, Wayne Dyer, and others have done an excellent job of advancing the research and helping people reach their full potential. It is due to their research, writings, and advancements in the field that today's learners are able to analyze and determine their best learning styles. Although personality surveys cannot be, and are not, absolute indicators of one's learning style, the well-designed surveys and inventories can help pinpoint general tendencies in certain situations.

Table 2.   Left Brain Activities

People use their left brain for:	*Left brain dominant people:*
• speaking,	• are rational and logical,
• reading,	• are verbal,
• writing,	• solve problems through structure,
• analyzing,	• remember names,
• categorizing,	• make objective judgments,
• logic,	• prefer multiple choice tests,
• reasoning,	• prefer hierarchies in formal structure, and
• mathematics, and	• "see the trees."
• managing time.	

Table 3.   Right Brain Activities

People use their right brain for:	*Right brain dominant people:*
• awareness without description,	• are intuitive and open-ended,
• seeing whole things at once,	• are visual/spatial,
• recognizing similarities,	• are fluid and spontaneous,
• understanding analogies and metaphors,	• solve problems through synthesis,
• intuition,	• make subjective judgment,
• insight,	• remember faces,
• synthesizing,	• prefers participating informally,
• visualizing,	• prefers essay tests, and
• spatial perception,	• "sees the forest."
• recognizing patterns,	
• "feeling" your way, and	
• relating things to the present.	

Saving and Remembering Information

People store and recall information to and from their short-term and long-term memory. Short-term memory is like the refrigerator where one stores food that will be used soon. On the other side, long-term memory is like the freezer which keeps things in good shape for a long time when wrapped appropriately. Short-term memory is also called the "working memory" because it contains the information people are presently using. Short-term memory can hold roughly seven unrelated pieces of information for about twenty seconds. When information in short-term memory is needed for more than twenty seconds, one must decide whether it will be needed in the future or just for a short time. When people need the information soon, they use retention techniques like repetition or written notes to keep track of it. For example, when a person looks up a number in the phone book, s/he may repeat the number several times until s/he is able to recall it without any hesitation. However, often s/he may forget the number once the dialing is finished and the ringing of the telephone on the opposite end is heard. If people need the information for longer periods of time, then they must study and learn the information and then transfer it from short-term memory into the long-term memory.

The more common studying or learning tactics include rehearsal, mnemonics, note taking, and self-questioning. Also, putting more importance and finding strong reasons for having to commit the information into the long-term memory can be very valuable. This way the information becomes meaningful and with ongoing rehearsal and attention, one will better remember the information. The long-term memory has an unlimited storage capacity and the information is stored for an indefinite period of time. Although the information is stored indefinitely, the information can be difficult to retrieve at times when it is needed urgently. How well one recalls the information in long-term memory depends on how well it has been stored.

One can better store and recall information by interconnecting new information with previous experiences or stored information. The process of interconnecting new information with previously stored information is often called pigging, associating, or linking. For example, one can associate hearing a poem to a certain experience of the past such as a song, a friend, a parent, the home, the family life, or even the first romantic occasion with the spouse. When one hears the poem, the sensory register alerts him or her to the song that is playing and compares it to the experience that has been stored. The experience is remembered because the song triggered the memory. The ability to link new information becomes easier as one gains more experiences. Just as having more assets or money can produce more money and more assets when used effectively, people need experience to link, associate, and store more information for better recollection at a later date.

Everyone has different experiences that he or she can relate information to and store it in his or her long-term memory. Since people base new learning on their experiences stored in long-term memory, every person can interpret the same experience in a unique way. In other words, people recognize and pay attention to information from their surroundings differently according to their paradigms. The more a person's life experiences differ from others, the more likely the person will experience things differently from others. Being aware of the fact that every person has different life experiences better equips one with an understanding of how an individual learns from and interprets his or her surroundings.

Theories of Learning

As previously stated, there are three main learning theories, which researchers have been discussing since the 1800s: the behavioral, the cognitive, and the humanistic. Even though these theories have developed over time, the three theories are valid and useful in today's changing environment. The behavioral learning theory is similar to Sir Isaac Newton's First Law of Motion, "For every action, there is an equal and opposite reaction unless acted upon by an outside force." According to behavioral learning, the learner reacts because some kind of stimulus has been provided to cause the action. The cognitive learning theory is more of a problem solving approach. The learner collects as much information as possible and then makes a decision. Whatever the decision, it is calculated and structured which can minimize the risk of making a bad decision. The humanistic learning theory is much like a nurturing parent. This "human" approach involves understanding the emotional needs of the learner and helping to develop those needs. Table 4 provides a brief description of the three learning theories.

Understanding and effectively utilizing the learning theories can be very advantageous to one's progress in his or her career. Using the theories can help to direct people toward a desired outcome that is favorable to the company or the individual. Just like other philosophical theories, these three theories have their strengths and weaknesses. The use of any of the theories depends on the personality style of the person involved and the situation at hand. See Table 5 to identify the strengths and weaknesses of each of the learning theories.

To better illustrate the differences between the learning theories, let us apply each of the learning theories to solve a common problem dealing with a challenging customer. As an employee, you are confronted by an

Table 4. Behavioral, Cognitive and Humanistic Learning Theories

Theory	Key Element(s)	Common Methods	Example
Behavioral	stimulus creates a response	rewards punishment time-out imitating other's behavior	When a child makes a bad choice, he or she is immediately sent to time-out.
Cognitive	information processing learning tactics learning strategies	problem solving techniques reasoning memorization comprehension	When a student needs to read a chapter from a text book, he or she takes notes, outlines, and re-reads the chapter.
Humanistic	emotional and interpersonal aspects of learning student's needs and emotions	I-messages clarification of values pass/fail grading systems empowering the learner by providing learning choices	When learning a particular type of information, the teacher lets the student choose how to learn the information (e.g. reading, discussing the information, watching a video, computer, experimentation, etc.).

Table 5. Strengths and Weaknesses of Learning Theories

Theory	Strengths	Weaknesses
Behavioral	• easy • quick results	• may be too aggressive, considered "bossy," coercive
Cognitive	• long lasting results • can be extended to many learning situations	• takes time • not easy, often considered the "hard way"
Humanistic	• empathetic • considers the learner's emotional needs • nurturing	• takes time to understand the learner before acting • not all personality types are receptive to nurturing • learner may feel intimidated by revealing too much of himself or herself

irate customer. You ask the customer if there is anything you can do for him or her to make the trip more pleasurable. The customer says that s/he is very upset about a product purchased from your organization and served to important guests the night before. Refer to Table 6 for an example of how each of the learning theories can be applied.

As can be seen from Table 6, all three learning theories can solve the problem and each is effective at different situations. Similar to the concept of situational leadership, as demonstrated by Paul Hersey and Kenneth Blanchard, one's personality style and the personality style of the other person(s) in the situation will determine the theory best suited for the case. This can be easily applied with co-workers, peers, students, suppliers, family members, and others on a regular basis.

Table 6. Application of Learning Theories

Theories	*Examples*
Behavioral	I'm sorry that you were disappointed with the product. Would you like the product replaced, or would you like your money refunded?
Cognitive	I'm sorry that you were disappointed with the product. How did you prepare the product? How long did the product remain un-refrigerated? When I prepare this product, I like to.... Would you like the product replaced, or would you like your money refunded?
Humanistic	I'm sorry that you were disappointed with the product. I understand how you feel, you must have been embarrassed. I want to assure you to that I will do whatever can be done to make you feel better. Would you like the product replaced, or would you like your money refunded?

SUMMARY

Extraordinary teachers often can and do take care of their students like they take care of guests when it comes to being responsive to students' collective and individual learning needs as well as their educational goals, while enforcing the university policies with high academic rigor. Treating students as "a star" or as "a guest" does not imply that schools should drive students to classrooms in a first class limousine, or that faculty members should bring goodies/food to class, or to cater to students' suggestions or requests for fewer or less demanding assignments, etc. What treating students like "stars" and "guests" should mean is that adult students should be respected for their maturity and they should become active participants in their learning journey while they receive timely and qualitative feedback on their progress from the faculty. The faculty member's responsibility becomes actual "facilitation of learning" that may include "lecturing" when needed. Gone should be the days of just lecturing and asking students to memorize the book for the mid-term and final exams. Such old paradigms of education and antiquated systems based on "memorization and examination" alone should be replaced with teaching skills and facilitation styles that encourage independent thinking and active participation of students in the learning process. Effective facilitation of the learning outcomes should have more assessment methodologies and feedback mechanisms built into the process on a continuous basis to see if the faculty member is achieving the learning outcomes before it is too late. Timely feedback through the built-in assessments will afford the faculty opportunities to adjust (facilitation and lecturing styles) to the learning needs of his/her students before the term ends. Seeing students as "stars" and "guests" requires a student-centered paradigm where the faculty member serves as a "facilitator" in the process rather than a purveyor of information. This facilitation paradigm requires that students become active participants in their roles as "stars" and "guests" in the class. If you, as a faculty member, do not buy in to the concept of seeing students as "customers" because it may imply exchange of grade for money, then you are welcome to see students as guests to dissociate that typical perception of a retail customer from students in your class. Traditionally speaking, we welcome our guests, we call them by their names, we take care of their needs, we thank them for coming, and, often times, we invite them back. Perhaps, many of the same concepts can be applied to students as well (welcome them to the class, call them by their names, take care of their individual educational/learning needs, and thank them for participating qualitatively in each session).

People learn in different ways. Just because a person learns differently from someone else does not mean that his or her learning style is better than another. Learning is storing in memory, and thinking is the use of information in the mind. Thinking about something does not always translate into, or mean, storing the information in long-term memory. Today's business world requires all individuals to become self-reliant learners in order to function successfully. Becoming a life-long learner (self-reliant learner) requires taking personal responsibility and the initiative to learn voluntarily. Understanding the internal and external learning conditions that are within one's circle of influence and those conditions that are outside one's circle of influence can help during the learning process. The key is to use one's strengths appropriately while strengthening one's weaknesses. Twenty first century adult educators can greatly help students learn more by using collaborative learning strategies, and by encouraging students to become self-reliant learners.

CHAPTER 2

FACULTY DEVELOPMENT IN DISTANCE EDUCATION

Developing and training faculty members to integrate cyberspace technology into the classroom for student learning is basically a necessity in today's competitive world of education, but many educators fear or resist it due to lack of effective training. As such, administrators should focus on the effective development, training, and retaining of qualified educators to teach in various distance learning modalities (online, on-ground, and blended formats) using cyberspace technology while focusing on effectively achieving learning outcomes. The next section will introduce an emersion model of training used for "training-the-trainers" in the corporate arena as well as for faculty development.

Administrators must ask for participation and interaction of experienced educators in order to glean and highlight their successes as well as challenges they face currently in serving the needs of diverse student populations in distance education. Both means and processes for effective faculty development and training in a just-in-time basis with least cost should be implemented by the administration.

Adult Education in Academia, pages 37–57
Copyright © 2006 by Information Age Publishing
All rights of reproduction in any form reserved.

TRAINING AND DEVELOPMENT PRACTICES
IN ADULT EDUCATION

Many traditional and non-traditional universities have integrated online education into their delivery systems to enhance their offerings and student learning. Many of the universities such as Carnegie-Mellon, London School of Economics and Political Science, Columbia University, and University of Chicago have created partnerships with suppliers such as UNext to aid with their online initiatives in course development (Barnes & Blackwell, 2004). Some of the for-profit institutions that are successfully using commonly available platforms in cyberspace technology include Walden, Kaplan University, University of Phoenix, Capella University, Jones International University, and Unexus just to name a few. Some of Nova Southeastern University's internal schools have used their own custom-built platforms such as their Huizenga School of Business and Entrepreneurship which used e-University while their undergraduate programs used the standard WebCT package. Other universities and colleges may be using software and courseware programs such as Outlook Express, Blackboard Course Info, Web Courses-in-a-Box, Top Class, Web Mentor, Lotus Learning Space, Groupware, and/or many other user-friendly packages entering the market. Hearing about such new software programs and their usage can be scary to traditional faculty members who have been effectively teaching classes in a face-to-face format without the integration of advanced technology. As such, many of the aforementioned schools have developed standardized training programs to make sure their faculty members are trained, developed and successful using cyberspace technologies as they compete to survive and hopefully capture a fraction of the market share in education using online modalities. Peter Drucker, the father of modern management, said universities will not survive if they do not adjust to distance learning. Drucker also said that the future is outside the traditional classrooms and the traditional campuses. Training and development programs may vary in terms of skill and pedagogy but many schools are creating programs that use online training as its basis, due to its low cost and flexibility of scheduling, in educating qualified faculty members throughout the globe so long as they have access to the internet. Distance education and distance learning are realities of life and educators should embrace it in order to create a healthy learning environment for diverse students. Educators must use distance education technology to enhance their offerings. However, they need continuous training and development opportunities to keep up with the changes in the application of technology.

Developing and educating faculty members are today's necessities as new technology to enhance learning is being introduced periodically so everyone can stay updated and skilled in their usage. A major element of effectively assisting faculty members' develop is to understand the nature of how adults learn best and then create an environment and processes that are conducive to learning effectively. Some administrators may be of the mindset that educators are already developed and they learn by osmosis; as such, they do not require formal development. A colleague in the corporate training world used to say that "people learn differently and facilitators of education are people too." Faculty members, just like other adults, need to be involved in the learning process in order for the learning to be enjoyable, effective and long-term oriented. Just-in-time education, learner participation during the session and interaction are critical to effective facilitation techniques that increase learning and retention with adult learners. A major element of being or becoming an effective educator involves understanding how each group of participants learns best and then integrating activities that best suit their learning styles regardless of teaching modality. Adults are *autonomous, self-directed, goal-oriented, relevancy-oriented,* and *practical* since they tend to focus on the aspects of a lesson most useful to them in their work. Furthermore, they have accumulated a foundation of *life experiences* and *knowledge* that may include work-related activities, family responsibilities, and previous education. An effective facilitator must remember that, as do all learners, adults need to be shown *respect.*

While considering the aforementioned characteristics of adult learners, facilitators should acknowledge the wealth of experiences that adults bring with them that can be integrated into the learning modules. These adults should be encouraged to take initiative in their learning and they must become a part of the learning process through effective facilitation by the facilitator and appropriate administrative processes that allow learners to become a part of the learning experience. There are many elements that should be considered with adults in the educational environment and one is that adults are likely to engage in learning activities before, after, or even during any challenges facing them (which are described as "teaching moments or opportunities") and they are likely to engage in learning that promises to help them cope with the transition. Furthermore, adults are concerned about their self-esteem and ego which influences their behavior. Facilitation should respect their dignity and self-esteem concerns. Facilitators must remember that the average adult can effectively focus on a limited number of concepts at a given time. The facilitator or trainer should effectively balance the presentation of new material, discussions, sharing of relevant experiences, and the time allotted. Trainers and facilitators should recognize that adults want their learning to be problem-oriented, personalized and appropriate to their need for direction and personal responsibility.

PEDAGOGY OF LEARNING
AND EXTRAORDINARY TEACHING

Learning is about the enhancement of one's capacity for effective action both immediately and in the near future. Learning is about building knowledge that brings more joy and opportunities to make better and more valuable contributions to one's field, industry and profession. Knowledge is not just the ownership of information but rather knowledge is one's capacity for effective actions, and the more immediate the need for relevant action the greater the need for learning. Human beings are designed to learn by nature. Each person has the natural drive, capacity and hunger to learn. We have the capacity to create the kinds of jobs we want to be in as well as to create the types of communities and societies in which we want to live. Unfortunately, many ineffective training and development sessions at many institutions do not encourage this because they are and have always been very "controlling." Top officials think and lower level employees act as done in most traditional or centralized organizations. Traditionally in schools, educators lectured and learners memorized to the best of their abilities in order to reproduce correct answers on the examination. This system has not been very effective in our society and it certainly will not be very effective for adult learners that teach others. As such, facilitators must work with each individual faculty or groups of faculty members in effectively developing them in the appropriate and timely use of advanced technology in the achievement of course learning outcomes with extraordinary results.

Mahatma Gandhi once said that you should "*Learn as if you will live forever, live as if you will die tomorrow.*" Extraordinary teachers continuously learn and pass on relevant (updated) information to their students. Michael Jordan, the extraordinarily successful basketball star, said "You have to expect things of yourself before you can do them." The same can be applied to faculty members' teaching styles and expectations as they assess or reflect upon their own current performance in the class and expect higher levels of success with their students in achieving the stated learning outcomes by becoming an extraordinary teacher.

ONLINE EDUCATION AND PEDAGOGY

Faculty members wishing to teach online should become online students first and learn the pedagogy of online education along with the school's electronic platform. This immersion model of training has been used to train corporate trainers and to develop faculty members in distance education. Understanding its practical application, successes, challenges, and best practices can be of great assistance as a starting place. Some suggestions offered for beginning online faculty members are:

- Learn and understand the mechanics of how the online environment of education works.
- Collect best practices and tips for beginning online faculty members to be effective in their initial online experience.
- Discover what learning strategies work best for teaching and learning the course material.
- Know how to best engage students, keep them interested and on track to achieve course and curriculum learning outcomes.
- Learn how to best manage time to adequately show presence on the discussion board. The minimum number of times faculty members should log on to their courses each week must be clarified for a foundational standard and consistency.
- Find out how to best manage discussion threads with large quantities of comments.

There are many best practices that new online faculty members can absorb, perhaps through osmosis, and benefit from as they observe an actual class facilitated by an experienced online educator. Furthermore, online administrators and facilitators should discuss and integrate some or all of the following suggestions for online courses:

1. Use the basic technology available to everyone in the market and the sophistication of technology requirements should be kept simple or to the lowest common denominator (Barnes and Blackwell, 2004).
2. Software, content links and "self help" training sessions should be regularly updated and made available asynchronously. Technical support experts should be available for online learners and educators seven days a week and 24 hours each day as online education is about learning at one's own pace and time.
3. Ask for contributions from faculty members, staff and students on ways to improve the system. Involve everyone that is impacted by the process, hear their concerns and, when possible, integrate their suggestions.
4. Rules, policies and training material should be formal and standardized. However, the training and facilitation of the content should be personalized, to the extent possible, based on learning styles and the individual needs of each learner.
5. For best results and when possible, effectively and appropriately use both asynchronous and synchronous formats depending on the learning objectives. Because adults like to learn at their own pace

and time, synchronized online learning and assessment requirements should be limited to the bare necessities when used.

6. Communicate regularly with online faculty members and students
   about the technology usage, software updates, and overall program
   objectives. Also, questions submitted through emails and bulletin
   board postings should be answered within a 24-hour period or as
   determined by the needs of learners and the availability of resources.

7. Create a standardized mechanism for documentation of feedback
   and development for each learner. This helps the faculty member to
   effectively observe, monitor, evaluate, and develop the progress of
   each learner. Similarly, such a process can greatly assist the learner
   understand his/her learning gap and do what is possible to close the
   gap between where he/she is and where he/she intends to go at the
   end of each term or module.

8. Compensate facilitators fairly while considering the amount of work
   that goes into preparing for the class before its beginning, interaction time and content preparation while the class is in session (asynchronously or synchronously), and communication time or follow
   up needed with learners once the session has ended.

9. Periodically measure and assess the actual learning to make sure
   it matches the intended learning objectives. Online groups can be
   compared with each other or with groups that meet face-to-face
   learning the same content through similar facilitation. Statistical
   analysis can be performed for data over time and relevant conclusions can be drawn. Make appropriate adjustments as needed.

Cyberspace Education

Pedagogy in online education requires the application of learning techniques and facilitation that works in the on-ground environment using different mediums or modalities of delivery. For example, students take tests
to show their understanding of the concepts, theories, cause and effect relationships, etc. to the faculty and the institution. In the traditional classroom, students can complete their exams using a computer, the paper and
pencil format and/or through oral examinations. Online faculty members
can do the same things using online mediums both asynchronously and
synchronously using proctored formats when needed. Computerized cameras and teleconferencing technology has made the impossible possible
and yesterday's vision into today's reality for online students and faculty.

For effective learning of students, online faculty members should be
involved in class interactions each week (four-five days per week) and re-

spond to questions within 24-48 hours since the new generation of learners are being conditioned to expect feedback instantly through the widespread use of "instant messaging" software. If one is not able to adhere to such simple guidelines by providing feedback to students in a timely manner due to other responsibilities, then one should not teach in the online modality. Online classes should achieve the same outcome as on-ground courses using online modality. Often students will spend more time on online courses than they do at the on-ground courses because there is no face-to-face interaction. Generally speaking, online courses have more assignments submitted than on-ground courses. This also means more work for the faculty. Online education is and should be convenient (as is the case with evening and weekend programs) but should not be lenient with its academic rigor. The following are some general guidelines and best practices for online educators.

- All assignments should be posted with clear directions, expectations and due dates. The evaluation methodology should be mentioned to students as well.
- Post a comprehensive lecture each week for students the day before the week starts. The lectures should be related to the assigned readings and the faculty member's personal experiences and thoughts about the material. The lecture should not just summarize the assigned textbook and article readings but it should offer more examples and personal experience with the literature. Faculty members may supplement weekly lecture with PowerPoint slides and links to relevant online articles, websites and newsgroups. One should make sure students know that they are to read their assigned textbook readings since faculty lectures are supplementary material to reinforce and/or enhance their learning.
- Discussion Board should be monitored every other day (if not every day) and used by the faculty member in all classes. Faculty members should post and respond to students' postings regularly to monitor learning, guide interactions toward course objectives, to show presence, and to encourage effective participation. Furthermore, faculty members should post appropriate cases and topics to reinforce the weekly assignments and objectives when needed and appropriate. One should be involved and post something related to the weekly objectives of the class at least four to five days each week to raise student contributions, interest in the content and learning. One can post relevant weekly questions, dilemmas, problems, cases, etc. to achieve the stated objectives of the course and to involve students in the interaction each week.

- Holding synchronized chat sessions is a good idea to either clarify content or to test everyone's comprehension of material on a real time basis. For example, Huizenga School encourages that each online faculty hold several chat sessions during the term with students and require students to attend at least two of the assigned chat sessions by awarding points (which can be a small portion of the participation grade). Attendance to two chat sessions should be mandatory; while, attendance to the remaining chat sessions should be encouraged by linking them to awarding of weekly participation points. Chat sessions can be about one hour and they should be conducted at reasonable times to accommodate working adults. Determine chat session times and dates during the first week of class to accommodate as many of the students' schedules as possible. Chat sessions should not be confused with online office hours since effective chat sessions can be used to evaluate students' comprehension of the material by asking them direct questions related to the content of each week's objectives. Although, having online office hours is not a bad idea either to answer any questions for students. *Online office* hours often range from 10-15 minutes at a specified time each week (or day) in case students have questions about course content, assignments, or team activities.
- Presence of the faculty and requesting relevant contributions from students to specific assignments (discussion questions, case studies, article summaries, debates, etc.) each week will increase participation, interaction, student reflection, the quality of learning in each class, and the program effectiveness. Again, the faculty member should be involved with the students each week in the online class; at least four to five days each week to facilitate the learning objectives.
- Quality feedback for all assignments should be provided to students within one week of original assignment due date (or submission), if not earlier. Timely and quality feedback is critical to student learning and progressive improvement.
- Participation feedback/grade should be given each week (if grades are awarded on a weekly basis) or at mid-term and final week (if participation points are cumulative). If student grades are low because of lack of participation in the online classroom and nothing was communicated to them in a timely manner then they would not be aware that they needed to improve. So, proper feedback in a timely manner must be provided to students starting at the end of week one of the course!
- Individual email correspondence should be reserved for personal student issues and course feedback. All other course related discus-

sions should be conducted in the course newsgroup and/or course bulletin board.

- Deadlines and submission policies must be consistently applied and enforced to all students. All assignments must be received by the course deadline and grades should be awarded appropriately. Offering students extended time to complete assignments without a good reason (exceptional circumstances) is not a good practice in the online world either. Students need to discipline themselves to complete their work on time. Also, providing extra credit opportunities for students may not be a good practice as it conditions some of them to not worry about completing quality assignments in a structured manner which is very important for all students, especially in the online environment.

An important aspect of online education is the effective evaluation and feedback process that is ongoing for both students and faculty members. Online faculty members, especially those who are just starting to teach online, need quality feedback in order for them to improve their facilitation skills.

Faculty Peer Review Process

As we all know, timely and constructive feedback benefits the faculty, students and the institution itself; in that regard, a peer review can be one of the most positive features of the online teaching experience. The review program should be designed to provide online faculty members with personalized feedback, based on performance, as observed by experienced online faculty leaders/reviewers. The feedback should be designed to help faculty members in their continued development and to enhance their online skills in order to provide the finest educational experience for students. Let us discuss one example from the University of Phoenix's (U of P) Peer Review program, where each new online faculty member can expect to be reviewed after the fourth course, followed by annual reviews on the anniversary of the first review.

The peer reviews at U of P are randomly scheduled using experienced and certified reviewers. Based on the success of the Peer Review program, it is hoped that every online faculty will continue to welcome and embrace such important efforts. The following are the key elements of the Peer Review process used at the U of P and how the Peer Review program actually operated during 2003 and was continued into their 2004 academic year.

1. Each faculty member is reviewed every 12 months. All new instructors receive an automatic Peer Review following the fourth completed online course; subsequent reviews are scheduled on the anniversary of the first review.

2. After being identified by the selection system, the faculty member is notified of the upcoming Peer Review on the first day of the last week of the selected course. Upon notification, the faculty is asked to place samples of weekly student evaluation feedback notes and graded assignment feedback into a designated newsgroup. Since timely and relevant student feedback is such a critical component of online education, it is critical that reviewers have access to this essential information. Of course, placing the feedback in the designated newsgroup helps the reviewers to avoid disturbing the faculty members as they usually have a pretty busy schedule.

3. The Director of Training & Development has overall responsibility for Faculty Candidate Training, Mentoring, Workshop Facilitation, Course Development, Faculty Leadership and Peer Reviews. Each of these areas is staffed by some of the most experienced and respected Training and Development staff, who are also seasoned, full-time faculty members. The Peer Review Team and their excellent staff are dedicated to making this a valuable and rewarding experience for the entire Online Faculty. Their mission is basically to help each faculty become an extraordinary online educator.

4. All reviewers are faculty peers and colleagues, selected from among the most experienced and successful Online instructors. Each has undergone rigorous selection and training for this assignment and the reviewer will also be an experienced Faculty Trainer, as well as an approved Mentor and Workshop Facilitator. The reviewers not only represent the best of the best, but they also consider this opportunity to assist their fellow facilitators both an honor and a privilege.

5. Following the end of the course, the faculty that is going through the review process, will have seven days in which to post the required assignment feedback and weekly grade summaries to the designated newsgroup. At this time, the reviewer will be granted access to all the class newsgroups. During the next week, s/he will conduct the review of the entire course using a standardized format—the Peer Review form was carefully developed with the assistance of members of the online faculty team. Following submittal of the form, the Peer Review team will analyze the results and make appropriate notifications and follow-up contact. Selected faculty members may also receive an electronic certificate with the school's logo and words of appreciation for excellent teaching.

6. In order to avoid any possible bias or distraction, Peer Reviewers do not directly interact with faculty members. All notifications, feedback and follow up are handled by members of the Peer Review team. Since members of this team have access to all the answers, this provides the faculty with 'one-stop shopping', in the event s/he has questions or concerns about the review.

7. After completed forms are reviewed and processed by the Peer Review team, the faculty will receive feedback within just a few weeks following the end of the reviewed class. This feedback also describes any areas of reviewer concern, as well as suggestions and coaching ideas, as needed.

8. A chief reason for the Peer Review is to identify and reinforce excellence in the facilitation process; however, should the reviewer discover an area of facilitation that needs attention, the faculty will be offered whatever immediate assistance or follow-up action is necessary, to help him/her bring everything within online facilitation standards. Actions could include coaching and self correction, attending a faculty refresher workshop or, in some cases, referring the situation to an Online Instructional Specialist for more detailed follow up and assistance.

9. The Peer Review program is designed to ensure that all online instruction is in accordance with established faculty standards and best practices. In addition to the rigorous faculty training and mentorship materials, their *Faculty Handbook* is an excellent source of information on standard expectations. In addition, the faculty always has access to special resources designed to assist him/her in remaining current in these areas. In addition to the Faculty Handbook, rules about classroom facilitation and participation, student feedback, grading practices, course materials, instructor availability, or any other required practices are all available online in their website. Also, a copy of the standard Peer Review form is usually sent with the Peer Review notification message to the faculty at the time his/her review is scheduled.

10. As specified in the *Faculty Handbook* and faculty contract, the University reserves the right to monitor faculty performance, in order to ensure that the highest quality education is provided in the virtual classrooms. However, the campus routinely schedules only one annual faculty Peer Review.

This Peer Review model seems to work very effectively as it provides timely feedback for educators and shares best practices with them to enhance their repertoire of teaching skills. The following are a sample of actual feedback from faculty members who have gone through the Peer Review process during 2003:

1. This type of comprehensive report, suggestions and coaching is most helpful. I find it to be highly valuable as it gives me incentive to enhance my approach which will bring added excellence to my materials and facilitation. This will positively influence my future classes.

2. I would be remiss not to take this opportunity to say thank you for the recent Peer Review, and the constructive feedback provided thereto. It has been my observation, as a new faculty, that there is always someone available to help you learn, progress and achieve your underlying goal—which is to provide the highest possible level of facilitation for the students who attend this university.

3. Thank you so much for the review of my performance. I thought the reviewer was accurate, thorough, and kind. The suggested changes and improvements will be implemented immediately. I am captivated by this teaching modality, and I want to become better and better so I can best serve my students and the University. Thank you again!

4. Thank you for the feedback, this helps me focus on the areas I need to improve. I have already started to adapt my materials and approach accordingly before beginning my next course. Please thank my reviewer for the valuable feedback and for continued advice as I update my materials.

5. I know we all get a bit off the center line as time goes by, and we don't always recognize the slight off course track we are on from that original straight and narrow. I appreciated the comments which were made and received as constructive suggestions to improve the delivery of product and services.

6. I really appreciate all of your comments and suggestions. I am about to begin teaching another two classes and I will do my best to implement your suggestions immediately. This is a great help getting a handle on how I am doing as a faculty member and it also helps me focus my efforts as I prepare for future classes.

7. I just wanted to say thanks for such a supportive and positive experience! I am adding all the suggestions with each class and they are helping me to ensure the clarity needed for assignments, due dates and such. I was concerned about this since I had a couple of difficult students but the reviewer was very understanding and supportive.

8. I appreciate the feedback, and I cannot tell you how much the strokes are all appreciated. It really makes me feel all the time I spend with my students and providing feedback is all worthwhile!

9. Thanks again! I want to be a GREAT facilitator therefore I appreciate the feedback, and see it as a great gift.

The comments from faculty members that have gone through the process are very positive and they appreciate having such a standardized process for personal development and improvement. Integrated with effective development programs should be appropriate policies regarding teaching loads and compensation methods for online educators. Most traditional schools that are teaching oriented (as opposed to research oriented) tend to have about 20–30 students in the masters programs for on-ground courses and a teaching load of four courses per term seems normal when no other expectations are placed upon the faculty. However, many traditional schools have graduate assistants that help faculty members in course preparation, teaching, and examinations. However, because online education requires continuous and daily asynchronous interaction through bulletin board, chat sessions, assignment feedback, lectures, etc. with faculty (and not graduate students) it may be extremely challenging to teach four courses effectively for first time online faculty members when there are 30 students in each section. This may even be more challenging for the first couple of years when an institution is just beginning to offer and teach online courses. In such cases, institutions should reduce teaching loads because there is a huge learning curve for both faculty members and technical administrators in resolving day-to-day operational challenges while attempting to ensure learning of students is not hindered. Overall, institutions should limit the size of their courses with regard to enrollment based on such variables as the experience of the faculty, the number of technical administrators who can help students and faculty, the comfort level of beginning online students, the daily or weekly requirements for online interaction, the software availability for exams and quizzes, and other relevant considerations.

Also, faculty members who teach online may not appear to physically be in their offices often if they are using their home computers to access class and as such may not appear to be very busy teaching. While most people know that appearances can be deceiving, it is certainly true in the case of online educators since effective online faculty members are really teaching twenty four hours each day. Their online classes begin on the first day of the term, they continue every hour of every day/night, and finally classes end once grades are submitted. So, there is no break for online faculty. Even when they are on vacation classes continue and learning objectives are being achieved with and through students. The main point here is not to overload online faculty members with too many students in each section of their course; otherwise, quality will suffer. The enrollment in each course should be limited to a manageable number that provides a good diversity of ideas and a number that is conducive to effective learning and timely feedback from faculty. It is strongly recommended that experienced faculty members' input be considered and integrated in determining the appropriate size of online classes. Most faculty members do not want small size classes since they do not offer much student diversity; but too many students in a course may make it very difficult to facilitate the learning objectives effectively.

Institutions should create and design a fair compensation strategy for those faculty members who have more students in their classes than the average course enrollment. Institutions should also discuss and create effective criteria for fairly compensating faculty members for developing or updating lecture notes, exercises, cases, and other teaching tools for the online environment when such tools are made available for others to use. Intellectual property issues and concerns should be addressed and policies should be created according to the specific rules of the institution so there is clarity before asking faculty members to devote time into developing lectures that will be made available for others teaching the same course.

BLENDED MODALITIES OF EDUCATION

Blended modalities of education and distance learning have existed for many decades. For example, Nova Southeastern University has offered blended forms of courses and programs through distance learning since the 1970's. In the late 1980's and early 1990's doctoral students were using email to communicate with faculty members and then attended on-ground classes on a monthly basis for two full days each month or for six consecutive days through "national clusters" in Fort Lauderdale, Florida at the Main Campus. During the 48 face-to-face contact hours, faculty members could facilitate learning of the concepts through exercises or lectures and students could learn the material interactively with their peers. In the mean time, student groups could communicate with each other or with the faculty via email to prepare their assignments, conduct interviews and submit assignments for feedback and evaluation. Today, more sophisticated technologies are available to enhance such distance modes of learning while keeping the face-to-face aspect of education.

Today, online education is also making effective use of blended modalities to enhance student learning. The Huizenga School started a cluster of MBA students in Manaus, Brazil in 1998 using a "Hybrid" form of distance education. Students would start their courses using online modality and then the faculty members would travel to Brazil to conduct classes with students for 24 face-to-face contact hours. The on-ground format allowed lectures, exercises, student presentations, and a proctored examination. Such hybrid forms of distance education require experienced online and on-ground faculty members. Another version that the Huizenga School introduced again in 2003 was the "Hybrid MBA Program" which allows students and faculty members to meet face-to-face for six hours at the beginning of the term and then classes are conducted online for about one month. Once again, faculty members and students meet face-to-face for six hours in the middle of the term. Then, classes are held online for another month and students finally meet face-to-face for another six hours at the end of the term.

The University of Phoenix implemented a similar program in 2001 called "Flexnet." Students enrolled in the Flexnet Program would meet for four hours face-to-face at the outset of each course and then again for four hours at the conclusion of the course. The weeks in between would be conducted using online modality and requirements. The face-to-face contact hours are used for exercises, lectures, face-to-face teamwork, presentations, examinations, etc. and online formats can do pretty much the same things depending on the course and preferences of the faculty. However, the on-ground sessions seem to fit best for presentations and proctored examinations since most faculty members feel more comfortable assessing students using traditional means.

GETTING TO KNOW THE ONLINE FACULTY
AND LEARNING STYLES

Understanding one's natural or best learning style and trying to adapt other effective learning styles is a necessity toward good and quick learning for time-impoverished working adults that are going to school either in the evenings, weekends or online. A discussion with regards to understanding and becoming familiarized with online teacher's lecture style should be explored. So, the question is: how do students get used to and/or familiar with another person's style in the on-line world of education? Yes, most students will tend to have the same kind of online platform, syllabus outline, weekly discussions, and similar grading criteria for most of their courses in the program. However, the faculty members vary and that by itself will make everything else different. Some schools such as Nova Southeastern University and University of Phoenix do have a standardized process to make the format easier for online students. This is not necessarily the case in all schools, especially schools catering to traditional students, since some schools provide much more freedom for faculty to determine what works best for his or her classes. In those cases, the student has much work each term to get used to new styles, new requirements, and new technologies. While there may be much consistency in online programs, some faculty members are very advanced in online education/protocols and may very well be using advanced cyberspace technologies to enhance the learning process. So, in such cases, students will have to be able to adjust quickly to new methods. So, the challenge still remains, how do students bridge the on-line style gap between one instructor and the next in their progression of classes toward graduation?

That is a very good question and getting to know the faculty is critical to successfully completing assignments. One suggestion would be to get to know the faculty's syllabus and then see how s/he approaches the learning outcomes each week through lectures and assigned readings (students can see the faculty's first week lecture and compare with learning objectives for the first week of the course). In some courses, faculty members may put more stock on students reading the assigned textbooks/articles and some of their lectures will be short and to the point since each course may have one or more specific textbook(s) for that topic. In other courses, textbooks are tools that can and should be used throughout the course and research process but faculty members may provide more detailed lectures or articles for weekly readings.

For the past decade, online services have been conquering the education and training market like there is no tomorrow, and we see that consumers all over the world are throwing themselves over their keyboards. Why? We know that customer service is best delivered face to face otherwise it seems to be a bit mechanical or automated, but then again it is all about convenience. What this means is that communication has its routes and forms, adaptation on the other hand is only a matter of time. Fetching the style in writings can never be simple in accordance to the time span of electronics that we have been encountering lately. *Emoticons* are used in delivering messages whether with a smile, frown or cry... words talk and eyes listen! Typed or written words express what encounters a human being from the inside (emotions) and the outside (facial expressions) and yet it can best be used to communicate on a professional basis according to the purpose of its use. So in the case of online students, communicating with an online instructor and getting to know him/her without seeing the person and what s/he has to deliver all lies in his/her words and way of typing them and how fast they can penetrate thoughts rather than telling or dictating to students!

The following are actual student responses to surveys conducted in 2003 with forty online graduate students in terms of their best practices in adapting to the online learning world and the faculty members style of facilitation.

> Gapping the style differences between instructors online is no different than on campus style learning. I remember when in a physical college, I had to become accustomed to 4 different instructors in 4 different classes in the same quarter. I actually think that it is easier to acclimate to an on-line instructor because it is only one or two classes at a time for most adult students. However, being flexible and not having any preconceived notions of how class should be will help smooth out the transition between classes and instructors.
>
> So, adapting to an instructor's teacher style is no different from a physical classroom than an online classroom. While at the undergraduate program, I

took between 12- 18 hours a semester and each instructor was different, from their lecture style, how they presented materials, their tests, and how much time they allotted to assist students outside of the classroom. For instance some teachers lectured in class, and were not available outside of class. You had three tests and a final and that was your grade. If you got behind or needed assistance then you needed to find someone in class to work with, and/or get a tutor. Other teachers held regular office hours and assigned homework that was gone over during class, with questions being asked as you went over the assignments.

One major difference between the online and physical classroom would be that with a physical classroom you had a set time with the instructor. Online you do not, you just have to post your thoughts, ideas, questions and wait for a response. The same goes for the team assignments, you do not set up a time to physically meet to work on your team project. The bottom line was you had to get used to the style of the teacher and adapt to the changes you experienced from one classroom to the next. It is beneficial that as an adult student I probably will only take one class at a time, allowing me to focus on one instructor's style at a time.

I think in the online world of education the hardest part is finding time rather than anything else. The other element I have noticed with online is that one needs to read everything because it is all written on a piece of paper and if you miss something you are doomed. I was amazed when I first had to read the syllabus, then the lectures, then the electronic textbook, and then the daily postings. As an online student, you wake up, go to sleep and think ok, what day is it today? What is due and when it is constantly on one's mind since the online classes go so fast. On the other hand it is nice not to have to get in the car and drive for an hour, try to find a parking space and rush into class, sit for 2 hours minimum and then drive another hour to get home. A total of 4 hours of class and driving it would be for me never mind the exhaustion. I think it all comes down to preference of learning and style.

While I was reading the first lecture for the online graduate course, I could not help to think that undergrad would have been a better learning experience if I could have taken some courses online. In undergrad, I participated in two varsity sports that required travel almost every week, therefore I missed one quarter of all lectures. I do believe that getting to know some professors on a personal and social level enhanced my development as a student and a person. Some lectures and professors I wish I had missed. I guess what I am getting at is that each faculty member is going to use his or her own method of teaching. Some I will find value, some I will not. My plan is to go into each online class as if it was a new client. Some become great clients, some do not.

I have taken close to 20 online classes and invariably there will be differences with instructors. Many of the basics are the same from class to class. There is freedom given to the faculty in terms of when the assignments are due and to which folders. A scan of the syllabus is important to get a "feel" for the faculty.

I had the same concerns myself in developing a learning style in regards to online learning. To me, being a recent college graduate, it will take some adjusting to figure out how to plot my path in the online environment. During my undergraduate studies, I never took an online course. I do see that it will not be as easy as the picture that was painted to me by others who were taking online courses. My biggest task will be disciplining myself with time management to complete assigned readings, written assignments, and discussion questions in such a fast and intense pace. I do feel though, through reading everyone's (peers) biographies and responses to discussion questions each week, that I am not the only one with these issues. Through each other's help, I think we will all make it.

I think adjusting to different teaching styles is part of being a student. Being flexible is the key. We, as adult students taking one or two classes at a time, are somewhat fortunate in the online program because we only have to "master" one or two instructor's style at a time. It is definitely easier than learning 4–5 styles per semester as we had to in the traditional undergraduate program. I had professors whose emphasis was testing while other professors emphasized homework. You just have to figure out what the professor finds important and gear your work accordingly. It was not always easy but it did prepare me for the real world. As a contractor, I have several bosses I report to for different aspects of my job: my company boss wants things as brief and concise as possible, the government person who oversees the helpdesk likes things fluffed up, the parts and software manager is a big procedure person, etc. It is the same game with different players. So, the online and on-ground classes both equally prepare students for their future (or current) job responsibilities as they will have to adjust to the learning and communication styles of their colleagues, peers, customers, suppliers, and bosses.

Online students should quickly condition themselves to the platform used by the cyber faculty and adjust to the teacher's requirements. This is very similar to the on-ground platform; however, online modality may be new to many adult students and they do not yet have the requisite experience with it. As such, faculty members should do what they can to familiarize students with the requirements at the outset of each course. This can eliminate much undue stress, frustration and negative student-faculty evaluations which are traditionally completed toward the end of each course by students.

Many schools have switched the student evaluation of the course and faculty procedures to the online format because of its convenience and timely processing for improvement. The purpose of this new system is to create a paperless student-faculty evaluation process that can be forwarded to faculty members as soon as their course grades are submitted. Also, administrators can take the necessary steps in improving the service for students if needed and appropriate. Oftentimes, administrators send emails to both faculty and students so they can complete the online evaluations. The student completion rate of course evaluation through the university's website or intranets seems to be low for most on-ground and many online courses. In one example during the fall term of 2003 in the undergraduate program having approximately 5,000 students, only 25% of the students responded. This meant an average of 2–8 students (from an average of 20–25) per class completed the evaluation. Of course, the 25% could be only those students who were either very happy with the class or not pleased at all. So, there is the non-response bias present which must be taken into consideration as well. If you are like most faculty members, you want the feedback from students, because it helps improve or change teaching techniques to enhance the overall goal which is learning. There are other benefits besides improving one's teaching style or techniques. Evaluations help administrators with merit promotions for fulltime faculty, and they may increase the opportunities to teach more classes for part-time faculty. Furthermore, and more importantly, good feedback keeps everyone in touch with the learning environment and the learners by providing timely feedback.

THE STONE SOUP LEGEND AND THE SPIRIT OF SYNERGY

The Stone Soup story is one of the best metaphorical examples of the objective of facilitation in the online classroom. In the story, the main character's purpose is to help the community see how they could create something wonderful that would benefit everyone, if they would each just put into the pot what they had to offer. The same holds true for the discussion in the online classroom and online teaching within an institution.

According to the Stone Soup Legend (2003), there existed a tale, handed down from times long ago, of two travelers on a pilgrimage. Hungry and tired from a long day's journey, they come to a small, impoverished, medieval village, where they decide to rest by the side of the road. One of the travelers builds a small fire, upon which he places a large pot, while the other, having drawn water from the town well, fills the pot and places into the vessel a simple stone. As the two men sit by the fire, bringing their "stone soup" to a boil, the local villagers become inquisitive of the curious antics of these strangers. Eventually, several townsfolk decide to investigate the matter and approach the two travelers to engage them in conversation. Shortly thereafter, there is heard the sound of merriment, as the visitors, who turn out to be quite friendly, share their tales of the lands and people they have met throughout their journey and pilgrimage with the local villagers. Finally, a young boy asks the travelers "But why, pray thee, are you boiling a stone?" One of the pilgrims replies, "So we may eat stone soup." "It must be terribly bland!" says an old woman. "But I have a cabbage, which will add some flavor!" "And I, some carrots, which will add color!" says another villager. "Some potatoes!", offers another, until, shortly, *by the contribution of a little by many*, a hearty stew was made, upon which the entire village and the weary pilgrims dined... and while doing so, shared their tales, talents, and camaraderie throughout the night. The very next day, the travelers (who by now could be called "strangers" no more), continued their journey, leaving the little town, and its people, behind. But the villagers never forgot them, and the lesson they had learned. In fact, during the hardest of times, in such a time as this tale, that little village thrived, because the townsfolk never forgot how to make "stone soup". Such is the legend of the "Stone Soup Story".

The legend of "stone soup" applies to the education arena as well when the input of everyone is sought, valued, appreciated, and implemented to enhance the process of facilitation and learning. For example, from your own experiences in the classroom, you can reflect upon some of the specific ways that faculty members can get students to contribute to the discussion(s) in a way that will enhance learning of the material and its practical application. In other words, reflect upon discovering the "ingredients" of a dynamic, interactive classroom discussion that illustrates the "Stone Soup Legend"? Think of how other peer faculty members can get involved as well as how adult students can integrate their experience into the discussions. Then, together with colleagues, you can begin "cooking" and effectively facilitate learning in all modalities of adult education.

SUMMARY

The adult world of education, using blended formats of distance learning delivery, has achieved a special market in the adult world by offering quality educational programs both nationally and internationally at times convenient to students. Through professional faculty members committed to student learning and their ability to combine academic theory with successful practical tools as well as their ability to effectively adjust to the changing educational needs of working professionals, online educators have and can offer great value to their students and their community at large. As such many schools have enjoyed increased enrollment over the past five years due to their quality, convenience, and satisfied stakeholders.

Over twenty-five years ago, when few other institutions proactively considered their students' needs, the distance educators, such as NSU, strove to accommodate working professionals by creating innovative programs to meet the needs of adult students. Today, that tradition continues at the

Huizenga School of NSU with better and more innovative teaching features using internet and cyberspace technologies. Online's unique feature has been and continues to be its flexibility to tailoring delivery of educational programs to the particular needs of corporations. Administrators and faculty are keenly attuned to the complicated demands placed on today's employees, managers, and leaders. Online courses can continually and easily be refined to the most current and relevant practices. Administrators, in conjunction with faculty members, must integrate fair and consistent policies with regard to minimum standards and professional development guidelines for all faculty members who wish to integrate cyberspace technology to enhance student learning. Furthermore, equitable compensation strategies must be established for online educators since they do more work and must constantly stay abreast of new technologies needed to keep up with the cyberspace generation of students. Online students can encounter some of the most exciting, enriching course work available anywhere in education today... courses designed to challenge critical thinking skills... to widen perspectives on traditional business practices, and to foster an entrepreneurial spirit due to the unique skills of the individual faculty who can reside anywhere in the world while teaching courses online.

No matter the program or format, each program should utilize all the tools technology and management have to offer, giving students an unprecedented opportunity to acquire skills that will enrich their knowledge base and leadership abilities, while learning to add value to their company and to their lives.

CHAPTER 3

FACULTY DEVELOPMENT

As most university administrators know, the challenge of recruiting, developing and retaining competent faculty is a moral imperative for quality assurance and improvement purposes in today's competitive world of higher education. As such, administrators should focus on the effective orientation and development of qualified educators to teach in various learning modalities (online, on-ground, and blended formats) using cyberspace technology, while focusing on effectively achieving the course's learning outcomes. Therefore, integrating cyberspace technology into the classroom for student learning as well as quality assurance and continuous improvement purposes is basically a necessity. Unfortunately, many educators fear this development due to lack of availability and effective training. This chapter provides an overview of faculty training and orientation program used at the H. Wayne Huizenga School of Business and Entrepreneurship of Nova Southeastern University. The emersion model of training and orientation used for indoctrinating and socializing new faculty members is presented. Prior to discussing the immersion model of training and orientation, this section presents an overview of the basic guidelines and suggestions from the regional accrediting bodies pertaining to faculty qualification, orientation, and development elements.

Adult Education in Academia, pages 59–80
Copyright © 2006 by Information Age Publishing
All rights of reproduction in any form reserved.

THE HIGHER EDUCATION SYSTEM AND ACCREDITATION

As a faculty member or an administrative staff person moves up or laterally on the "ladder" of academic success, one is likely to, sooner or later, become increasingly involved with the world of accreditation. For effective leaders and administrators, it will be a necessity that they become aware of what accreditation is, how it works for accountability and credibility, and how it can be used, or abused, by various stakeholders involved in the process.

Simply stated, accreditation is a comprehensive process for evaluation by an outside agency which can conclude with either the granting (or withholding) of certification or a seal of approval that demonstrates that an academic program or school meets quality standards established by professional peers (Greenberg, 2001). Greenberg continues to state that "The remarkable feature of this process in the United States is that it is done through the efforts of voluntary associations rather than, as is the case in most of the world, by a centralized ministry of education." Schools that seek accreditation do so voluntarily on behalf of their students and other relevant stakeholders to show that they meet certain standards in higher education. Since accreditation is not a requirement for the successful operation of a school, some institutions operate without ever officially seeking it. Generally, accreditation is conferred on entire institutions by one of the six regional accrediting bodies (Middle States, New England, North Central, Northwest, Southern, Western). Since Nova Southeastern University (NSU) is located in Florida, the school falls under the "umbrella" of the Southern regional accrediting body.

NSU is accredited by the Southern Association of Colleges and Schools (SACS), which in 1994 stated that "The library and other learning resources must be evaluated regularly and systematically to ensure that they are meeting the needs of their users and are supporting the programs and purposes of the institution" (Southern Association of Colleges and Schools; 1994, p. 54). As such, all SACS accredited universities are required to conduct "ongoing, integrated, and institution-wide research-based planning and evaluation processes that incorporate a systematic review of programs and services that (a) results in continuing improvement and (b) demonstrates that the institution is effectively accomplishing its mission" (pp. 12-13). Furthermore, the schools are required to provide students "collections and resources that are sufficient to support all its educational, research, and public service programs" (Southern Association of Colleges and Schools; 2003, p. 14). NSU's H. Wayne Huizenga School of Business and Entrepreneurship has done a very good job of keeping "their fingers on the pulse" of their students by surveying students and their employers to determine the best course of action in terms of program offerings and course content. Furthermore, appropriate individuals and departments conduct research to determine the operational needs of students, who are very widespread nationally and internationally at various locations.

Nova Southeastern University (NSU) has been offering classes locally at the Main Campus, nationally throughout the United States, and internationally in over ten different countries for the past four decades. For example, NSU has close to 800 active students in the country of Jamaica and the school's faculty members have been active in many countries including Bahamas, Trinidad, China, Brazil, France, Germany, Dominican Republic, England, Greece, Panama, Venezuela, and others, offering various programs at the bachelor, master and doctoral levels. While the locations and modalities of education tend to vary from group to group, the content and consistency of the subjects that are taught to each group of students tend to stay the same. As such, not only do the administrators meet the stated requirements of SACS but they also meet their own stated institutional mission statement which is:

> Nova Southeastern University is a dynamic, not-for-profit independent institution dedicated to providing high-quality educational programs of distinction from pre-school through the professional and doctoral levels, as well as service to the community. Nova Southeastern University prepares students for lifelong learning and leadership roles in business and the professions. It offers academic programs at times convenient to students, employing innovative delivery systems and rich learning resources on campus and at distant sites. The university fosters inquiry, research, and creative professional activity, by uniting faculty and students in acquiring and applying knowledge in clinical, community, and professional settings. (NSU, 2003)

According to SACS (2001), "Accreditation of an institution by the Commission on Colleges signified the institution has a purpose appropriate to higher education and has resources, programs, and services sufficient to accomplish that purpose on a continuing basis." Each institution creates its own reason for existence and has to make sure it lives up to the institution's own expectations by periodically measuring achievements against pre-established expectations and goals. Outside accreditation agencies simply "evaluate whether an institution maintains clearly specified educational objectives that are consistent with its mission and appropriate to the degrees it offers and whether it is successful in achieving its stated objectives" (SACS, 2001, p. 1).

PRINCIPLES OF ACCREDITATION FOR FACULTY DEVELOPMENT

The Southern Association of Colleges and Schools (SACS) is one of the six major regional accrediting bodies that provide guidelines for schools with regard to faculty recruitment and hiring practices. In its 2001 publication on "Principles of Accreditation: Foundations for Quality Enhancement," the Commission on Colleges provides the following guidelines for Faculty:

> The institution employs competent faculty members qualified to accomplish the mission and goals of the institution. When determining acceptable qualifications of its faculty, an institution gives primary consideration to the highest earned degree in the discipline in accord with the guidelines listed below. The institution also considers competence, effectiveness, and capacity, including, as appropriate, undergraduate and graduate degrees, related work experiences in the field, professional licensure and certifications, honors and awards, continuous documented excellence in teaching, or other demonstrated competencies and achievements that contribute to effective teaching and student learning outcomes. For all cases, the institution is responsible for justifying and documenting the qualifications of its entire faculty. (p.17)

The Commission on Colleges further provides specific credential guidelines for the recruitment, hiring, training, orientation, and development of all part-time and full-time faculty members, as follows (SACS, 2001, p. 17–18):

a. Faculty teaching general education courses at the undergraduate level: a doctoral or a master's degree in the teaching discipline or a master's degree with a concentration in the teaching discipline (a minimum of 18 graduate semester hours in the teaching discipline).
b. Faculty teaching associate degree courses designed for transfer to a baccalaureate degree: a doctoral or a master's degree in the teaching discipline or a master's degree with a concentration in the teaching discipline (a minimum of 18 graduate semester hours in the teaching discipline).
c. Faculty teaching baccalaureate degree courses: a doctoral or a master's degree in the teaching discipline or a master's degree with a concentration in the teaching discipline (minimum of 18 graduate semester hours in the teaching discipline). At least 25 percent of the discipline course hours in each undergraduate major are taught by faculty members holding the terminal degree—usually the earned doctorate—in the discipline.
d. Faculty teaching graduate and post-baccalaureate course work: earned doctorate (terminal degree) in the teaching discipline or a related discipline.
e. Graduate teaching assistants: master's in the teaching discipline or 18 graduate semester hours in the teaching discipline, direct supervision by a faculty member experienced in the teaching discipline, regular in-service training, and planned and periodic evaluations.

Since Nova Southeastern University is accredited by SACS, the program directors, faculty coordinators, and program managers adhere to their rules and policies that pertain to the achievement of the school's mission. NSU has over 500 full-time faculty members and thousands of part-time faculty that assist them in the delivery of up-to-date education to adult students. NSU's schools and colleges keep track of their hiring and teaching data for faculty members in order to make improvements. For example, NSU's H. Wayne Huizenga School of Business and Entrepreneurship (Huizenga School) keeps track of student credit hours that are taught by doctorally qualified faculty members. As can be seen from Table 1, about 40% of the undergraduate student credit hours and over 76% of the masters level student credit hours were taught by doctorally qualified faculty members during 2003. As demonstrated in Table 7, the percentage of undergraduate credits hours taught by doctorally qualified faculty members at the Huizenga School exceeds SACS' requirement of 25% for such programs. Accordingly, in this case, the Huizenga School is exceeding the requirement by making sure that a larger percentage of its courses are taught by a diverse group of terminally degreed educators. Of course, hiring qualified faculty members to teach in their areas of specialization is one of the initial steps in ensuring student success in the program. Other measures (such as outcomes assessment, student satisfaction surveys, observation of content application, oral presentations, etc.) must also be taken to make sure students are achieving what they should be attaining as a result of completing the program.

Since the criteria for success are determined on whether students are achieving the learning outcomes of each course and the curriculum, it is necessary for the administration to periodically measure the success of each faculty member as well. As a matter of fact, in one of its guidelines in the 2001 Principles of Accreditation, SACS states its expectation by saying that "The institution regularly evaluates the effectiveness of each faculty mem-

Table 7. Student Credit Hours Taught at the Huizenga School in 2003

Year 2003	Undergraduate Hours	Graduate Hours (Masters)
Total student credit hours taught by faculty members at the Huizenga School (HS)	46,401	50,609
Total credit hours taught by Doctorally qualified faculty members at HS	18,800	38,897
Percent of total credit hours taught by Doctorally qualified faculty members at HS	40.5% (SACS requirement is 25%)	76.9%*

* Non credited prerequisite courses taught by non-terminally degreed faculty members are included.

ber in accord with published criteria, regardless of contractual or tenured status." Furthermore, the Commission on Colleges requires that each institution (SACS, 2001, p. 17–18):

- Provide evidence of ongoing professional development of faculty as teachers, scholars, and practitioners.
- Ensure adequate procedures for the safeguard and protection of academic freedom.
- Publish policies on the responsibility and authority of faculty in academic and governance matters.

Besides being accredited by SACS, the H. Wayne Huizenga School of Business and Entrepreneurship has been a member of the *International Assembly for Collegiate Business Education* (IACBE) and the *Association for the Advancement of Collegiate Schools of Business International* (AACSB) which provides additional levels of "programmatic" accreditation for business schools. AACSB (1999), in their Standards for Business Accreditation, stated that "The school should demonstrate continuous efforts to achieve demographic diversity in its faculty" (page 11). This objective is why NSU's Huizenga School always attempts to hire and retain a diverse group of practicing faculty members from various fields and specializations. The school currently has 45 full-time faculty members and over 400 part-time faculty members that reside in the United States, Jamaica and the Bahamas. One reason for having such a large number of part-time faculty members is that they are mostly employed practitioners and teach in their areas of academic and practical expertise. As such, these practicing educators are fully qualified to discuss the latest "best practices" with their students. Since many of Huizenga School's students are working adults, the presence of practicing faculty members facilitating specialized courses can enrich class discussions, learning, and content retention. Similar to most schools that have their own graduates teach in their programs, Huizenga School attempts to balance the percentage of their faculty with the diversity of educators from various institutions.

Table 8 shows the number and percentage of student credit hours at the Huizenga School during 2003 that were taught by educators who earned their highest degree from NSU versus those who have graduated from other regionally accredited schools in the United States or abroad. Again, the goal at NSU is to have a mix of diverse faculty members from various institutions that can enrich the learning experiences of students through innovative teaching and facilitation skills at times and modalities convenient to students. While securing a diverse group of faculty from different institutions can be a great asset to an institution, these individuals should also be inculcated and oriented with the rules and policies of the school if

Table 8.   Credit Hours Taught by NSU Graduates versus Other Institutions

Year 2003	Undergraduate Hours	Graduate Hours (Masters)
Total student credit hours taught by faculty members at the Huizenga School (HS)	46,401	50,609
Total student credit hours taught by full-time faculty members that earned their highest degree at NSU	2,490 (6.5%)	4,087 (8.1%)
Total student credit hours taught by part-time faculty members that earned their highest degree at NSU	15,121 (32.7%)	19,152 (37.8%)
Total NSU Graduate Faculty	17,611 (39.2%)	23,239 (45.9%)
Total student credit hours taught by faculty members (part-time and full-time) that earned their highest degree at other institutions	28,790 (60.8%)	27,370 (54.1%)

they are to deliver consistently educational values of superior value in each course from the outset.

On page 11 of the Standards for Business Accreditation, AACSB mentions that "The school should have appropriate practices for the orientation of new faculty to the school." On page 12 of the guidelines, AACSB continues to state that "Processes should be in place to determine appropriate teaching assignments and service workloads, to guide and mentor faculty, and to provide adequate support for activities that implement the school's mission." Such rules and guidelines are designed to ensure fairness and integrity of the system, while continuously providing a diversity of thoughts for enhancing each program.

As such, the Huizenga School administrators, Chairs and faculty members also follow the suggestions and rules set forth by AACSB and IACBE to ensure they have the best curricula in each program and the best qualified faculty members. The IACBE's Accreditation Manual (2002) links the characteristics of excellence that pertain to the faculty in business education to being current in one's field. Some of their characteristics are as follows (IACBE, 2002, p. 19):

- The business unit has meaningful and effective linkages between the classroom and practitioners in the business community, thereby providing assurance of relevancy and currency in the academic programs.
- Faculty members in the business unit are effective teachers who are current in their fields and active in their professional contributions to their institution and discipline. Further, the faculty members are

positively engaged within their business unit and contribute to the mission and broad-based goals of the business unit through appropriate faculty development and faculty evaluation processes.

- The mix of academic and professional credentials of the business faculty is worthy of the respect of the academic and business communities.

- The institution provides adequate resources to the business unit to accomplish its mission and broad-based goals.

- The content of business courses is delivered in a manner that is appropriate, effective, and stimulates learning.

IACBE further stated that "Each institution seeking IACBE accreditation must, therefore, (1) have an effective method for recruiting faculty; (2) evaluate faculty based on defined criteria; (3) provide support for faculty development and scholarly activity; and (4) foster an academic climate conducive to excellence in teaching and learning." The IACBE organization and their personnel believe that "quality teaching should be supported by highly-qualified faculty who are capable of providing opportunities for student learning and who are active in professional and scholarly activities." Such expectations go beyond academic preparation and include current or recent business-related field experience in one's area of teaching. In order to meet the expectations of various accrediting bodies and effectively meet its mission statement, the Huizenga School's Undergraduate Business Programs created and implemented a comprehensive faculty training and orientation program, which is discussed in the next section, and many of the supplementary forms are attached in the appendix.

FACULTY TRAINING AND ORIENTATION MODEL

Faculty development and retention are critical elements of a successful institution. Effective faculty members always have been, and will continue to be, an important and mission critical asset to any University, as the facilitators of learning have the most important job in the world—preparing future leaders of the society! Therefore, one essential educational institution goal must be to recruit, develop and retain faculty members with the required skills to compete effectively in global industries, because students seek to learn from them the skills required to compete with the very best in their professions. As the Associate Dean of Academic Affairs (Dr. Preston Jones) at the Huizenga School, has stated for most institutions today, the only true sustainable advantage comes from out-innovating the competition. It matters not which particular organization stays alive, rather, it's only essential that competition among them is fierce and fair—and that the fittest survive. Therefore, educational institutions can neither survive nor prosper without extraordinary faculty members who can be innovative and globally competitive. Consequently, all institutions need to have a standardized process to consciously recruit, hire, orient, develop, and retain extraordinary faculty members for all education modalities. Having a standardized faculty orientation and development process is even more critical for institutions involved in distance learning. A formalized training program requires an annual budget for each academic unit. For example, Nova Southeastern University (NSU) has been involved in distance education for over 40 years now. NSU had approximately 25,000 students in early 2005 and nearly 5,000 of these students are registered to pursue degrees in business at the undergraduate, masters, and doctoral programs. As stated on Table 9, about 28% of NSU's institutional credit hours in 2003 were taught by the Huizenga School and this trend is expected to continue for 2004 and 2005. This also means that the business school can also secure an appropriate budget for faculty training each year.

Table 9. Educational and General Expenditures for NSU and Huizenga School

Expenditure and Student Credit Hours	Academic Year 2003 (ACTUAL)	Academic Year 2004 (BUDGET)	Academic Year 2005 (BUDGET)
Total educational and general unrestricted expenditures for the institution	300,212,000	309,511,000	347,256,000
Percentage of academic expenditures allocated to the School of Business.	10.2%	9.7%	11.2
Total student credit hours for the entire institution	371,892	389,898	410,900
Total student credit hours- School of Business	105,553	106,170	100,128
Percentage of institutional credit hours taught by the School of Business	28%	27%	24%

The Huizenga School of NSU has traditionally been recruiting and hiring faculty members to teach its classes, mostly based on "word of mouth" advertising for the past few decades, since there really has not been a shortage of qualified people who wanted to teach in this non-traditional format of adult education. However, enrollment has substantially increased in the last decade, which has required the school to have a large group of qualified part-time faculty members from diverse institutions.

In 2002, the Undergraduate Business Programs at Nova Southeastern University had about 2,100 students and nearly 300 part-time faculty members with 14 full-time professors serving as mentors and lead faculty for courses in their areas of specialty. While the program was large, the hiring of adjuncts was being conducted mostly through one-on-one socialization with the Lead Faculty members, Faculty Coordinator, and/or Academic Director. While this process can be done effectively with a large number of Faculty Coordinators, the Undergraduate Business Program only had one official Faculty Coordinator who recruited, hired and trained all part-time faculty members for classes each term. Naturally, this is too much work for any one person, as there were over 200 sections of classes each term. Based on a thorough analysis of how things were being done with regard to faculty training and orientation, recommendations from the accreditation team at the University Council of Jamaica (UCJ) when the Business and Professional Management (BPM) program was reaccredited, the shortage of faculty coordinators for the program, and the growing enrollment at the Undergraduate Business Programs, the new Director of Undergraduate Business Programs (Dr. Bahaudin Mujtaba) decided that a comprehensive faculty training and orientation program was needed for incoming part-time educators. This idea and concept of developing a comprehensive training and orientation program at the Huizenga School was further welcomed and supported by the Associate Dean of Academic Affairs (Dr. Preston Jones). As such, the Program Director with assistance from selected full-time faculty members prepared a manual titled "Faculty Training and Orientation Guidelines" for an eight-hour session for all incoming part-time faculty members. The manual was designed to be a part of the comprehensive assessment and orientation program for implementation in late 2002. The program was scheduled for pilot implementation at the Main Campus in Fort Lauderdale, and then at four other locations including Tampa, Orlando, Nassau (Bahamas), and Kingston (Jamaica). See the attached email in Appendix F which provides the date and location of each "training and orientation" session that were scheduled and implemented in the early part of 2003.

The comprehensive faculty training process developed in 2002 for the Undergraduate Business Programs, discussed in this document, can be a good way of socializing and preparing incoming educators at the Huizenga School or at any other center in Nova Southeastern University. As a matter-of-fact, the faculty training and orientation model can be applied at any academic or non-academic institution. The visual representation of faculty training and orientation model is presented in Figure 1 of this document. Each element of this ideal immersion model of training (Figure 1) can further provide more specific institution-related policies and links to the organization's policies, guidelines, and mission as follows:

- Hiring
  - ➢ Considering required academic credentials.
  - ➢ Professional experience and teaching flexibility.
- Orienting
  - ➢ Education on learning and facilitation.
  - ➢ Pedagogy of adult education.
- Modeling
  - ➢ The faculty experiences learning as a student.
  - ➢ The faculty observes and teaches a mock class.
- Mentoring
  - ➢ Evaluating and enhancing lesson plans, lectures, and activities.
  - ➢ Making sure the content is being facilitated to achieve learning outcomes.
- Teaching
  - ➢ On-going training and development is offered on a just-in-time basis.
  - ➢ Faculty is monitored to make sure technology is being used effectively to achieve learning outcomes.
- Evaluating and Developing
  - ➢ Evaluation should be an ongoing process.
  - ➢ Development should be focused on student learning.

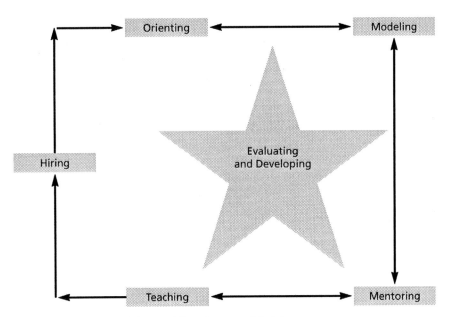

Figure 1. Faculty Training and Development Model.

As part of the immersion model of training and orientation, the following is the general process that the Undergraduate Business Program communicated to everyone for the formal faculty assessment and orientation at the Huizenga School starting in 2002:

- *Interview:* Résumés are reviewed to see if the academic achievements and practical experiences of each candidate meet the Program's needs for subject areas that will require more instructors. See Appendix A for a typical response that prospective faculty members received when they submitted a resume for teaching opportunities in the Undergraduate Business Programs. Qualified candidates are often screened and/or interviewed (by phone) to discuss possibilities for a face-to-face interview and assessment. Face-to-face interviews are conducted and those who match the school's needs (and the needs of accreditation criteria) are invited for the assessment, which is inclusive of a presentation by the candidate and other exercises to assess each applicant's ability to facilitate discussion and style of teaching with adult learners. In the case of prospective adjunct faculty members, living outside of Fort Lauderdale—Florida, who cannot attend one of the scheduled assessment and orientations at the Main Campus, other options (such as online training and orientation) might be considered and implemented. See the attachment in Appendix B for sample interview questions with prospective candidates.

- *Assessment:* Assessment is often inclusive of a presentation on a topic (about 10–15 minutes) in the applicant's area of academic expertise to see his/her teaching and lecture style. Candidates will also become aware of the institution's mission, vision, philosophy, and overall expectations from faculty members during the initial hour of the assessment session. See Appendices C and D for the evaluation criteria and forms used as part of the assessment. These forms are used to screen out candidates who are not a good match for the Huizenga School's culture, and the information on these forms are also used for providing appropriate training based on the weaknesses and strengths pointed out by the observers. As such, this information is very helpful for the facilitator of the orientation session. Those who successfully complete the assessment process will be invited for the hiring and orientation session. While the initial part of assessment is complete after the first session, the assessment really continues until the successful completion of the faculty member's first course. Instructors who do not have a successful teaching experience in their first course may either receive more mentoring/coaching or may be de-activated (if the situation cannot be improved), and consequently will not be able to teach at the school.

See the letter in Appendix E that details the invitation information for assessment and orientation.

- *Hiring and Orientation:* Hiring and orientation training are scheduled on a separate day for qualified applicants who have gone through the assessment process. After the successful completion of the above steps (including the orientation) and the required paperwork, new faculty members can be scheduled for courses in the coming semesters (or year) with an assigned Lead/Senior Faculty serving as a mentor/coach for the first course. The candidate may actually sit in classes with his/her mentor or other experienced faculty members to observe best practices while preparing teaching notes for the upcoming scheduled class. Online faculty members may be asked to actually observe an online section of a course from the mentor or other experienced faculty members. Based on the readiness assessment and first teaching experience of the candidate, the mentor may recommend future course assignment possibilities and/or more training for the newly hired faculty to the Program Director (or Chair) based on the teaching effectiveness of the newly hired faculty at the first course assignment.

- *Mentorship:* Once a course and mentor has been assigned, the new faculty member would need to submit electronic copies of his/her syllabus for the scheduled course (along with possible exams, quizzes, and teaching plans) to the Lead/Senior Faculty (mentor) for approval at least three weeks prior to the start of the course's first official session. So, the mentorship starts with the approval of course syllabus and teaching content. Once this material has been approved (or revised as needed) by the mentor/coach (Lead/Senior Faculty), then it can be submitted to the Program Director/Coordinator for archiving purposes (records are kept for auditing needs) if these items are not available on the online course servers. Newly hired faculty members can call on their mentor/coach for directions and guidance as well as on the Chairs, Academic Director and Program Coordinators when needed. See the email in Appendix I that provides more information on the mentorship process to both mentors and mentees. Also, see Appendices L and M for the "Mentoring Evaluation Form and Mentoring Checklist" used by mentors.

As can be seen on Appendix F, there were a total of six different training and orientation sessions scheduled, and eventually successfully implemented as planned, for the first few months of 2003. Appendix F also shows that all current full-time and part-time faculty members were invited to participate in one of these sessions. Actually, over 120 full-time and part-time faculty members were able to participate in one of the eight-hour orientation sessions.

Motivated by professional curiosity, prospective faculty members often wanted to know what would be covered in the assessment and orientation sessions. As such, they were told that the assessment sessions, which usually last about four hours, were inclusive of passing on relevant information to everyone about the university and the school's expectations from all faculty members, introduction of the school and academic directors along with faculty members present, a presentation by prospective faculty members (about 10-15 minutes), and other exercises to evaluate each person's teaching and grading style. The presentation by prospective faculty members should be in their area of academic expertise to assess their knowledge and facilitation style. The presentations usually took place in a classroom setting, while other prospective faculty members (and the evaluators) served the role of students/audience. Since working adults who are not necessarily experts in each person's area of expertise were the audience, candidates were encouraged to prepare their presentations accordingly so it would not be too complex or boring for the audience. They were encouraged to present academically "published" materials relevant for the audience. The key was to make their presentations interesting for a diverse audience. Presentations could have been made using lecture, blackboard, transparencies, activities, questions and answers, and/or handouts to achieve the proposed presentation objectives in the time allotted.

The orientation session, which usually lasts about eight hours, may include completing the hiring package during the first thirty minutes. As such, candidates are asked to bring the actual and copies of their Social Security Card, Driver's License, Green Card, two forms of picture identification, two professional letters of recommendations, copies of certifications and licenses, and/or other relevant items needed for an employment application and academic credentials. The remaining time is spent on faculty familiarization/orientation with the university policies, expectations from all faculty members, grading criteria, preparing standard syllabi with the same outcome competencies, evaluating student performance (see Appendices G and H for evaluation of written papers and oral presentations), familiarity with the American Psychological Association's (APA) writing style, dealing with different learning styles, effectively handling students' concerns with regards to academic rigor or grade complaints, managing diversity in the classroom, and other such topics so as to better equip everyone for a successful teaching experience at the university. After the successful completion of the assessment and orientation sessions, faculty members can be assigned mentors and a course in a prospective term once they complete their Course Approval Requests (CARs) based on the Course Profile and Teaching Qualification Requirements (see Appendix J for a sample of the profiles and teaching requirements). The Undergraduate Business Program's lead faculty members developed a comprehensive document known as the Course Profiles and Teaching Qualification Requirements which is initially used by Faculty Coordinators to recruit and hire the right faculty members by matching the credentials of prospective candidates with the qualification requirement of the courses which need more teachers. These qualifications are usually discussed during the initial interview sessions, so the candidate knows what s/he is being asked to teach if hired. Once the candidates complete the assessment and orientation sessions, they are asked to electronically complete a Course Approval Request (CAR) within the next few weeks for courses that they are willing to teach as per their academic (or practical) qualifications and the requirements of each course. As such, the comprehensive Course Profile and Teaching Qualification Requirements form is made available for all faculty members so they can match their credentials with the right courses. For a completed sample of a CAR, see Appendix K. The newly hired faculty members are asked to electronically submit their CAR to the academic program office, which is reviewed by the Academic Director, Associate Dean for Academic Affairs and/or Chairs in order to grant approval or deny approval for teaching the stated courses. If the person's qualifications match the requirements for teaching the course, then approval is granted. Otherwise, approval is denied. Once approval is granted, then the person can be scheduled for a course in one of the upcoming terms.

Course assignments in the Undergraduate Business Programs are usually completed about one to two semesters ahead of schedule when enrollment is known. If a faculty member is selected for a course during a given term/semester, then someone from the Program Office would contact him or her immediately to see if he or she is open, willing, and available to teach it. If the person agrees to teach it, then he or she will be scheduled for it. If one cannot teach it because of other commitments, then another faculty member will be contacted to see if s/he can teach the course. Periodically, the Undergraduate Business Program holds Faculty Development meetings/sessions to gather information about the curriculum and its improvement, provide updates, network with other faculty members for discovering best practices, etc. and faculty members are expected to attend at least one each year along with all the required meetings. Of course, the main purpose of such a formalized process is to make sure each person is able to be successful as a faculty member and achieve extraordinary results with his or her students in the class. The pedagogy of adult education, as well as expectations and characteristics of being an extraordinary faculty member are discussed with everyone during the assessment and orientation sessions.

DEVELOPING EXTRAORDINARY FACULTY MEMBERS

No faculty orientation session would be complete without a good discussion and dialogue on the characteristics and best practices of extraordinary educators. Mahatma Gandhi once said that you should "Learn as if you will live forever, live as if you will die tomorrow." Extraordinary teachers continuously learn and pass on relevant (updated) information to their students. There is an interesting book, titled "Extraordinary Teachers: The Essence of Excellent Teaching," by Dr. Frederick Stephenson, Associate Professor of Marketing and Distribution at the University of Georgia's Terry College of Business. The book is basically a compilation of about thirty six papers written by teachers that are considered to be extraordinary, and have also received the Josiah Meigs Award for Excellence in Teaching (the highest teaching honor given by the University of Georgia). Throughout the book, six characteristics of extraordinary teachers are discussed. Extraordinary teachers:

1. Have great passion for their work.
2. Know what to teach, how to teach, and how to improve.
3. Excel at creating exciting classroom environments.
4. Connect exceptionally well with students.
5. Challenge students to reach their full potential.
6. Get extraordinary results using a variety of skills.

Dr. Stephenson goes on to mention the applicability of the six characteristics, no matter at what level one is teaching. New faculty members may want to obtain the book as it makes for excellent reading. The papers are all extremely inspiring. The goal for faculty members at the Huizenga School is to be, and keep on becoming, extraordinary teachers. We want our students to say that "my professor had great passion for the subject area, knows how to teach, created an exciting environment where I wanted to learn and participate, connected my experience to the learning objectives of the session/course, challenged me to stretch and learn beyond my known abilities, and assisted me in achieving extraordinary outcomes." Michael Jordan, the extraordinarily successful basketball star, said "You have to expect things of yourself before you can do them." The same can be applied to our own teaching styles and expectations as we assess our current performance in the class and expect higher levels of success with students in achieving the stated learning outcomes by becoming an extraordinary teacher. One characteristic of extraordinary faculty members is that they treat students with respect and dignity as if the students were the "biggest stars on earth" while expecting them to perform with excellence in everything they do.

Extraordinary faculty members should involve their students, to the extent possible based on their individual learning styles, in order for learning to be long-term and memorable for adult students.

The vision statement at Huizenga School states that we need to become a "...*world leader...using personal relationships and leading-edge technology to provide superior educational value for students...*" so, we can "*...provide superior educational value to students...*" by showing a positive attitude toward them and by treating them as mature adults as one would do with honored (and mature) guests and family members. Thus, faculty members can welcome students to the class, call them by their names during the sessions, take care of their individual learning needs (academically and connecting with them based on real-world experience), thank them for participating in the classes and submitting quality assignments on time, and by inviting them to (and encouraging them to) continue using their knowledge both academically and practically. Faculty members should remember that a person who has the knowledge to do something, but chooses not to use this knowledge, may not be much better than a person who does not have the knowledge. Knowledge is not power (nor useful) without application and results.

Distance Education Online

One of the modes used to facilitate distance education is online teaching/learning. Nova Southeastern University, for instance, offers a compulsory online course in Management Information Systems, which must be successfully completed to graduate from the graduate business programs. This type of online course requires the student to attend classes online, access resource materials online using electronic libraries, facilitate all student-teacher interactions online, and take exams online. Other universities may facilitate or require some *traditional* type of online learning, whereby the Internet is a required source for references to be used in research assignments. Some universities also engage in a somewhat *transitional* approach to online interaction (via email) between teachers and students. Assignments and exams may be sent by email and "feedback" on performance may also be provided by email.

With the current trends towards distance education, the need for flexible class schedules for both students and lecturers, and the astounding advancements in technology, there can be no doubt that online teaching will continue to become more popular. Eventually, most if not all schools will be forced to facilitate some form of online teaching. Therefore, teachers who want to remain relevant should acquaint themselves with at least the basics of online teaching. Faculty members wishing to teach online must become online students first and learn the pedagogy of online education along with the school's electronic platform. The immersion model of training, discussed earlier, has been used to train corporate trainers and to develop faculty members in distance education. Its' practical application, successes, challenges, and best practices should be comprehensively explored, presented and discussed in the development process. Some suggestions offered for online faculty members that complete the orientation process are:

- Learn and understand the mechanics of the online environment.
- Collect best practices and tips for beginning online faculty members to be effective in the initial online experience.
- Discover what learning strategies work best for teaching, understanding and learning the course material.
- Know how to best engage students, keep them interested and on track to achieve course and curriculum learning outcomes.
- Learn how to best manage your time to adequately show presence on the discussion board. The number of times faculty members should log on per day/week should be decided based upon learning outcomes.
- Find out how to best manage discussion threads with large quantities of comments.

Furthermore, understanding and clarifying the following areas in distance learning are crucial elements of faculty development process:

- Hybrid Style of Teaching Courses (Online & On-ground)
- Online Course Size Management
- Weekly Lectures and Activities—Intellectual Property Concerns
- Syllabus & Assignments for Discipline
- Asynchronous Interaction and Participation
- Weekly Assessment of Learning and Feedback
- Online Exams, Evaluations, and Final Grades—No Surprises!

Each program office at the Huizenga School should provide their specific rules and policies to faculty members before they begin teaching. This can be best done during the orientation program or through follow up sessions in order to best develop or prepare faculty members that can achieve extraordinary results using cyberspace technology in any modality of education.

SUGGESTIONS FOR LONG-TERM SUCCESS

While successful completion of the immersion model of faculty training and orientation is necessary for newly hired part-time faculty members, faculty members wishing to teach online need to also go through an extensive technical training for the WebCT platform through the Innovation Zone (I-Zone) or Huizenga School's designated personnel. They need to shadow a class (preferably) in their area of teaching with the mentor or an experienced online faculty member.

The following are some general recommendations for Program Directors of various centers and/or large schools that wish to duplicate this Faculty Training and Orientation process in their departments:

1. Create an experienced committee made up of faculty, staff and administrators to design, prepare and implement the faculty training and orientation program. The leaders and senior faculty members must continuously support and feed the program. Not many things can exist productively for very long without periodic quality nourishments. So, the leaders have to "plant the seed," provide sufficient nourishments for it, and then watch it grow.

2. One of the first things that must be done by the committee and faculty members is to create a complete list of course profiles and qualification requirements for all courses in the program. Then, educate everyone on how this document can be used to recruit the right persons for teaching the courses. As such, the faculty coordinators and program managers must be thoroughly educated in the process so they can be empowered to use and improve it.

3. Clarify and communicate the program's vision, expectations and orientation process to all faculty members and administrative staff so they can both support and promote it.

4. Schedule at least one faculty assessment and orientation session each quarter, or as needed, so the new faculty members can be indoctrinated to the school's culture on a just-in-time basis for teaching in the upcoming semesters (as per the school or college's needs).

5. Once the sessions are scheduled, each program should review their projected (or actual) enrollment for the coming few terms to assess their faculty hiring needs. Then they can select resumes for interviewing.

6. Interview qualified candidates and invite those who match your needs to the assessment session.

7. Conduct the assessment and orientation session for all newly hired faculty members.

8. Once the candidate's hiring paperwork and orientation session are successfully completed then schedule a course for this faculty in the coming term and assign a mentor to work with this person.

9. Follow up to make sure the person is ready to teach his/her first course. Offer any assistance that the candidate or the mentor needs.

10. Once the newly hired faculty member's class is over, speak with the mentor and the newly hired faculty to assess the success of the new faculty.

11. All faculty members should be given "feedback" on their performance on a regular basis. It might be best to implement a formal and standardized program where each faculty goes through a peer review process annually. Corporate and government employees often receive a formal appraisal each year and the same should be true of academics as everyone can use quality "feedback" to set goals and improve their performance.

12. Learn from the experience, improve the orientation program and continue this process each term or year as needed.

It is also important to mention that an effective faculty training and orientation program qualitatively involves relevant staff, faculty, advisors, administrators, and students. Furthermore, the success of this process requires commitment and resources to effectively compensate mentors and lead faculty members for developing newly hired educators. As part of service requirement to the university, it might be fair to expect full-time faculty members who are not involved on other committees to mentor two new individuals each year. When mentoring more than two mentees in a given year, full-time faculty members should be compensated fairly or given some sort of a reduction in teaching load as appropriate. It is important to note that mentoring requires work and its long-term success depends on appropriate rewards and recognitions for all relevant parties. When resources are available, and to fairly reward each person's commitment, it is recommended that new faculty members should be given a stipend of $500 for successfully going through the assessment and orientation process. This stipend should be paid, along with the contracted compensation for the course, once the person finishes teaching his or her first course. Furthermore, it is recommended that mentors (lead faculty, full-time faculty or senior part-time faculty members) be compensated a sum of $500 for working with each mentee as they teach their first course at the university. In such a case, when mentors are given a stipend, then they should also be required to physically observe the new faculty in the class for a period of two hours on the first session and then once again for another two hours during the term as appropriate. Each mentor should also complete formal evaluation forms that need to be submitted to the program office for documentation and processing. When the new faculty member is assigned to teach an online class, the mentor should observe and monitor all interactions (in the background without students being aware) while providing regular feedback on the performance of the faculty. Of course, the specific amounts of compensation, reward and recognitions may vary depending on the teaching load or student numbers in each course, compensation for each course, contact hours with students, benefits offered, and other such variables. So, each program should discuss and design strategies that are appropriate for their program and faculty. Furthermore, the program directors should design effective documentation strategies for properly monitoring progress and performance, while continuously improving the process as needed.

The program directors and administrative leaders must also reward and recognize the assistance and contributions of everyone making the process successful. See Appendix N for one formal way of recognizing everyone's contributions to the success of a process. This type of a formal email or letter to recognize everyone's contributions can provide feedback (information) to everyone, appreciate everyone's contributions, encourage others to become a part of the process, and provide a document that faculty members can proudly attach to their portfolios as part of their service to the university during annual reviews or when seeking rank promotion. Of course, this is just one very sincere and inexpensive way of recognizing everyone's contributions when sufficient resources for tangible rewards cannot be secured or don't exist. Other means of rewarding everyone for their contributions can include taking them and their significant others to a dinner, a play, or a theme park for a day or two as per their preference. Sometimes, the entire team along with one or two family members can be taken to places like Disney World, Epcot Center, Universal Studios, or Busch Gardens where everyone can enjoy the day with each other because of their hard work and synergy as a team. The author used to take such trips with the entire team and/or departments when he worked in the corporate arena and this can be a great way of further developing groups and creating loyalty, while increasing the probability of effective communication among diverse team members and groups.

SUMMARY

Global trends towards the removal of cultural, geographic, social, and economic boundaries are providing endless options and opportunities to individuals worldwide. The field of academia is fast catching up in this regard. Various forms of distance education, including the phenomenon of the virtual classroom, are now being explored and developed. New challenges are presented by these developments, both for educational institutions and their various stakeholders.

Distance education provides one opportunity for institutions to compete effectively in the global marketplace. However, structured training and orientation approaches must be developed and maintained in order to achieve success. Participants in this new era of distance education have many factors to consider including cross cultural challenges; the availability of the various infrastructural support systems; and the hiring, training and development, compensating, and retaining of the human resources (i.e.

faculty members) needed to facilitate this development. Additionally, the needs of students, as well as the organizations that will be "purchasing" faculty skills, must be considered. Advances in technology have to be monitored and incorporated into the education system in order that universities remain relevant and continue to produce graduates that can fit into a corporate world which is characterized by fierce competition, disappearing global boundaries, and information technology. Accordingly, this section presented an immersion model for faculty training and orientation that can prepare new faculty members for successfully facilitating the learning objectives of each course and curriculum in the program.

CHAPTER 4

BECOMING A WORLD-CLASS FACILITATOR OF LEARNING SESSIONS

T here are many keys to becoming an outstanding facilitator of learning. The focus of this chapter is to synthesize the most important means of creating and conducting effective learning events. A requisite for any successful training facilitation is love of the job. That cornerstone is covered, followed by the authors' ideas about three key aspects of the facilitation of learning: design, set-up, and delivery.

It is possible to build your skills as a world-class facilitator to meet the current universal challenge to improve everyone's knowledge and skills (Preziosi and Preziosi, 2001). As skills build, so do credibility and reputation. Learners will seek you out and look forward to sessions with you. In this section we share some key building blocks from our experience of training and consulting with learners at all levels of business and government agencies around the world. Portions of the material on the next few pages have been adapted from Preziosi and Preziosi (2001), and the full version of their article titled "How to be a World Class Facilitator of Learning" can be viewed in the *Training Annual* published by Jossey-Bass (2001).

Adult Education in Academia, pages 81–103
Copyright © 2006 by Information Age Publishing
81

LOVE THE JOB

To be really effective and ultimately successful in a job-no matter what it is-a real love for the work is a strong propeller. To be an educator of adults, you must love what you are doing. The nature of our work is to help others be successful. If we do not love the work, our help and facilitation will not seem sincere and the outcomes will not be fruitful for the learners. The love for your work must be clearly telegraphed in everything you do, inside and outside of the classroom. "Love Your Job" is thus the cornerstone for anyone wanting to be a superior facilitator of learning.

Loving your job, however, is just the jumping-off point. In order to be an effective facilitator, you must pay careful attention to three aspects of training design: design, set-up, and delivery, all of which are covered in the following sections.

DESIGN THE IDEAL LEARNING MOMENTS

First, you must *be aware of learners' motivations and needs.* People come to a learning situation for a variety of reasons. Some come because their boss directs them, some come because of their own achievement orientation, and others come for a host of other reasons. We as facilitators of learning must find out *why* they are there and what they expect to gain. We must be careful not to project our own needs on the learning population, but must focus on what learners require from the learning environment to be successful.

Second, *be aware of learning styles.* We want, of course, to teach in a way that is most comfortable for us. However, the focus should be on the learners and their preferences. Some people learn best when they hear (auditory learners), some when they see (visual learners), and some when they do (active learners). As a matter of fact, most adults probably learn better when they see *and* do. Several learning style instruments are available for determining learners' styles, including the Learning Style Inventory (Kolb, 1985), which identifies four learning styles.

Third, *consider the learners 'stages of life development.* All of us are probably familiar with the stages of human development that we have studied or heard about. In her popular book, *New Passages,* Gail Sheehy (1995) reminded us again that adults go through developmental stages also. Sheehy also said that adults have different needs at different stages. We as trainers have to be sensitive to developmental stages. Another resource for understanding developmental stages and their impact on adult teaching and learning processes is Keegan (1982). Become a student of your own and your participants' developmental needs. Ask the learners to complete a questionnaire prior to your session so you can discover their needs.

Fourth, *consider differences in values.* Design for differences. People have different value systems, the result being that they frame educational experiences in different ways. Be familiar with and comfortable with this process, whether it is conceptual or abstract, hands-on or theoretical. Help learners understand their own values with regard to the topic. Drive home the point that there often is more than one way to approach and/or analyze any situation and the people involved. There may be more than one valid perspective. We as facilitators also have to be comfortable with multiple value systems.

Fifth, *use learners' past experiences.* When you introduce a new concept, a new behavior, or a new skill, anchor it to something learners know. This gives the learners a frame of reference, without which it will take much longer for them to learn. The key is to identify a generic experience or bit of knowledge that learners can relate to their own past experiences. These may not always touch every learner, so provide other experiences, examples, or pieces of knowledge to help those who cannot relate to the first one. Whatever program you are doing, whatever kind of session, the content and material must be tied to past experiences. Adult learners must have a starting place.

Sixth, *plan meaningful activities.* As we clearly know, the adult learner must be *engaged* in order to learn. The activities used in the learning event must be relevant for the audience. Each audience has different characteristics. For example, a group of thirty-year-olds has a different perspective from a group of twenty-year-olds; a group of executives has a different context than a group of twenty-year-olds; and a group of supervisors or a group of front-line employees. Learners must be able to relate to and learn from our examples and activities.

Seventh, *make training immediately applicable.* Make sure that whatever you teach can be integrated into learners' jobs or into their lives. Show how learners can immediately use what is being presented. "Immediate" can mean different things, but we interpret it to mean that learners will be able to *use a* concept, a skill, or a behavior as soon as the session ends. *Immediate applicability* creates added value and makes your participants more receptive. For example, if you are training learners to use a new software package, its use in the workplace should be imminent. Otherwise, the new knowledge or skill may be forgotten and the training will have to be repeated.

When learners leave the training room, they must take something that they are capable of integrating into their activities. It is a mistake to assume that their active participation in the learning event means that they will use the learning on the job as intended. How can you tell? You developed, you designed, you delivered, but how do you know that learners are able to integrate the learning afterward? You can help ensure after-class application by asking probing questions of the participants, asking them how they will use the knowledge gained. You can use "applied learning forms," a one-page tool that requires learners to commit to actions they will take after they leave the learning session. (An example is shown in Figure 1.) When learners return for another learning event, it is very important for them to discuss how they integrated their previous learning into their work or into their personal lives.

Last, *take advantage of visual learning.* People can learn a lot from what they see, even if they are not visual learners, so visuals are very important. We know that adults remember best what they see or hear first and what they have seen or heard most recently. Thus, the material presented in the middle of your program is less likely to be remembered. At the midpoint we as trainers should be more involved with the participants and have them become more involved with each other. The more visuals-overhead projection, flip charts, etc.-during the training, the better chance of participants retaining the content.

SET-UP FOR SUCCESS

A Comfortable Learning Environment. Some learning experts have suggested that unless the environment is comfortable, people will not learn anything. We strongly agree. It can be relatively easy to create a comfortable physical environment; however, trainers do not always do the things necessary to ensure that participants are comfortable. For example, we have known for at least twenty-five years that incandescent lighting is better in a classroom or training room than fluorescent lighting. However, to conserve energy we more frequently use fluorescent lighting. We sometimes find that the seating is not appropriate. The chairs may be so uncomfortable that no one can sit in them for more than five or ten minutes. Often there are barriers that we cannot overcome because our client organization has limits. But we must do everything that we can to make the setting physically comfortable for our participants.

A High-Impact Beginning. The first few minutes of interaction set the tone for the entire session. A high-impact start includes a touch of humor, some eye-opening data, a brief and focused statement of the expected outcome(s), complete attention to each person's introduction, use of everyone's name, a twenty-second (or less) answer to any question, positive eye contact, and a friendly but firm interactive style (Preziosi, 1994). If an icebreaker is used, it should tie in directly to the expected outcome(s) of the session (Preziosi, 1999). Avoid devaluing the session by apologizing or making excuses for the unimportant things.

Energy and Interaction. Keep yourself energized physically, mentally, and emotionally. Your participants will likely follow your lead and feel more energized themselves. Solid interaction is the result of your warm, friendly interactive style from the first contact with your participants. Even a welcoming statement on the overhead or flip chart generates interactivity. Make it easy for participants to interact by using nametags.

Starting on time is energizing because your participants' energy is rising toward the published start time, and that energy will only dissipate when it is not put to use.

A very important, but often overlooked, concern is the refreshments or meals that are provided. Foods that keep energy high in the morning are coffees, teas, juices, and fruit, not bagels, muffins, or doughnuts! At the noon hour provide chicken, salads, vegetables, and clear soups. Fish is great, but some do not care for it. Be sure to avoid turkey, beef, heavy starch, and anything fried. If you provide dessert or snacks, fruit or a small amount of something made of chocolate works well.

Transfer of Learning. What good is the time spent with you in the training if the learning is not used later? There is tremendous opportunity to impact the business through your training programs if you work hard to ensure transfer of learning.

Your first task is to meet with your learners' supervisors to discuss their expectations of the learning and to set forth some tasks for them. These would include such things as a supervisor-learner pre-training conference to reinforce the value of the training program and a supervisor-learner post-training conference to discuss what the participants learned and how it will be applied on the job. You would also discuss with the supervisor ways to incorporate the learning applications from the training into the performance management and appraisal processes.

Throughout the training, ask learners how they will apply their learning. Include small-group discussions with reporting out as part of your learning design. And, of course, use applied learning forms.

Job aids and other learning tools can be valuable for learning transfer. Online job aids can also be tremendously useful. For example, use an e-mail attachment to send a brainstormed list or other products from a learning session to an entire training group. You could also provide your participants with audiotapes of the session or of other relevant information.

Fun. Everyone likes to have fun. Games provide a wonderful opportunity. You can create greater learning success by integrating games into your session (Salopek, 1999; Sugar, 1998). They are also energizing. However, before using games, be sure your corporate culture is accepting of the idea.

People also enjoy music. You can use it in a variety of ways. One of the most popular is using classical music for "concert (content) review." We have also found it useful for "concert preview." Energizing music is useful when participants are returning from a break. You can also find great music to inject into specific training content. For example, one of the authors used segments of "The Best" by Tina Turner, "One Moment in Time" by Whitney Houston, and "Wind Beneath My Wings" by Bette Midler during a program on self-esteem for nurses.[1]

Finally, there are props and toys. Here you can be very creative. One of the authors currently uses small stuffed animals in discussion of certain leadership practices. Another idea is to use a full-size plastic bowling pin to emphasize the importance of hitting targets during a class on performance management. Visit stores that sell toys and/or party supplies. Wander around the store, letting your mind replay your instructional design as you look at things and ask yourself: "How can I use this to make or reinforce a learning point?"

DELIVER WITH IMPACT

Meet Expectations—Theirs and Yours. Any time a trainer introduces a new program, it is essential to establish learning expectations. What do you want your learners to do? Do you want them to be involved a great deal in the classroom activities, or do you want them merely to sit quietly and listen to you? In ninety-nine cases out of one hundred, passive yet attentive listening will not suffice for adult learners. It is necessary for the participants to be involved in the learning experience. We want participants to have a positive frame of mind-to be told that this will be a positive learning opportunity for them. In contrast, we would never tell them: "This is going to be difficult," "It's a tough course," "It'll be a tough three days," or anything like that. We want to begin on a positive, upbeat note. This increases the probability of successful learning outcomes.

Ask the group what they expect. What do they want you to do? Do they want you to challenge their ideas? Do they want you to guide discussions very specifically? Do they want you to provide specific learning aids or job aids, or do they expect you to just talk and allow them to listen? Find out early what they think and what they want you to do. That will help you integrate their perspective with your perspective. It will help you decide who needs more independence as a learner and who requires more guidance and direction.

"Hands-On" Learning. In everything you say and do, emphasize that learning application is hands-on. Without that strategy, the learning outcomes may be construed as knowledge for knowledge's sake, and the participants may

---

[1] Always be aware of copyright issues when using music and obtain permission prior to your session if necessary.

feel no real responsibility for doing something with what's learned. The participants must know it's going to be "hands-on" learning and that they are expected to do something differently as a result of the learning event. Hands on is often thought to be physical only. But it can be "hearts on" (dealing with affect or attitude) or "heads on" (dealing with cognitive elements).

Nudge Your Learners. We know from learning masters such as Malcolm Knowles (Knowles, Holton, & Swanson, 1998) that adults are self-directed, so approach adult education as a self-directed process. Of course, our experience has shown that not all adults are self-directed learners, even though we may want them to be. Do what you can to nudge adults along, to help adults develop, to help them move from one developmental stage to the next so that they are indeed self-directed learners. After they become self-directed, it is much easier to teach and train them, so determine each person's perspective and work from there.

Create a Positive Environment. Create a supportive environment. People want a trainer who welcomes them, someone who is there with a smile, someone who is pleasant to talk to, who enjoys talking with them. People don't want trainers who frown because they've had an unpleasant experience just before arriving. It is important that you be as positive as you possibly can.

Deliver to and for the Learner. Know what the benefits of the learning are for every person. The adult learner says: "Okay, here I am. What am I going to get out of this? Will I receive a promotion? Will I be in consideration for a promotion? Will I get a raise? Will I become better able to compete in the marketplace? What will I get out of this?" Maybe the answer is as simple as personal satisfaction for completing a learning event. Frame for people what they are going to get out of the training. Some organizations provide financial incentives for those who complete certain training programs. That is wonderful motivation, but it is not available to everyone, so you will have to find other ways. Find other options for helping each person to define what the benefits of a particular program are going to be for him or her. Without knowledge and acceptance of those benefits, a learner attains less valuable outcomes.

Use Summaries. As leaders of the adult learning process, summarize the learning for the participants often. Pull things together for them. This helps to reinforce the learning and enhances the chance that it will be retained. You must have complete and total grasp of the material in order to summarize it well. Summarize as often as possible-the key points, the behavioral parts, the conceptual parts, everything. Learners consistently report that this improves closure and application.

Address Requirements. While in the classroom, individuals have professional needs, personal needs, or a combination of the two, so the material or the content that you are addressing must be related to both. Understandably, it is not always possible to build a relationship of content to current needs for every person publicly in the classroom. You may have to spend time individually with the learner, which can be as important as the public process with the entire group. Working with each individual is essential; it is fundamental. Tying the material in to individual needs adds value to the process.

Use Learners as a Resource. Use the experience of the learners as a resource. Involve them in discussions. Ask them to exchange experiences. Emphasize how important their experiences are to what they have learned, what they are learning, what they will learn. This will give the learning episode much greater impact. Remember, each of us carries around an invisible sign that states, "I am important. Listen to me. Let me tell you about my experiences." New trainers often make the mistake of believing that they must do all the talking. The irony is that the best adult learning environment involves the learners as active contributors to the process. This enhances participants' self-esteem and validates the utility of these experiences.

Control the Classroom. Create and maintain a positive learning environment in the classroom. Control is a part of it. "Control" is not always a negative word. You have to have control. You need to know what is going on in your classrooms. Give some direction, even though you are dealing with many adults who may be totally self-directed. Control the situation so that they form peer learning networks. Maintain control so that you can nudge them along when they need to be nudged along.

Maintain Participants' Self-Esteem. Always protect minority opinions the opinions that are not shared by many people in the classroom. When you have discussions in class and ask for opinions, many people will support one perspective, and a small group will not. It would be very easy to say: "Okay, it's all right. There can be disagreement." In reality, that small group that is not aligned with the larger group may feel a drop in self-esteem, although it may not be apparent. Therefore, it is very important to ensure that everyone's self-esteem is maintained. Protect the minority opinion by protecting their perspective, because nothing is more important in your training room than self-esteem. If training or education is going to be successful, then trainers must do everything in their power to maintain or enhance self-esteem of participants. Esteemed learners are more successful.

Be a Role Model. Be a model of everything that adult learning and organizational training stand for. For example, if you are leading a discussion about the importance of participation and respect for each individual, be a model in that process. Allow for complete and total respect for each of the individuals who are present. Whether the issue is respect or something else, encourage learners to reflect critically on their attitudes, beliefs, and/or behaviors. This will help them confirm or realize a need for change. By being a model, you can challenge individual attitudes, beliefs, and behaviors. People must come to grips with what they see and what they hear, with what they understand and with what they learn. And the best vehicle for that challenge is the trainer's behavior. So challenge learners through your thought patterns and your behavior. Also, model the values and performance that your organizational culture supports. For example, if timeliness is an organizational value, then start and end all sessions on time.

CHARACTERISTICS OF AN EFFECTIVE LEARNING ENVIRONMENT

Assessment is important for learning, improvement and the delivery of an effective learning environment. Through assessment, educators acquire evidence to meet responsibilities to themselves, to students, and to the public. Thanks to McEnerney and Webb, California State University–Dominguez Hills, and to the Teaching in the Active Voice Institute, University of Prince Edward Island, Canada, the following are some characteristics needed for the creation of an inclusive and an effective learning environment:

Effective Facilitation:

1. Focuses on teaching the audience, not just the subject.
2. Has a title or topic statement.
3. Contains a brief review of the main ideas covered in the previous class session and relates the present material to them. May also ask students to summarize the main ideas.
4. Provides a preview of information prior to the explanation.
5. Provides an outline in several formats (*e.g.* visible, audio, handout) so as to engage the different learning styles of students.
6. Engages the attention and interest of the audience, often around a question.
7. Organizes information logically for audience comprehension.
8. Reinforces new or specialized vocabulary and important points in visible as well as audio formats; employs synonyms and descriptors; avoids jargon, slang, and undefined acronyms.
9. Reinforces core information with audiovisual aids; repeats for reinforcement.
10. Gives many concrete examples to illustrate information points.
11. Uses analogies, metaphors, and/or stories frequently so that student can conceptualize concepts in more familiar contexts.

12. Relates information to assigned readings and sites the location where students can find the information.
13. Speaks clearly and loudly enough to be heard comfortably; uses a microphone or sign language interpreter as needed.
14. Stops often within a lecture (*e.g.*, the punctuated lecture) to check for comprehension.
15. Clearly signals topic shifts and transitions by using verbal and non-verbal cues.
16. Clearly signals digressions and indicates how a digression relates (or doesn't relate) to main points.
17. Contains a visual and audio summary of main points at the end.
18. Reserves time for student questions and comments.
19. Respects audience needs by ending on time.
20. Assesses student learning at multiple levels and intervals throughout the semester.
21. Attends to fundamentals of public speaking and adjusts style to make language comprehensible
    - Speaks slowly and enunciates clearly so that all students can hear, understand, and write. Allows adequate pauses (count to twelve) to facilitate the decoding process so that listening becomes active and students can process information and generate questions.
    - Recognizes individual students and makes regular eye contact with them.
    - Modifies pace when audience behavior indicates changing needs.
    - Uses appropriate gestures and facial expressions to emphasize main points.
    - Doesn't let voice trail off at the end of a sentence or idea.
    - Uses transition phrases to link information.
    - Avoids nervous use filler words ("Okay..") and non-words ("Uh... Um...").

Effective Questioning:

1. Asks clearly-worded, focused questions that contain indicators for how to respond.
2. Conveys to students a genuine interest in hearing what they have to say.
3. Allows ample time (count to twelve) for a response before restating, modifying, or moving on.
4. Makes eye contact with individuals and does not ask questions to the back wall, the blackboard, the video screen, or one individual repeatedly.

5. Calls students by name when eliciting responses from specific individuals.

6. Either restates the response or politely asks students to restart inaudible responses so the entire class can hear.

7. Does not remain primarily in one place or engage in repetitive one-on-one questioning.

8. Does not pester or hassle; aims at eliciting information flow and not at embarrassing individuals.

9. Moves around the room so as to engage and retain group interest.

10. Frequently asks a question before naming a respondent in order to encourage all students to listen and decide how they would answer.

11. Does not allow a minority of more confident or impulsive students to dominate.

12. Gives students who do not normally respond a chance to enter the conversation.

13. Is egalitarian in order to capture a diversity of views.

14. Uses a variety of strategies to allow different kinds of learners a chance to answer comfortably: students call out answers, a student is selected to answer, students raise their hands and volunteer to answer.

15. Does not limit more challenging and stimulating questions to students perceived as having higher ability or knowledge.

16. Asks students to justify and further explain responses.

17. Encourages students to answer each others' questions.

18. Allows time to consider different points of view and multiple responses.

19. Does not overtly or covertly invalidate students' responses by unnecessarily changing their wording or meaning.

20. Creates a safe and supportive atmosphere for student questions by answering them immediately and politely.

21. Does not make students feel assailed, threatened, and passive by asking them too many questions.

22. Invites questions as if they are a normal part of the teaching/learning process (*e.g.*, "Now is a good time to hear your questions," instead of "Anybody come with any questions at this point?").

23. Employs multiple formats and Classroom Assessment Techniques for questioning, such as the Unanswered Question and Muddiest Point.

24. Uses "think-pair-share" in which students think of an answer, pair with another student, and discuss their answers before sharing with the entire group.

25. Asks in a voice, tone, and manner that correspond to the accepted principles of public discourse.

Effective Group Work:

1. Creates or selects an activity that lends itself to group processes.
2. Clearly explains the purpose and expected outcome of group activity.
3. Gives clear expectations, and accountability for the activity orally and in writing.
4. Models the task in whole or in part.
5. Breaks group activities into clear, manageable sequences or process.
6. Assigns specific roles for each student, or allows group to assign specific roles.
7. For each role, identifies specific behaviors necessary for completion of the task.
8. Provides locations, times, and resources for group activities and for task completion.
9. Allows an appropriate amount of time to complete the task satisfactorily.
10. Assesses group progress early through Classroom Assessment Techniques or other methods and intervenes appropriately.
11. Takes a facilitative rather than a dominating or disruptive stance while monitoring groups in process.
12. Allows sufficient time after group work to integrate the activity as a unified class.

Effective Assessment: (Modified from Angelo, 1999, and AAHE Assessment Principles)

1. *Assesses what matters most.* Assessment makes a difference when it illuminates questions people really care about.
2. *Focuses on processes as well as outcomes.* Attention is given to main outcomes and also, equally, to the experiences that lead to those outcomes.
3. *Operates at key points in the educational process.* Programs recognize those keys as having visible, clearly defined, explicitly stated purposes.
4. *Uses multiple measures over time.* Assessment works best when it is ongoing, not episodic.
5. *Generates feedback for improving learning.* Assessment of student learning begins with educational values.
6. *Provides feedback and development to those most affected.* Improvement arises more easily when assessment operates in conditions where change is likely.
7. *Actively involves students and members of the teaching staff.* Assessment fosters improvement when it engages the wider educational community.

8. *Is embedded in teaching and learning.* Learning is understood as multi-dimensional, integrated, and revealed through performance over time.

GENERAL GUIDELINES FOR NEW FACULTY

Often, Deans, Program Directors and Program Managers in higher education institutions get a number of calls related to what are coined "classroom management" issues. They include grading but, also faculty deviating from the course objectives and the standard syllabus, starting and ending times, use of textbook, providing students timely and meaningful feedback, turning in grades on time, using inappropriate language or remarks, grade inflation, as well as plagiarism and cheating. This section addresses each of these issues because proper handling of these matters greatly increases our professionalism and reputation in the field.

New faculty members should thoroughly read and enforce the relevant suggested guidelines along with university policies and rules in each of their courses. It is also very important that faculty members keep a complete record of attendance, syllabus for each section of the course, exams used in the course, and feedback provided to students as their course might be audited in the years to come. If your course is audited, then the administration will likely need an electronic version (or hard copy) of the course syllabus (if they don't have it on file), exams and activities used for the course, and a sample of actual outcomes produced by students as a result of the teaching/facilitation. The results from such academic audits may be used for many purposes including but not limited to the following:

- For the assessment of academic standards in the course,
- To assess student learning outcomes and progress along with their consistency across different modalities and locations,
- For accreditation or "major" review,
- To see if there is a relationship between exams and activities used for student assessment and grading patterns,
- For determining faculty training needs,
- To evaluate faculty effectiveness in the classroom, and/or
- Gather best practices that can enhance the overall curriculum.

Academic standards and expectations can be fully enforced if the expectations are clearly documented in the course syllabus and fully explained in the first session. Faculty members should make sure to fully explain their assessment requirements (both orally and verbally) in the course syllabus which must be provided to students in the first session of the course. Course syllabi may be available online and one can provide them for students on the first session of the course in the hard copy format as well. Remember, if specific rules are not in the syllabus that is provided to students in the first session then the faculty may not be able to enforce them since the school may not be able to support it. So, it is best that faculty members include all the specifics (rules, policies, and guidelines) in their syllabus and fully explain their expectations to all students in the first session.

Assessment and Course Objectives

Academicians know that taking the strategic plans for measuring and assessing student achievement, analyzing them for improvement purposes, and implementing the resulting analysis throughout the university can present many challenges for colleges committed to a process improvement philosophy. Universities use a variety of tools that support the model of planning, delivery, assessment, reflection, and continuous improvement of student learning. However, none of the tools can take the place of the faculty member's key role in effective deployment, improvement and documentation of student learning in each session of each course.

Assessment can be seen as the process of establishing and/or understanding the learning outcomes that meet the learners' needs, assessing students to determine whether or not the learners have met the learning outcomes through factual evidence, documenting those results, and reflecting on how to continually improve the process of teaching, learning and learner assessment. The purpose of the assessment process is to continually improve and document or credential learning. A structured review of the assessment model can enhance the assessment process by providing a framework that supports thoughtful planning, communication to relevant stakeholders before and during the learning process, deployment of valid and reliable assessment strategies, informed reflection on the results, as well as improvement of teaching, learning and assessment.

When it comes to personal reflections for improvement, faculty members and trainers tend to have three formats for facilitation of learning: one, the facilitation they plan to do; two, the facilitation they actually do; and, three, the facilitation they wish they had done. This type of reflection can certainly lead to improvement when the third format is put back into the loop thereby improving the next facilitation they plan to do. This closes the loop and improves the learning process for the students. It has been said that some universities have three undergraduate curricula: The one that appears in the catalog, the one that professors teach, and the one that students actually learn. It is the faculty member's moral imperative to find out the degree to which the curriculum asserted on paper or imagined by academic leaders accurately portrays what goes on in the minds of students.

Making the curricula visible so their usefulness in terms of demonstrated learning and results through students can be documented as evidence is the business of *assessment*, an activity practiced by each faculty teaching the course.

So, as faculty, it is your responsibility to make sure students learn the stated course objectives and learning outcomes. It is also each faculty member's responsibility to assess student learning, provide timely feedback to students for improvement purposes and to be able to demonstrate or provide evidence of student learning for those who successfully complete the course. Most schools try to accommodate a certain amount of academic freedom in the facilitation of learning objectives; however, every deviation from the syllabus and its learning objective should be evaluated in terms of meeting the stated course objectives and academic performance of the students once they complete the program. All successful students are expected to achieve the stated objectives and/or exit competencies regardless of location or delivery modality. New competencies gained as a result of academic freedom cannot be substituted for those stated competencies described in the course outline/syllabus. All exit competencies and outcomes must remain the same as per the standard syllabi.

Class Contact Hours

Faculty members must dress professionally when teaching classes at the campus and/or national and international clusters. All academic interactions and discussions related to school must be conducted professionally between faculty members, local community members, students and local administrators.

Faculty members should not and cannot miss classes or have others teach the class for them without prior approval of their Program Director/Dean. Also, guest speakers should be approved by the Program Director or Associate Dean for Academic Affairs prior to attendance and they should be limited to being a guest speaker since they cannot be replacements for the faculty. Each school or college may have specific rules related to this and these thoughts are just one perspective. Because many of the distance education courses for adults are offered through an accelerated program, faculty members must use all contact hours productively. So, faculty members should make sure students are productively involved with them in the class during ALL the required/scheduled class period. Classes should not be dismissed earlier than scheduled; so, it is important that faculty members come prepared to share additional material with the class for the entire period, including the last session. It is better to prepare too much and not use it than to not have enough material or activities for the entire length of time that the class is scheduled.

Course Textbooks

Sometimes, publishers are out of the books temporarily or the bookstore might be behind in shipping textbooks to students. If this is the case, faculty can go forward with their lectures, activities, and assignments as planned; however, they could be flexible not to punish those who could not get the books because of the university's or publisher's delays. Faculty can encourage students to check out similar books from the local library on the topic so they can study while the books are coming to them. If educators notice that such delays are caused by the system and not the students then they exercise good judgment in communicating with these students and work with those students who may have been impacted by such system-related delays. Perhaps, one can allow these students to complete the work and assignments by the next session, if and when appropriate.

Often times, phone calls are received by administrators regarding the issue of textbooks. Students pay about $50–$100+ per textbook for each course and would like to see these books be used in the classes. So, make effective use of these textbooks in each session—this does not mean that faculty members should read verbatim from the book as that would be extremely boring and not very effective. Remember that faculty members are required to use the textbook stated in the syllabus, and there are no exceptions in most adult education programs. A process exists for recommending textbook changes, beginning with sending those recommendations to the Director and/or Lead Faculty for consideration of new material into future courses. Otherwise, all courses taught are likely to require and use the same textbook as stated in the syllabi, as prepared by the University/ Lead Faculty Member.

Participation and Attendance

An official course roster can be used (often times downloaded through the online account provided by the institution or the school) to take attendance at the beginning of each session. It is good to require students to stay in the class for all the required hours by productively involving them in the interaction and awarding participation points to those who bring value-added information to the course/session objectives. Students who come in late to class or leave the session early should not be awarded any participation points. Partial class attendance should not be given any credit toward participation points, unless a faculty sends the student home because s/he is ill. As a general rule of thumb, one suggestion is to distribute about 10% of the course grade toward participation points for all on-ground sessions. It is critical to state personal policies with regard to participation points clearly in the syllabus and consistently enforce them for ALL students.

Faculty members should make it clear to students in the first session that they will not accept any assignments after the last class/session. Do not extend assignment due dates beyond the last session. Not submitting grades within the required time period may delay payments, registration and it may also create difficulty for students' financial aid status, thereby preventing them from receiving reimbursement and/or continuing their next course.

Plagiarism

Most universities will not compromise on this issue and any student caught plagiarizing or cheating will face severe consequences, up to dismissal. As part of classroom management, faculty members need to address this issue during the first session of class with strong words related to student conduct. Strongly recommend that students consult the school's recommended writing book/style, the catalog, the school's writing lab/literature, and the APA (American Psychological Association) web site for information related to citations and references. In addition, exams should be proctored to reduce and/or eliminate the potential for cheating. Guard exams so they do not get out into the student population; and don't forget to change exam content and/or style frequently. The use of alternate versions of exams can be an effective method of guarding against cheating in crowded classrooms. Should a faculty be confronted with the problem of cheating use every professional means to deal with the problem and never make accusations about, or to, a student in front of other students. If one suspects a problem during an exam, then the faculty can confidentially ask the student by use of a note, that he/she would like to see him/her outside the classroom for a moment.

On matters of papers being copied, recycled, or prepared beyond the academic ability of the student, please use your judgment in terms of what needs to be done and/or call the Program Director for more information. If you wonder about proper referencing techniques, simply ask the student to submit the reference materials used in the paper. These reference materials should be received prior to your issuing a grade for the paper. Scheduling the term project to be due at week 7 (one week before last session) or earlier allows time for a re-submission of reference materials. Students should include their telephone or email contact information along with their paper so that the instructor can call or email if there is a problem with the paper. Down-grading a plagiarized paper is not acceptable. Plagiarized papers are worth zero points and possible referral for academic dishonesty. If you judge that the plagiarism is unintentional, then the paper must be corrected before a grade can be issued. After all is said and done, all we have is our integrity and commitment to quality education. If this is compromised, the university will eventually be doomed. Please help the education institutions do all they can to make sure *all* students earn their grades.

As a supplement (in later chapters), there is extra content regarding academic misconduct, plagiarism and some helpful links for the faculty's consideration. In addition, we have included a list of websites where faculty members can check papers for possible plagiarism. Many other new websites become available all the time that might be of some use to your course content. Look for them online or ask your school administrators to see if they have an account with any of the websites. Some are free while others cost a small fee. *Hint:* Use the free links. It is often a helpful plagiarism deterrent to require students to submit an electronic version of their papers along with the hard copy so that you *could* use these websites.

Providing Feedback

Most courses have some type of an assignment due on a weekly basis. We encourage a variety of learning modalities and testing methods; thereby eliminating the option of having three exams for a course and nothing else. Students learn differently and we must incorporate a good diversity of assessing their skills through written assignments, tests, activities, group work, presentations, projects, etc. Each course must have exams and assessments that are objective and application oriented. Make every effort to grade papers and *provide feedback by the next class meeting or as early as possible in the course.* In most accelerated courses with 32 contact hours, students should submit an assignment by the second week/session (if not earlier) and receive quality feedback with a grade by the third session/week. It is difficult to defend against a grade dispute if the student never received any meaningful feedback on the assignments in a timely manner. Most students may not want to see their final project or exam unless their grade is less than an "A" or if they can get some helpful comments to make it stronger. Nonetheless, it is best to proactively provide them clear and succinct feedback, even on the last assignment. Furthermore, it is your responsibility to provide that feedback on a timely basis if and when the student requests it.

Some faculty members do not want to return the exam to the student because they wish to re-use the exam questions at a later date. We respect this practice, and ask that you communicate the results to the student in a way that does not compromise your need to re-use the exam. Most students do understand this practice and as long as a reasonable attempt is made at communicating how the student did and why they got certain problems wrong, the students generally will feel their questions and concerns have been addressed.

Let students know whether and how you are going to send final feedback to them with sufficient and clear content on how they did. Students need to get feedback from you with regard to their final assignments/exam and possible suggestions. Please make sure that you send (email) appropriate feedback in a confidential manner to the student. This is to insure that no one violates FERPA (Family Education Rights and Privacy Act) directives. *Feedback must remain confidential.*

If faculty members are unable to adhere to these guidelines by providing feedback to students in a timely manner due to other responsibilities, then please do not accept the course for that specific semester so another faculty can be assigned. The same is true, in terms of responsive and timely feedback, for all modes of course delivery. Online faculty members are to be involved in class interactions each week (four-five days each week) and respond to questions within 48 hours.

Grading Fairly

Quality grading requires each faculty member to be academically honest with the student. Many of our students enter the program with less than a 3.0 GPA. Although adult students tend to put more effort in their education, all of them may not be "A" or "B" students and grading should reflect the true variation in abilities that exist among students. Allowing additional work to substitute for demonstrated knowledge is a poor practice by many (and should be reserved only for extenuating circumstance), as is group grading (beyond the pre-determined group assignments which should not exceed 20–30% of the overall course grade.) When applicable, it might be appropriate to make team/group assignments on the average about *20–30% percent of the final grade.*

In order to avoid grade inflation and meet the university's guidelines, closely read the following sections and the university's policies. Higher education institutions appreciate your cooperation, immediate and appropriate proactive actions to prevent such issues from happening, and assistance in this important matter.

The highest purpose served by the grading system, as often stated by researchers in the academia, is that of making distinctions, distinctions between excellence and competence, various levels of competency and understanding, and between competence and incompetence. In order to help eliminate grade inflation in our American higher education system and meet the university's guidelines, here are some suggestions:

1. Tighten up the requirements in your course, both the general educational expectations and the quality of students' performance.
2. Radically revise your existing system of students' oral and written project/assignment evaluations so that any evaluation focuses exclusively on the academic quality, academic seriousness, academic literature, use of strong and credible references, and practical application to the workplace.
3. On the first session of your course, explain to students that "A" grades are reserved for great performance that meets the level as articulated in your syllabus.
4. Dispense academic honors to only the very top students; those who achieve the standards of an "A" as expected by you and/or the university.
5. Continue to show you care for your students by taking a critical eye to their work. Tell them that you will conduct the course and grade so as to provide them with the opportunity to grow and become as quickly as possible graduates who can make a difference through great leadership and quality output.
6. Do not drop or throw out exam questions that only one or two students answer correctly. These questions help to differentiate excellent students from very good students.
7. Do not curve midterm or early assignment grades. This leads to student expectations that they will not have to work harder to achieve good marks. Students should receive what they earn.

Hopefully, these suggestions are helpful as you try to meet your own and the university's high expectations. Meeting these expectations is critical in order for our department to continue to be successful which will enable our adjunct faculty members to continue receiving teaching assignments. The department will uphold grade appeals and give you our full support regarding the assignment of grades as long as you are fair and consistent with all students. All we ask is that you are fair, impartial, and have supporting documentation that can be provided to students for their growth in the next course. Remember, it is your responsibility to grade performance and not necessarily effort. This will prepare us, and the next faculty member, to raise the standards in order for students to be challenged in their educational journey. Use concisely-written grading criteria that are stated in your course syllabus, to differentiate among students' performance. Here is one example that has been used in grading.

- **A** = *Clearly stands out as an excellent performer.* Has unusually sharp insight into material and initiates thoughtful questions. Sees many sides of an issue. Articulates well and writes logically and clearly. Integrates ideas previously learned from this and other disciplines; anticipates next steps in progression of ideas. Example: "A" work should be of such a nature that it could be put on reserve for all students to review and emulate. The "A" student is, in fact, an example for others to follow.
- **B** = *Grasps subject matter at a level considered to be good to very good.* Participates actively in class discussion. Writes well. In on-ground environments, speaks well. Accomplishes more than the minimum requirements. Produces high quality work. Example: "B" work indicates a high quality of performance and is given in recognition for solid work; a "B" should be considered a high grade.
- **C** = *Demonstrates a satisfactory (or below average) comprehension of the subject matter.* Accomplishes only the minimum requirements, and displays little or no initiative. Communicates orally (on-ground environments) and in writing at an acceptable level for a college student. Has an acceptable understanding of all basic concepts. Example: "C" work represents average work. A student receiving a "C" has met the requirements, including deadlines, of the course.
- **F** = *Quality and quantity of work is unacceptable.* Academic credit is not earned for an F. Example: "F" work does not qualify the student to progress to a more advanced level of course work.

SUMMARY

There are many opinions about what can make the difference in design, setup, and delivery of a learning event. If you have a love for your job as a facilitator of learning, you can adopt these tips to help your learners achieve relevant, vibrant, long-lasting learning.

SAMPLE APPLIED LEARNING FORM

Reinforced Learning

The most valuable things I was reminded of during today's class session were:
  A.

  B.

  C.

New Learning

The most valuable new concept(s), techniques(s) or strategy(ies) that I learned about during today's class session were:
  A.

  B.

  C.

Applied Learning

I will apply one new concept, technique, or strategy at work to add value in the following way:

Learning Need

Something I would like to learn more about after today's class session that would add more value at work is:

Learning Plan (What, from Whom, Where, When)

I will learn more about the above by:
  A.

  B.

  C.

CHAPTER 5

SUGGESTIONS FOR EFFECTIVE TEACHING

In a recovering and developing economy filled with undesirable surprises, lack of effective security and much uncertainty, being an effective government or business leader means being a good teacher and thus an effective communicator. But how would one lead and teach simultaneously? Who are a leader's students and how can one best meet their demands more effectively and most efficiently?

This section, and many of the suggestions that are prepared through physical meetings with business faculty members at Nova Southeastern University, explores some of the answers to the aforementioned questions in the context of adult education, and it further discusses the role of leaders in effectively facilitating learning to adults. Then, it offers practical suggestions for current and first time educators of higher education.

BUILDING SMART TEACHING TECHNIQUES

It is known that many government and business leaders have a selection of their favorite well-worn books that relate to their profession or content area that they go back to occasionally for inspiration or ideas as they facilitate the finer points of discussions with employees, students and/or their followers. One of the books on the first author's shelf in the corporate environ-

Adult Education in Academia, pages 105–121

ment used to be that time-honored favorite "The One-Minute Manager" by Ken Blanchard and Spencer Johnson (1983). While flipping through it back in the late 80s, the first author came across the point that managers should catch their people "doing something right" and praising them for the specific behaviors in one minute. Educators, unlike most government and business employees, probably receive the least amount of praise or feedback from their superiors. As such, it becomes their responsibility to continually learn new facilitation skills and obtain feedback for continuous improvement. This section explores and offers practical suggestions for leaders, managers, teachers, and trainers who are all educators either directly or indirectly as they assist, guide and coach people's development.

It is important to provide a quality learning experience to students, employees and one's colleagues. If necessary, one should also let them know of the materials and resources available regarding current best practices and training and development opportunities so they can continue to develop their skills. George Bernard Shaw coined the famous maxim, "He who can, does; he who cannot, teaches." Well, he was wrong because today's leaders and managers teach and perform various tasks very successfully. In a fast-moving economy that is driven by new ideas, an essential part of being a leader is being a good educator or facilitator of learning experiences. Teachers and leaders alike need similar skills regardless of whether they are teaching the concepts to traditional students, adult students, working adult students, or simply to adults in the workplace. For example, managers often need to effectively persuade employees, colleagues, peers, and bosses in an organization in such matters as adopting a new marketing strategy or a new selling technique to become more competitive. They may also need to refocus everyone around a new and more aggressive strategy to survive an economic slump or to move ahead of their competitors in a new market. They also need to effectively communicate so that employees at every level understand the priorities for both short and long term strategies in order for them to become the leaders of tomorrow. All such tasks can be performed effectively by teaching and facilitating the learning experiences. In such cases, teaching and facilitating are different from giving a speech in a companywide meeting or giving orders to a subordinate (Salter, 2001). A speech is not teaching; speeches are top-down information spreading which basically amounts to commanding and dictating. Telling people what to do doesn't guarantee that they will learn enough to mentally develop and think for themselves in the future. Instead, it may mean that they'll depend on the leader or their peers even more and that they will stop taking chances to be competitive. Even worse, they may even stop innovating because of the fear and they may stop learning, unless they are required to do so by their superiors.

So, what do great teachers do that government and business managers should be doing in their roles as leaders? They all have a diverse repertoire of skills that enable them to situationally match their skills with their audience and learning objectives. Salter (2001) states that effective teaching is universal as facilitation skills are to be focused on the audience and not necessarily the presenter. Salter further stated, "Whether the topic is a new-product launch, social studies, or a triple bypass, the same principles—and many of the same techniques—apply." The following are a few of the principles offered by Salter (in the article titled "*Attention, Class! 16 ways to be a smarter teacher*") and other educators (see the 100 suggestions in the last part of the document) that all good teachers and educators must understand and consider as they develop people to their maximum potential.

1. *It's not about the teacher; it's about the audience* (students or employees). The best teachers see themselves as guides, coaches, and facilitators to lead and get learners to think for themselves. They share what they know, but they understand that they are not the focus.
2. *Study and understand the students.* Teachers need to know the people they are teaching—their talents, prior experience and needs. Then adjust the teaching style to their learning preferences and needs while integrating them into the process.
3. *Students take risks when teachers create a safe learning environment.* Get students to acknowledge what they don't know, take risks, and rethink what they thought they knew. That can be an uncomfortable—even scary—situation for anyone.
4. *Great teachers exude passion as well as purpose for each course and session.* The difference between a good teacher and a great one isn't expertise. It comes down to passion. Passion for the material. Passion for teaching.
5. *Students learn best when teachers can show them how much they need to learn.* Be ready to surprise them and stretch their imaginations to new heights.
6. *Keep the lessons or teaching objectives and concepts clear even if you can't keep it simple.* One of the chief attributes of a great teacher is the ability to break down complex ideas and make them understandable.
7. *Practice vulnerability without sacrificing credibility.* To some people, being a teacher or a leader means appearing as though they have all the answers. Such mindsets are more the case in the collectivistic societies such as Japan, Korea and Afghanistan where signs of vulnerability are seen as weakness. Educators or leaders with such a paradigm make the worst teachers because they end up focusing on themselves rather than keeping their eyes and their hearts on the audience or students. Sometimes the best answer a teacher can give

is, "I don't know." Instead of losing credibility, s/he can actually gain students' trust. That trust is the basis of a productive relationship. Acknowledging what a person does not know shows that s/he is still learning, that the teacher is, in fact, still a student.

8. *Teach from the heart and based on personal experiences, likes and thoughts.* Share your successes and your failures as they can all be a learning experience.

9. *Repeat the important points for understanding, reinforcement and long-term retention.* If you want everyone to remember that new vision or strategy, you need to give it to them more than once and discuss its importance. Three times is usually recommended.

10. *Repeat the important points again with a new focus and check on their understanding, views and thoughts.* Make sure they are with you before moving on to new points.

11. *Extraordinary teachers ask good questions to keep everyone involved and thinking for themselves.* Effective teachers understand that learning is about exploring the unknown and that such exploration begins with open ended questions and personal reflection.

12. *Teachers are not just passing out information.* Educators are teaching people how to think and arrive at conclusions. The last thing you want to do is stand up and tell people what to do or give them the answers that you want to hear. The best instructors are less interested in the answers than in the thinking behind them.

13. *Stop lecturing periodically and listen effectively.* When it comes to teaching, what you do is nearly as important as what you say. After all, students are watching your behaviors and actions. Effective learning is a two-way street: It's a dialogue, not a monologue. Learn to listen for important items that help you assess learning and lead students to higher levels of thinking.

14. *Let students teach each other in dyads, triads, and small groups.* You're not the only one your students learn from. They also learn from their peers.

15. *Avoid using the same approach for everyone since students and their learning styles may vary greatly.* Good teachers believe that every student can learn, but they understand that students learn differently. Some students are visual; some grasp the abstract; while others learn best by reading. So the instructor might adopt a multidimensional approach, something along these lines: lecture or facilitate for 10 minutes, then pose a question to the class for the assessment of learning and to involve them. Next, ask everyone to write down an answer to the question and then have people take turns explaining it to someone else in the class.

16. *Never stop teaching as it is the best source of learning.* Effective teaching is about the quality of the relationship between the teacher and the student. It doesn't end when the class or the workday is over. One should remember that effective teachers must be like effective coaches that coach their players before the game, during the game, and after the game for future success. It is a continuous learning process for both the coach and the players.

LEARNING MODES FOR ADULTS

Designing training or a facilitation session is different from designing an organizational learning process. Training will always be needed to help people and their organizations enhance their capacity to create knowledge that produces results. Learning happens through action and by doing. In knowledge generating institutions, the human aspect of knowledge is a necessity. Basically, effective leadership is about tapping the inspiration that exists in the organization because people want to learn more and not necessarily because they need to due to survival. Today's learning institutions are made of diverse learners and effective organizations understand, acknowledge and use such differences to their advantage by equipping faculty members with more information about the learners.

Learners can be categorized in at least one or two of the following four basic sensory modes of learning: Somatic, Auditory, Visual and Intellectual (SAVI). Everyone uses all four modes when learning, but most people tend to have one or two dominant modes. A few people are balanced between differing modes. The four modes are defined as follows:

1. *Somatic:* Learning by doing, moving, getting physically involved, and actively using the body in some way.
2. *Auditory:* Learning by talking, hearing, feeling, and engaging in human interaction.
3. *Visual:* Learning by observing, listening, and picturing.
4. *Intellectual:* Learning by thinking, reflecting, analyzing, and problem solving.

Adult students and facilitators can read the full descriptions of their most dominant mode(s), and they are likely to find themselves in all of the four categories below. But, chances are, they will have a single dominant mode regardless of whether they are a learner or instructor.

Somatic: Learning by Doing

Somatic learners tend toward a practical, hands-on approach to learning. They prefer to be physical while they learn and get things done quickly. Somatic learners are often impatient with lectures, presentations, and computer-based learning programs that give them no opportunity for physical action. "Theory is fine," they feel, "but let's get on with practical applications." When engaged in a phone conversation or listening to a presentation it often helps them stay focused by doodling, manipulating objects with their hands, or moving their bodies in some way. They are direct and to the point and want to do what works. Their orientation is: "Don't make me just sit there, I want to do something!"

Auditory: Learning by Talking and Interacting with Others

Auditory learners are also affective learners. That is, they tend to be sensitive to the feelings and emotions in presentations and learning environments. As such, they tend to be more intuitive than rational. They are simultaneous processors (as opposed to sequential processors). The "feel" of a learning experience is more powerful for them than the "logic" of it. They rely on feelings and hunches rather than rational analysis. They tend to "live in the moment." And, for them, talking and writing is a way of thinking and a necessary adjunct to optimal learning. The more they can talk about what they are learning, the more their learning tends to integrate and stay with them.

Visual: Learning by Observing

Visual learners tend to be astute observers and have the ability to create knowledge for themselves by watching and listening. They like to look before they leap because the looking is the initial learning. Strong visual learners can take their time in observing several sides of a situation before acting. They can think visually and are helped by learning programs that start by giving them something to observe, whether words, pictures, computer screens, or real-world examples. It helps them learn new skills by first observing how something is done before doing it themselves.

Intellectual: Learning by Thinking and Analyzing

Intellectual learners are rational, logical and thoughtful. They tend to want to engage their full intellect while learning. They are sequential processors (as opposed to simultaneous processors) and prefer learning things systematically in a step-by-step manner. If given disjointed learning mate-rial, they must first put it into some logically coherent form. They often enjoy solving problems that test their thinking and are the first to reject playful learning exercises that have no intellectual depth or rational coher-ence. They tend to dislike indecisiveness, and their learning is likely to be driven by reason rather than emotion.

PRACTICAL SUGGESTIONS FOR HIGHER EDUCATION

Over the past decade, there has been a consistent pattern in the requirement for the development of a systematic approach to outcomes assessment and continuous improvement of student learning by the accrediting agencies. Accrediting bodies tend to focus on the inclusion of demonstrated literature on the achievement of learning outcomes and strategic planning to enhance student learning. College educators know that adults need to be more in-volved in the learning process in order for the learning to be effective and used. Learner participation and interaction are critical to effective facilitation techniques that increase learning and retention with adult learners. A major element of being or becoming an effective educator involves understanding how each group of learners learns best and then integrating activities that best suit their learning styles regardless of teaching modality. Dr. W. Edwards Deming has been quoted as saying "Learning is not compulsory. Neither is survival." Adults understand this concept and learn because they want to use the learning to achieve their personal and professional goals. The field of adult learning was pioneered by Malcolm Knowles as he emphasized many characteristics of adult learners. Adults are *autonomous, self-directed, goal-orient-ed, relevancy-oriented, and practical* thereby focusing on the aspects of a lesson most useful to them in their work. Also, adults usually have accumulated a foundation of *life experiences* and *knowledge* that include work-related activities, family responsibilities, and previous education. Furthermore, as do all learn-ers, adults need to be shown *respect*. The implications of this for teaching are very clear in the discussion of specific behaviors for set-up, design and deliv-ery (Preziosi and Preziosi, 2001).

Learning institutions tend to generate knowledge by empowering their employees to become continuous adult learners rather than being passive doers based on what they know from their certification or degree upon hir-ing. There are many significant changes happening in business education both nationally and internationally. Such changes will have a profound im-pact on education, training, human resources, and in all areas of business leadership. Besides being learner focused, chairs or lead faculty and school administrators are required to provide systematic and formal development opportunities for their faculty members. The following is a list of 100 suggestions initially generated by the School of Business and Entrepreneurship faculty members based upon their own teaching successes at one of the annual faculty retreats. It was compiled and edited by Dr. Robert Preziosi, the Interim Dean, of the business school in 1993. For many years, Faculty Coordinators used these suggestions for training new adjunct faculty members as they were being hired and oriented with business programs and the school's rules and policies. The document was enhanced and used in 2003 by Dr. Bahaudin Mujtaba, Director of Undergraduate Business Programs at the H. Wayne Huizenga School of Business and Entrepreneurship. In February and March of 2003, over 150 full-time and Part-time faculty members from the undergraduate business programs attended one of the one-day faculty development sessions held in Fort Lauderdale, Tampa, Orlando, Kingston-Jamaica, and Nassau- the Grand Bahamas. So, these suggestions were further enhanced as a result of the faculty development sessions with these diverse and experienced educators throughout Florida, Nassau and Jamaica. The list, updated once again for this publication, is organized under various categories to assist both faculty and academic administrators as they educate students in each program. This list of one hundred facilitation and teaching suggestions focuses not just on enhancing learning outcomes in each course and program, but also on boosting student satisfaction. Research continues to support the belief that teacher behaviors play a significant role in the level of student satisfaction (Brokaw, Kennedy and Merz, 2004).

First Class Session

1. Delay class introductions during the initial session until after the first break. Allow the group to form preliminary conclusions about the instructor, group and/or each other and course before being formally introduced. Then discuss the impact of the pre-break session and the conclusions formed.
2. As a way to handle student introductions during the first class when students already know each other, have individual students give name only—allow classmates to then state three things they know about that student. This combines humor, participation, and fun for the professor to learn about the group.
3. Set up goals, expectations and structure during the initial session, leaving no loose ends or misunderstandings.
4. For introductions, you can place two students together to interview each other and subsequently introduce each other to the large group. This method immediately establishes rapport. For those who are shy or unwilling to disclose, this makes it easier for them to talk (on a one-to-one basis).

5. Develop an "opening" class participation exercise that will serve as an assessment tool of class level and background. Reveal to the class how you will utilize their respective backgrounds and needs. Refer to specific progress throughout the class. A variation could be to ask the class to assess progress from their viewpoint. Also, solicit the class for input on "how" to use group diversity/needs/etc. Part of the value of this process is to help students accept responsibility for management of the learning environment.

6. During the first session assess the group through self-introductions, and assure the group that the material (including the presentation of that material) will be tailored to their needs (within the parameters of the course syllabus, of course).

7. Having set the framework properly, follow-through in delivery is essential. If you stray from the framework, be sure to make note of it and provide an explanation.

8. When first meeting a new group of students, realize you are not just teaching another course. You are meeting a group of individuals with unique strengths, anxieties and expectations. Make a conscious effort to understand their uniqueness.

How to Get Started

9. Thoroughly explain the syllabus and any addenda or amendment that you make.

10. Before the first class session begins, review handouts to make sure that they are customized and current.
    - Get students to do most of the talking during the first 25 minutes.
    - If anyone asks a question, provide a direct answer in 20 seconds or less.
    - Be friendly, but firm.
    - As each person introduces him/herself, give your complete attention.
    - If you must be humorous, one relevant statement will suffice.
    - Keep your statement of course objectives short and directly to the point.
    - Make sure that every student receives positive eye contact or one positive comment from you.
    - Be sure to use everyone's name at least once.

Adult Student Esteem

11. When you recognize competence and experience in a student, welcome and encourage their participation based upon that competence and experience.
12. To behave in a manner conducive to enhancing student's self esteem, you must first have a high level of self-esteem. Always keep yours in excellent working order.
13. Ask basic questions to stimulate discussion among students and draw them into discussion on basic concepts and allow the students to achieve a feeling of competency before going forward.
14. Use formal address (Mr. Majboor or Miss Jamasi) to emphasize respect for students as adults.
15. Maintain student self-esteem with body language and eye contact. Show students that they are important by personally coming up to them (look at them with sincerity). Through total body language and spatial relations, indicate that they have your total attention. Focus in on them for the moment.
16. Use the student's name frequently. Show you know who they are as individuals.
17. The way and the manner of the response is often more important than the response itself. Give assurance to the student that it is quite alright that he/she may not know something at this point in the course.
18. Provide individuals the opportunity to become experts in a topic or issue that will recur throughout or later in the course. Refer others to that person as appropriate—to increase self-esteem … working adult students can be recognized experts, also.
19. Differences in learning styles should be acknowledged, and teaching styles should adapt so that all learning styles are accommodated.
20. When possible, review students' profiles before the course starts. The profile might include such items as the student's learning style, his or her work experience, etc. You can also develop your own profile during the first session.
21. Make every student believe that you have a direct line to his or her concerns and that you want to address those concerns. Then make every effort to address their concerns.
22. Protect every student from other students' criticism. Remember, the objective is to get them talking and thinking about the material, presenting their understanding and views, thereby leading to the achievement of the session's objectives.
23. Avoid sarcasm and defensiveness in your communication with students.
24. Be flexible on whatever issues allow for flexibility or individual student need.

25. Stay in control using appropriate facilitation techniques. For example, if a few students are talking among themselves (and disturbing others), you can walk next to the talkers as you continue lecturing to the class. Oftentimes this will get their attention. At other times, you can stop talking, remain calm, and see if they would like to share their thoughts with the entire class.

Student Participation

26. Regarding the "first hour of the session or later afternoon/evening sessions" and to add stimulation to the class during first hour or later evening hours, have students report on (course related content):
    - Personal experiences
    - Professional experiences
    - Readings
    - Viewings
27. The student knowledge base is formidable. DEMAND and REWARD participation.
28. Recognize that groups will be cohesive and relatively homogeneous after the first few terms together. This will be true no matter how diverse and cosmopolitan their profession, backgrounds and interests.
29. Demand student participation (take advantage of their varied experiences). This may require that more than 10% of the grade be allowed for participation.
30. When experts are in the class, use them to reinforce/support your content accuracy.
31. Get each student to respond to a question on the text at each session, to assure that they are keeping up with their reading requirements.
32. Maintain "control" through leadership (followers have the opportunity to be leaders and leaders have the opportunity to be followers).
33. Facilitate, don't dictate. Capitalize on students' resources.
34. To help people with various learning levels enjoy and learn from a class or session, pair experts with novices.
35. The expert designs strategies and the novice learns to implement tactics and develops vocabulary and conceptual skills.

Group Considerations

36. Assess the peer clusters so that balance occurs as far as personalities (right brain vs. left brain), thereby adding to potential stimulus with group interaction. Random grouping may cause one-sided stimulus.

37. A suggestion for group projects is to establish a leader in the group to evaluate each person's performance. Also, place people into groups by diversified backgrounds in order to increase group learning. Another option is to have every person in the group evaluate each other. This would model shared leadership.

38. A suggestion for the barrier of multiple levels/backgrounds is to subset the large group into 3-4 groups. Now you have three or four subsets of people to reach—similar to market segmentation—grouping according to like variables that have meaning.

39. When students exhibit different levels of capability, assign students to groups so that they can complement each other, rather than grouping homogeneously.

40. Have students form study groups and have them call the faculty as a group during arranged office hours using a speakerphone so that you can be more accessible.

Evaluation

41. Halfway through the term, the instructor can have an open discussion evaluating what has been happening and setting guidelines for the remainder of the course.

42. Student identification cards should be made out at the first class meeting (index card—3x5 with name, phone number and email). This card can be used as an interim roll, random selections for participation, and recording grades for participation.

43. At the midpoint of the course use an open forum in the classroom to allow students to evaluate the course and voice individual concerns/problems with the course or the instructor. Try to address as many of their relevant concerns before the end of the term when possible.

44. Give the final test in groups that have worked together during the semester. The group that gets the most correct answers gets the highest grade.

45. Provide choices for demonstration of mastery of competencies and completion of assignments; i.e., written/oral presentation, test, exercises, etc.

46. Provide opportunities for peer evaluation of term project presentations. When appropriate or when some students are involved in social loafing with team activities, provide confidential peer evaluation opportunities for each team member.

Attitude, Style and Technique

47. Provoke students to engage in meaningful dialogue, both in and out of class.

48. An effective instructor of adult learners is more of a facilitator than a lecturer.

49. The education industry is one of the noble fields of endeavor. A wise person once said, "If you give a man a fish, he will eat for a day. If you teach a man to fish, he will eat for a lifetime." So, teach them to think for themselves.

50. Your own expectations can mold the class. If you are dynamic, if you are demanding, you can raise the energy level of the classroom. You owe your students that kind of performance. If you are dry, if you are dull, if you will settle for mediocrity, you'll get it. You'll deserve it. Do your students? So, have high expectations from *everyone*.

51. Always be well prepared, but if you get a question from a student that you aren't sure of, never FAKE or BLUFF an answer. Admit that you will need to research an answer. Then follow up and deliver a superior answer at the next session.

52. Maintain your "focus" at all times, to include:
    - What is my purpose here?
    - Why are the students here?
    - What do I want them to get from the course when they are finished?
    - What does the school expect from me as an instructor?

54. By teaching consciously, you should be able to avoid the appearance of a "canned delivery," and should be able to deliver a fully and carefully personalized presentation.

55. No matter how beaten up you may personally feel, do not be a carrier of pain. Be jovial, positive, upbeat, and enthusiastic. Instructors are not allowed to have a bad day in the presence of students.

56. Remain positive even when students are experiencing difficulty in understanding the concepts or material being facilitated.

57. Do not take teaching for granted, even if it is your tenth time teaching the same course this year. Remember, students are new and they are different than any other group.

58. A professor needs to be an actor/actress, producer, stage manager, and director all at once. Educators should entertain to teach, even if the "act" is outrageous. If one can keep their attention, and entertain at the same time, it will create interest and excitement. If one can get their attention, entertain them, create interest and excitement, they will learn something, and they will remember.

59. Use color on the chalkboard, whiteboard or flipchart to separate ideas, points, and concepts.
60. Teach to attain learning objectives, not to impress.
61. Love thy students, for they are the sole reason for teaching.
62. Calibrate to the low end, vector to the high side.
63. Constantly reinforce that they are adult students and not in high school or middle school. Encourage them to be creative, take risks and not be afraid to challenge either what they may read in the textbook or what the professor may say.
64. If the class needs "additional stimulation" (in afternoons or late evening sessions), present a controversial issue related to the course content and take the unpopular side. This will stimulate debate and even argument; both are better than drowsiness. You may not want to use this method the first session since students are often getting to know each other and may feel uncomfortable taking sides. Also, be careful with this method when teaching abroad or with international students whose cultures may vary drastically than yours.
65. Because of the method of presentation on evenings and weekends with working adult students, two sets of students are often encountered. The dress is different, the attitude is different, and the ability to absorb appears to be different as well, compared to traditional full-time students. These differences should be addressed and instructional methods should reflect the differences.
66. Relate the information in the course to the real world. Use examples from the workplace. Mention current, new topics. Ask for student comments. Have they read articles or encountered situations related to the coursework?
67. In each course that you teach, experiment with at least one new teaching technique or learning activity. This "new" technique or activity may be something innovative or just something different from that which you have done in the past. By evaluating these "experiments" and keeping those that work well, you can constantly improve your effectiveness as a teacher and prevent burnout, boredom, or the feeling of getting into a rut when teaching the same course term after term.
68. You're more than a tape player, and you know more about your subject than the book gives the student. Don't be afraid to interpret or to interpolate. Add a little color—underline, italicize, tell a story, even a true story—make the subject more real. Include your experiences.
69. Use visuals, color, and anything that enhances excitement without degrading professionalism.
70. Often educators teach more effectively by asking thoughtful questions than by giving brilliant lectures. The most impressive instruc-

tors use the technique of only asking questions, never stating opinions. Think of Socrates.

71. Consider every session taught to be a significant and positive emotional event resulting in a natural "high."

72. Establish expectations early with regards to: Goals, Rules/Boundaries, Justification for the subject matter and its linkage to other courses.

73. Keep presentation material (particularly personal examples) current, contemporary, and up-to-date.

74. To excel in teaching—you have to learn how to improve. Are you thinking of your future? Are you planning for the future of your profession?

75. Use email, newsgroups, bulletin boards, or even a fax machine to receive written work from students on a regular basis and send the work back to them with specific and detailed comments as quickly as possible. This provides for more responsiveness than the regular mail or waiting for class sessions.

76. Encourage student learning networks with current students as well as those who have gone before them and those who are coming after them. Also, contact with alumni of the program can be a great connection for job opportunities.

77. Combine superb preparation with a high degree of energy and make it contagious.

78. For all written projects, spell out clearly the information to be included in each section. This makes evaluation much easier.

79. When utilizing overhead transparencies, use reverse negatives with color. Duplicate the information on the transparencies and provide as hand-outs.

80. Use verbal encouragement positively as a way of motivating students.

81. Research suggests that adults learn best when they are treated like adults.

82. Avoid using red for written feedback....use blue or green.

83. Research suggests that a break in long sessions should occur every 50–60 minutes, especially in the afternoon or evening.

FOLLOW-UP

84. There is a need to keep or re-establish continuity and thought after a several week hiatus/break.

85. Instructors must provide access to themselves after class so that students can call for help when needed. The use of email, telephone,

Internet websites, newsgroups, bulletin boards, and fax machines are good ideas.

86. Leave time during each class meeting for random and off-the-wall questions. The end of a class meeting is best suited for this. When time is up, class can be adjourned and those who wish to stay can, and not hold up the whole group.

87. Follow-up—If you can't answer a question fully, get back with the response in a timely manner.

Spatial Room Environment

88. Change room layout, move chairs, move podium, and break down the seat selection to bring about a change. For example, after class is assembled, sit in back of room and turn entire class around so students see things differently, and/or hopefully with a different paradigm.

89. Update classrooms to provide more working space. The biggest complaint from students especially in quantitative courses is that there is not enough space for notebooks, textbooks, and calculators. Also, provide more board space and switch to white boards when available.

90. It is much better for the classroom to be a bit too cold in temperature than a bit too warm. It helps everyone stay awake.

Instructor Development

91. Continue to hold and/or attend "faculty retreat" workshops with colleagues to energize and refresh faculty.

92. Provide more opportunities for faculty to learn from each other, especially personal interaction to share teaching techniques. Create a community of practice.

93. Have instructors teaching similar courses (quantitative methods, finance, cost accounting) broken into think tanks to ferment ideas.

94. One barometer for a successful class is that if the faculty has covered all the material, and s/he has learned more than students, then it has been a successful session.

Curriculum/Syllabi

95. Use updated textbooks, especially books with CDs and website supplements from the publishers to take advantage of the new technologies for up-to-date learning.

96. Allow the electronic world to enter the classroom—permit students who must miss a class to submit their exam, project, or in-class presentation via video tape, audio tape, CDs, or DVDs as appropriate.
97. Provide a general computer literacy course at the beginning of the program mandatory.
98. An idea to add quality to term/research paper: Have students turn in the first five pages of the paper at the mid-term session. The professor reads this, comments on content, style, etc. and submits back to student. This encourages students to start on their paper early, do their own work, get past content problems at an early stage, and receive added guidance from the professor (make this worth a certain percentage of the final grade).
99. If one of the syllabus activities is no longer meeting the needs of the course due to external changing forces, notify administration that a re-assessment is necessary. Include recommendations for change.
100. Remember, first there is the course that a faculty prepares to teach; second, there is the course that the faculty actually teaches; and third, there is the course that the faculty member wished s/he had taught. Everyone goes through this process which actually means that the faculty is always improving his/her facilitation and teaching methods. So, don't forget to assess the learning of your students and make sure the course learning objectives are achieved each term. Measure your students' understanding on a regular basis through having objective and subjective assessment tools. Compare students' learning assessment across different groups over several terms and try different techniques to enhance learning for your students.

SUMMARY

Educators (teachers, managers and leaders) have an important job and need to be aware of individual differences as they have the power to mold each individual's perception of the organization through knowledge. Educators teach not only the necessary material to get started on the job, but they also introduce new employees to the organization's culture. They assist in the current employee's career advancement opportunities and it is their duty to make certain that information is transferred successfully.

This section presented many practical techniques for both formal educators and industry leaders to successfully facilitate learning to adult audiences in school, government and businesses.

CHAPTER 6

ONLINE AND CYBERSPACE ESSENTIALS

In the twenty first century, Internet Technology has been one of the most remarkable developments that has made ground-breaking progress and has influenced every aspect of modern society. In particular, advances in the use of the Internet Technology have enabled online education to transform and redefine the field of education. This form of education has offered students, especially working adults, an opportunity to get involved in the learning process, bridging the gap that once existed between the busy lifestyles of working professionals and their goal of obtaining a University degree. Similar to the conventional module of face-to-face interaction, online education has required learner participation and interaction in developing and initiating effective facilitation techniques to help increase learning and retention among adult learners. This section outlines certain skills and nuances required for the successful participation and completion of online courses such as the effective interaction and communication techniques necessary to correspond with colleagues, administrators and faculty members. In addition, unlike other literature on cyberspace learning, this chapter provides a simple format on the essentials of online learning, chatting and emailing without inserting too much academic literature, while serving as a manuscript for the "know-hows" and "how-tos" of online education for prospective online students. Some of this material was prepared by

Adult Education in Academia, pages 123–140
Copyright © 2006 by Information Age Publishing

Mujtaba and Salghur (2005) and presented at the Teaching and Learning Conference at Disney World Resort in Orlando, Florida.

ONLINE PROGRAMS AND DISTANCE LEARNING

There are certain similarities and differences that exist with online and on-ground (face-to-face) education formats. Table 10 shows the various attributes of both the educational structures. As indicated, in terms of the grading criteria (i.e. participation, exams), plagiarism and available administrative and registration support, both education formats share similar approaches. Additionally, within both formats, students are required to closely follow the class syllabus and be on par with the pre-assigned readings and assignments. Therefore, both online and face-to-face formats share parallel class structures and formats. However, the two formats vastly differ in their modes of delivery. More specifically, while instructors in both edu-

Table 10. Differences between Face to Face and Online

	Face to Face	*Online*
Similarities		
Transcripts	Courses not identified whether its online or ground on transcript	
Grading	Participation and preparation accounted for in grades	
Withdrawal	There are specific times to withdraw from classes	
Plagiarism	Plagiarism not accepted in both cases	
Credit Transfer	Transfer of credit possible	
Differences		
Modes of Delivery	Direct interaction with professor and students	Online interaction with professor and students via different modes such as Scheduled Chat Sessions, Bulletin Boards (discussion), online timed exams; Use of Graphics and visuals to present material
Readings and Assignments	Pre-assigned readings as noted in class syllabus	Pre-assigned readings as noted in class syllabus
Subject Matter Experts/Guests	Class Room guests	"Virtual Guests"
Access to Support	Access to registration and administration support "online" or via personal visits	Access to registration and administration support "online"
Office Hours	"Walk-in Office Hours"	"Virtual Office Hours"

cation modules utilize guest speakers and maintain specific office hours for their students, online courses utilize "virtual guests" and have "virtual office hours" since all aspects of online courses are conducted via the Internet. Online courses also depend on email conversations, online chats and discussion sessions (asynchronous and synchronous) to compensate for the lack of face-to-face interaction and class-room discussions (Salghur and Mujtaba, 2005).

Online education, an educational format that enables an individual to complete a Master's level degree online in the comfort of one's home, has grown in popularity particularly given the flexibility and convenience that it offers to working professionals when pursuing a degree program. Nevertheless, this form of education requires students to individually develop personal discipline, exceptional management and communication techniques and technical capabilities, particularly a strong working knowledge of computer software and hardware. As a result, adult students are often advised to take a selective and cautious approach when considering their choice of graduate degree program preferably from an "accredited" institution. Online programs also have high associated costs wherein a Masters of Business Administration (MBA) program, for instance, can cost anywhere from $15,000 to over $100,000 depending on the school and the program curriculum. But it is safe to deduce that with the growing popularity and demand for online education and as it inevitably becomes highly competitive, the costs will fall, while the quality of online programs will increase. In fact, many institutions have already invested in expanding their programs to other locations beyond their main campus to reach a wider demography and area, which will be highly beneficial. Within the South Florida region, over 30 different universities now offer students an online degree program of their choice.

The term distance education has become synonymous to the term online education. The main component of online or distance education is the Internet and there are three different characteristics of Internet-based learning. For one, there are distance learning programs that utilize the Internet Technology as a support mechanism rather than as a primary medium of delivery. Second, the computer conferencing medium can use the Internet as the primary mode of delivery through the means of asynchronous discussions and emails. Third, virtually all courses or aspects of the courses can be delivered online (virtual courses). The H. Wayne Huizenga School of Business and Entrepreneurship of Nova Southeastern University, for instance, widely employs the first and the third types of cyberspace learning, providing students the distinct opportunity to complete the requirements of an entire program online while providing students the flexibility to undertake on-ground classes to diversify their course structure and closely match their interests.

Clearly, the nature of online learning is vastly determined by the flexibility and convenience it offers to a diverse population. In addition, this form of education also depends on the role and the qualifications of online instructors. Many institutions with distance learning education usually have a competent instructor that is an expert in the subject area who helps facilitate traditional classroom discussions, administer and conduct online programs and sustain the consistency and the quality of online courses. Online instructors directly discuss and communicate course objectives, while they administer the submission of course assignments, tests and exams. To facilitate the learning process, experienced educators often use a combination of colorful graphics, audio and video streams, and hypertext links as tools to advocate better understanding of the course material. Research comparing student outcomes between online and on-ground classes, in fact, suggests that there is a strong learning equivalency that exists in both online and classroom learning.

Just as instructors are expected to guide and be involved in creating the ideal setting to facilitate a productive online learning environment, online students are also expected to play a prominent and active role in the knowledge generation process through regular online interaction with their instructor(s) and their colleagues each week. Such involvement is critical especially since the materials being taught are learned, utilized and retained by the students themselves. Students are also often encouraged to provide constructive feedback that instructors can incorporate to enhance the online learning experience.

Therefore, when selecting a graduate online program, prospective students should consider the following components:

1. Assess personal learning styles, preferences and interests.
2. Assemble a list of various programs that best matches aforementioned needs.
3. Learn about the instructor's credentials and teaching techniques to make certain that the instructor is one that accommodates a student's dominant learning style.
4. Acquire information from interviews conducted with school administrators, advisors and student services, particularly on the resources and the level of technical assistance available for online students.
5. Determine a program's graduation requirements and anticipated graduation rate, post-graduation employability rates and the program's overall ranking.
6. Spend some time at the school that offers the intended program to become familiar with the school's culture and the overall quality of the program.

Undoubtedly, students have various options and choices in today's competitive environment. Hence, an institution offering an online curriculum should also appreciate the needs of its prospective clientele, particularly by offering the requisite tools required to ensure the successful and smooth completion of virtual courses. Just as it is the responsibility for students to have access to the necessary computer hardware and software components, an institution should also provide assistance by recommending and providing adequate information to obtain the needed technology. As is evident, being technologically savvy particularly in the area of Internet surfing and uploading and downloading files are critical. The following section expands on the requisite skills that have been widely acknowledged to be useful for online programs and education.

REQUISITE SKILLS FOR ONLINE EDUCATION

Online learning has seemingly become ubiquitous in today's higher education system. However, students and administrators are apprehensive about online education given that there are many nuances and challenges that exist within the education module. One challenge of online education that is often discussed is the lack of face-to-face interaction. In spite of this, supporters of online programs indicate that the alternatives to traditional learning such as designated real-time chat sessions, email interaction and telephone conversations provide equal opportunity to develop the essential communicative relationship between both students and professors. While most online courses are asynchronous, many educators hold synchronized chat sessions to assess learning needs and to ensure the steady progress of students in fulfilling the class requirements. Figure 2, created by Mujtaba and Salghur (2005), provides some of the requisite skills needed for online education. As observed, online faculty members particularly often provide some common rules for chatting during the first week of classes and give students an opportunity to clarify any doubts about the class objectives and the syllabus.

The following are some general chat session rules that Bahaudin Mujtaba, an online professor at Nova Southeastern University, utilizes when conducting his online courses:

- Discussions must begin and end as scheduled.
- When confronting difficulties with computer connections or technology issues, one can continue a discussion session upon computer reconnection.
- In cases of emergency, students are encouraged to engage in discussions without the instructor present by engaging in conversations re-

lated to the week's assigned topics. Each individual is given the opportunity to expand their thoughts and experiences. Each chat session's transcript is accessible to the instructor that can be used for grading and evaluation purposes. Chat session contents are not posted for general review by everyone. Therefore, individual presence is required.

- Certain general topics or specific questions are posed for discussion purposes that require active student participation and response. In the case where questions are directly posed to a specific individual, the person has 30 seconds to respond and based on the response, other members have the opportunity to comment on or pose further questions for clarification purposes.
- Assigned readings should be completed prior to each chat session as they complement the discussions.
- At times when topics that are not discussed during chat sessions, students have the option to use bulletin boards (newsgroups) to discuss issues and concerns which allow for more time and research opportunity before the next scheduled chat session.
- Maintaining a sense of professionalism at all times, particularly during chat and email sessions, is expected of all students. This also includes being careful of the "tone" of the message and avoiding the use of inappropriate and derogatory terms.
- Students are also expected to be non-judgmental and respectful of peer opinions.
- Students are highly encouraged to ask questions but, when doing so, should consider the questions they choose to pose publicly and/ or privately.
- Students should be both constructive and critical when responding to questions.
- To benefit from chat sessions, students should also attend and qualitatively participate in each chat session.

The latter designated rules on chat sessions act as a platform to assist students in understanding chat specifications and expectations to help initiate a healthy learning environment for students. The rules help create an environment that encourages all students to participate and voice their unique perspectives. In addition to "chat" that acts as an effective communicative tool, asynchronized bulletin board discussions, newsgroup interactions and emails are alternative and additional means in which students can interact with professors and other fellow students.

Hence, certain email protocols are commonly enforced when sending messages. Most instructors are often hesitant to open and/or acknowledge indistinguishable emails or files given the threat of computer viruses. Therefore, the protocol recommends that students state the course, the date

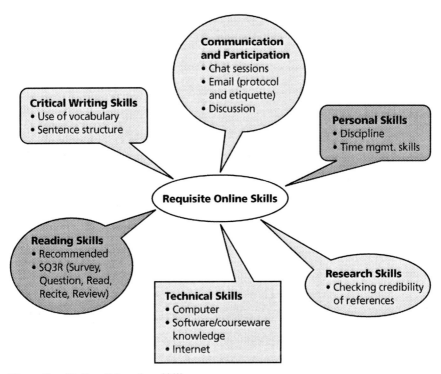

Figure 2.   Online Education Skills.

(week) and/or student information to help an instructor effectively pinpoint the purpose and subject matter of the email to be able to adequately respond to student queries. Equally important is the suggested "tone" of the email message given that certain messages can often be perceived or interpreted differently from what the sender had originally intended. To avoid potential communication barriers and conflicts, the following is a list of commonly used email protocols that online students should consider:

1. Include full name, specific subject title and a request for a response. Students can choose to provide additional contact information such as "telephone" number if required.
2. Include a subject line in every email message as this sets the tone and the purpose of the message.
3. Incorporate a brief, but clear message that expresses the intent of the email.
4. Avoid over abbreviating and being overly cryptic as this may result in an ambiguous message that an instructor may not be able to understand.

5. Relaying emotions, humor or sarcasm can be difficult. Hence, using emotions in the form of symbols such as : -) (smile) can help avoid potential miscommunication.
6. The use of uppercase letters often indicates or signifies that a person is screaming or shouting! The use of lowercase letters is recommended as readability studies have shown that it takes less-time to read all-lowercase messages versus an all-uppercase message. The use of asterisk to emphasize a certain word or phrase is more professional than the use of uppercase letters.
7. Proofreading a work and checking the spelling and the grammar of a text is a must.
8. Certain care and caution should be taken when providing confidential information such as social security number, student identification number, credit card, etc.
9. When replying, one should try and include the original message text as a reference point.
10. Beware of sending emotionally charged messages as this may ultimately have severe repercussions on relationships. When annoyed or angry, take some time to cool off.
11. Show consideration of people's privacy and therefore avoid the mass distribution of other people's email addresses. When sending an email message to a group of people it is courteous to list all of the recipients' email addresses in the Blind Carbon Copy (BCC) field. The Blind Carbon Copy field enables the intended recipient to get a copy of the email while ensuring that other email addresses remain invisible.
12. When forwarding email, deleting the prior trail of messages is recommended. It is an inconvenience for the recipient to scroll down through all redundant or irrelevant messages/email addresses to read the actual email content.
13. When forwarding jokes, seek permission first as certain jokes and/or contents may be inappropriate or even an inconvenience to people with restrictive inbox space.

Maintaining a level of email etiquette plays an important role and increases the chances of receiving a timely response from instructors. Besides the technical skills required for cyberspace communication, online students should also familiarize themselves with online study skills, preparation required for course assignments, time management skills, support mechanisms for technical assistance and the inherent benefits that online education offers that are not offered in the traditional approach.

Christ and Ganey's (2003) book, *100 Things Every Online Student Ought to Know,* (Cambridge Stratford Study Skills Institute) is a vital resource that current and prospective online students can use as it provides exceptional insights on how to successfully complete online courses (Mujtaba and Salghur, 2005). The following list highlights some of these two authors' ideas and thoughts, as well as those of ours, that online students should bear in mind when taking online courses.

Online Students Ought to Know That:

1. The number of online degree programs, distance education and their popularity have grown considerably particularly in the U.S. increasing by 72% between 1995 and 1998.
2. Not all programs are offered by a "Regionally Accredited Institution". Hence, it is the student's responsibility to find out about the credibility of the degree program and the usefulness of the program in a student's future.
3. Individuals have the opportunity to complete an entire undergraduate and/or graduate degree programs online hence making it possible for students with diverse lifestyles and professions to obtain degrees.
4. Various institutions have designated websites or web pages that contain important information that focus on online course work and support services for easy accessibility and efficiency.
5. Accessibility of an online course anywhere and anytime is an important feature of online programs.
6. Online courses have different and unique features compared to conventional "face to face" course structures and formats particularly in their "modes of delivery" and differences in their content and the level of self-discipline and time management skills required for each structure.
7. The convenience and flexibility of distance learning has been one of the key features and attractions of online courses.
8. Online courses are often fully "asynchronous;" therefore, one doesn't have to be at a computer at a specific time period or timeframe unless required. Ultimately, the student formulates his or her own schedule depending on the deadlines.
9. Online courses are also synchronous wherein communication between participants is synchronous and students are required to be present at certain chat sessions to interact with the instructor and fellow students.
10. Paying attention to the differences in time zones that may exist between an instructor and a student is important especially when completing online assignments on-time.

11. Given the expenses incurred toward the maintenance of technology and online instructors, online courses are relatively more expensive than traditional courses. But, as the number of courses and colleges offering distance learning increases, prices are likely to go down.
12. Various financial assistance and opportunities are available for students interested in taking online courses.
13. On the transcripts, online courses are reflected just as traditional courses wherein courses are not identified whether they are traditional or online.
14. Most online courses provide course information and requisite requirements (i.e. assignments) at the beginning of the course.
15. Just like traditional formats, there are specific dates for withdrawal from a course, guidelines for incompletes and even options for auditing a course.
16. Provides an opportunity to meet and interact with a diverse group of people from varying backgrounds, interests, education levels, genders, and professional levels.
17. It helps to enhance one's vocabulary and phrases especially those that are unique to online courses. Various online glossaries are available for students to use as references.
18. Special "virtual" guests are sometimes invited to enhance the understanding and knowledge base of a course. This form of interaction between subject matter experts, authors, and others provides students first hand perspective of the courses being taken.
19. The courseware for online courses (i.e. WebCT, eCollege, eUniversity) require some time for students to get oriented to and practice to be able to navigate with ease and effectiveness. Hence it is recommended that students attend a courseware orientation to become familiar with certain software.
20. The value of online courses and degree programs (i.e. distance learning) is immeasurable and is of high quality. According to a survey conducted by the Distance Education and Training Council that surveyed 1,300 online graduates from 21 accredited online schools, 54% reported a pay increase due to their online degrees, while 50% of the candidates were granted job promotions or had a career change.
21. In a highly competitive educational market, the options for accredited online programs and courses are different and number has continued to grow. Therefore, students have various options for selecting their preferred institution and program that best fits their needs and requirements.

22. To transfer credits of online courses from one institution to another, a student must acquire authorization and acceptance from the department or academic advisor.
23. Certain institutions have specific academic counselors and advisors for particular online programs that have the background and the knowledge to guide and assist students with their academic decisions.
24. Students can access registration and/or administrative support online.
25. Prior to registration, each student is given a unique username and password, which acts as a code to log on and access online courses.
26. Each student must take the responsibility for accessing their online course(s) and in completing their assignments and chat sessions as required by the instructor.
27. The type and version of the internet browser (i.e. Internet Explorer, Netscape) has an impact on the quality, speed and efficiency of a student's access to online courses.

Online Preparation

28. In determining a student's readiness and competence in distance learning, a pre-assessment can help assess certain skills such as computer, time management and organizational skills.
29. Many institutions offer orientation courses for online learning that help enhance a student's understanding in the courseware and certain challenges of online learning.
30. An online student must be a motivated self-learner to maintain the level of discipline required in succeeding in online courses.
31. A student's personal computer must meet the university hardware and software configuration to be able to successfully access online courses. Most distance learning institutions have a profile for hardware and software configuration.
32. Computer literacy particularly in the basic use of the computer and internet skills are critical when taking online courses.
33. A working email address that a student checks on a regular basis is critical when communicating with an instructor and fellow students. Many institutions offer free email addresses.
34. Prior to the start of an online course, a student should have a copy of the text book and other materials/resources on hand.
35. Certain textbooks are accompanied by CD-ROMs and resources (i.e. websites) that are useful in understanding the course materials.

Hence, students are encouraged to refer to other such sources for information and clarification of course material.

36. A student is recommended to allow anywhere between 9 and 12 hours every week toward a three-credit online course to be able to read, study and prepare the materials for the course.

37. It is a student's responsibility to carefully read the course syllabus posted online so that he or she can clarify possible ambiguity that may exist. Online syllabus provides deadlines and completion dates for assignments and has details on scheduled chat/instructional sessions.

38. All online course materials can be printed and stored in a binder for present and future off-line references and as a study-guide.

39. Students must schedule and allow certain timeslots in their calendars for the completion of online course assignments and other requirements before the deadline.

40. For the purposes of better online organization, it is highly recommended that students maintain a special diskette or zip drive to save as well as back-up existing work. Having a specific Microsoft Word folder, for instance, especially allotted for an online course can also be helpful in one's organization techniques.

41. A basic background and knowledge of the Internet, such as conducting research on search engines, doing reference checks and source validity are critical elements in the successful completion of online courses.

Online Communications

42. There are various online tools available for students to communicate with and amongst each other and the instructor making the online experience very interactive and providing the opportunity to network with each other.

43. Only certain people are permitted access to a student's coursework online including the instructor, the student and possibly fellow students. Therefore, a student's work is usually secure and confidential.

44. A student's course email system has the security levels and measures to disable spam emails from overloading their inbox. It is against an institution's protocol to sell and/or exchange a student's email address to other companies and businesses.

45. Creating a homepage may be one of the requirements for a course to increase the learning experience and in building and connecting with a diverse learning community.

46. A student must have the basic technical knowledge of how to use and "thread" appropriately on discussion boards. Discussion boards

provide a student the opportunity to reflect on certain readings and thoughts and the ability to exchange their points of view that makes online discussions very interactive.

47. Some of the critical elements that determine a student's success in an online course are their level of participation and interaction, which are reflected in their attendance, grading, weekly appearances online and contribution on the discussion boards. These are all part of being proactive.

48. There are certain specific times allotted for group discussions which provide students an opportunity to interact and socialize amongst one another. The discussion board acts as the module for student discussion and are sometimes known as "Arena of Discussion," "Water cooler," "Cyber Student Union," or "Around the Watch Tower" just to name a few.

49. Only the student is authorized (i.e. password protected) to access and view his or her grades on the online grade-book.

50. The careful management and organization of the email account that is used for an online course is equally critical. It is recommended that a student creates and labels specific course folders for organization purposes.

51. Communicating via email requires a basic understanding of email etiquette and protocol to be able to correspond with fellow students and instructors appropriately and effectively.

52. All email communications should be addressed properly and must contain an appropriate title in the "Subject line" to inform fellow students and instructors of the topic that the body of the email addresses.

53. Using MSWord to draft your email and discussion board messages is a wise habit to adopt for the purposes of checking spelling and grammatical errors. This is part of being professional.

54. To avoid misunderstandings and misconceptions that are sometimes common with email communications, it is essential that a student has a back-up of all email communications in the draft folder as reference points and to be able to clarify certain misunderstandings. This is all part of effective communication and in being professional.

55. Many colleges have an internal courseware system that provides internal email systems that can be used to send, receive and manage emails within a specific online course, which enables a students to manage their email accounts and communication effectively.

56. The majority of the communication that occurs between a student and an instructor will be asynchronous (at different times) via certain modes especially discussion boards and email communications.

57. There is a possibility that a student may not immediately receive a response for a question or a comment by his or her instructor and, therefore, it is important that the student is patient and understands that an instructor has additional priorities and online-courses. Most online faculty members, however, attempt to answer any question within a 24 and 48 hour timeframe.

Online Learning and Study Skills and Strategies

58. A student must be well aware of the time commitment, organizational discipline and management skills required for accessing courses and in completing off-line reading and writing requirements.
59. Reading is an essential ingredient toward the successful completion of an online course as it provides the background information for the course.
60. Completing assignments and research papers requires study-reading skills, which is essentially an "active form" of reading that helps students find the main ideas and supporting arguments. One of the recommended and preferred forms of study-reading is the SQ3R method—Survey, Question, Read, Recite and Review.
61. Critical reading and writing skills are important facets to the successful completion of online course assignments and research. It is equally important to know what to write as well as how you write so that a response or a reaction is communicated appropriately and effectively.
62. There needs to be a set plan and a suitable time-line when scheduling an online coursework so to better manage and schedule certain time periods to access the course online, studying the materials and completing assignments.
63. Keeping track of assignments and completing them before the deadline is part of good time management and organization skills.
64. Finding, reading and following directions are essential when completing course assignments as they clearly outline the instructor's expectations and assignment requirements.
65. Thousands of websites are available on the World Wide Web which provide a wealth of information and act as critical resources when completing assignments. Various search engines such as Google, Yahoo, Alta Vista and Excite provide easy access to such resources.
66. Institutions offer on-campus reading and study-skills assistance to improve individual skills. In recent times, there are certain computer software that provides essential reading and writing tools in enhancing student skills.

67. How-to-study books are available that act as a vital resource in gaining practical assistance for online learning and the methodology for answering study problems.

68. A student has the opportunity to visit on-campus learning centers that offer tutorials in math, writing and other subject matters that may better assist a student effectively complete online courses.

69. Besides on-campus learning support centers, the internet acts as a great resource and tool in finding websites and services that offer assistance in basic and advanced math.

70. Additionally, a student can receive online writing help via online writing centers that many institutions have established. Based on Purdue University's Online Writing Center, many of the writing centers provide websites that offer assistance in the use of the English grammar, punctuation, essay writing, writing styles and in conducting research papers. Certain online platforms have advanced features such as chat sessions that enhance student comprehension of the English language.

71. Grammar handbook and suggested writing manuals act as additional resources for students when writing assignments and research papers.

72. The Internet also provides a student with various learning and study skills resources that present specific applicable tips and tutorials in reading, math and writing.

73. Part of active learning is working in study groups that enhance student interaction, participation and understanding of certain questions and assignments from another point of view. Fellow students themselves act as critical resources when clarifying certain topics and issues that a student may not understand on his or her own.

74. There are tutors/tutorials available for many online courses. Some are available on-site at the institution, on the internet or from commercial tutoring services.

75. Most online tests and exams are completed online. Tests are either scheduled on specific days, at select specific times or can be taken at the time the student decides.

76. Using a word processor such as MS-WORD to initially type out course assignments is a good idea rather than directly typing answers or responses into courseware so that students have the opportunity to edit their work and have back-ups for all coursework completed.

77. Proofreading acts as an additional tool to the "spell checker" that often overlooks certain words or meaning of the word.

78. Some courses require students to have proctored computer examinations that may require early preparation, better management tactics and organization skills.

79. Most of the online course study and assignments can be completed offline hence it is essential that a student maintains a course binder that contain the study guide and course materials for offline preparations.
80. "Rewriting the question as the lead into your answer" is one of the best ways to answer questions.
81. Plagiarism—"the act of borrowing of facts, statistics, illustrative materials, and another person's idea without giving the author his or her rightful credit"—is unethical and irresponsible. Most institutions have stringent policies on the act of plagiarism that has vast ramifications on the student's future and credibility.
82. Students are required to send their assignments to designated course drop boxes and or instructor email addresses. It is, therefore, critical that the student follows the instructor's guidelines and instructions on the proper format and delivery mode of assignments.
83. Accessing journal databases for articles is critical for completing assignments and research papers. Finding, reading and using materials on online databases are important when analyzing information and preparing research papers.
84. "Distinguishing websites that have academic credibility" plays a significant role to the research materials and information students have gathered especially since with the growing popularity in the World Wide Web, it is important to differentiate between a fact and fiction. Double-checking references and cross-referencing are important to establish source credibility.
85. "Recognizing specialized sources of Internet information" via recognizing "domain" names (i.e. com, gov, mil, and edu) helps in determining the "origin and the authenticity of Internet information."
86. Certain instructors require assignments be submitted in certain formats and document type. It is, therefore, important that a student pays attention to the syllabus as well as the instructions to meet the expectations.

Online Student Support

87. A student that has previously been an online-student is another important resource for current online students. The first hand experience provides a student with an enriching online experience.
88. Students must remember that in order to clarify doubts, questions must be asked. Asking the instructor to clarify assignments and/or other questions acts as an important tool. There is no such thing as a dumb or stupid question.

89. Institutional libraries act as a vital resource for online students when gathering information for assignments and research papers. Understanding methods of conducting proper searches on online databases are critical. Certain instructors have a special arrangement with the college library to have specific text made available to the students of the course which are scanned and posted on the courseware.

90. Most institutions have a "help desk" that provide technical (computer) assistance. Students should make note of important numbers and contact information to receive technical support.

91. Various institutions have libraries; learning support centers and bookstores that have an assortment of how-to-study guides that are helpful to a student taking online courses. Asking a librarian or the instructor for certain references may act as critical resource points.

92. To address courseware problems, certain online courses have a help desk available for students. Usually FAQ's and Subject Matter Experts provide vital information to some, if not most, of the problems that students may face.

93. For convenience of the students, most online courses have an 800 toll free number for assistance in courseware and other online course information. Having such information handy may be both tactful and wise if and when certain unexpected problems arise.

94. A "virtual faculty office" is available wherein students can send inquires and concerns. Online faculty numbers have set office hours during which time they answer student queries and issues as well as check assignments and coursework. Many in fact host virtual office times for live chat and or synchronous communication.

95. Taking the time to investigate and efficiently navigate the online course is important. Having knowledge of the functions of certain tabs or tools on the courseware may save plenty of time in the future, particularly when assignments and projects are due.

96. There are manuals for courseware such as blackboard, WebCT, Desire2Learn, and eCollege which are made available online. Taking the time to research the manuals is highly recommended to master the skills required toward becoming a successful online student.

Online No No's

97. Instructors often place selective course materials on reserve for students from the course. Such agreements have certain copyright laws that the university and the instructors must abide by. In doing so, students registered in the course should not share copyrighted licensed materials with unregistered students.

98. Sharing a username and/or password is unadvisable and irresponsible given that this could potentially jeopardize an individual's ability to secure his or her online course information.

99. Being very selective with the word-choice and the suggested tone is a critical element to online course because they could potentially alienate fellow students and the instructors. Given the lack of face to face interaction, gestures and/or expressions, the words exchanged between people in a form on in an email is the only method of communication.

100. Conducting research that is relevant to the course is critical when completing assignments. Getting sidetracked with information unrelated to the course may lead to the loss of critical assignment points.

101. Maintaining email etiquette at all times is a basic rule that one should abide. Respecting other student's privacy, perspectives, certain copyright rules, instructor's mode of instruction, etc. are part of maintaining that level of decent etiquette.

102. Although the Internet acts as a vital research tool, it is important that a student realizes that it is not the *only* tool. Resorting to other sources and reference materials helps broadens a student's viewpoints and understanding of the course and makes it interesting. Some of the other tools include books and audiovisual materials.

SUMMARY

No longer is one restricted to delaying one's higher education dreams due to a work schedule, a peripatetic lifestyle, or distance because internet technology has made obtaining a degree a reality with unlimited possibilities (Mujtaba and Salghur, 2005). Although making a transition from the traditional face-to-face format into the conventional mode may seem challenging, while online and distance learning education share similar characteristics, it has also introduced new components that has elevated the standards of education, making online learning highly marketable and appealing to a large and diverse demography, particularly among working professionals. The flexibility it allows students and adults to study at home, the options it provides students in choosing to complete a program entirely online or via a mixture of online and on-ground courses (hybrid), the opportunity of obtaining a quality degree program and education as a result of highly-qualified and competent professors and the increasing investment that colleges have made in online education nationwide reflects the very nature and the course of online education in the future.

PART II

INTEGRATING CYBERSPACE TECHNOLOGY
TO FACILITATE LEARNING

CHAPTER 7

QUALITY ASSURANCE IN DOCTORAL PROGRAMS

Higher education, especially doctoral degrees, throughout colleges and universities has been in high demand and more schools are getting into this arena to fill the need. As such, understanding the needs of higher education institutions and current doctoral students has become especially important for success in the new millennium. Furthermore, understanding the common denominator of technology available to distance education students can assist administrators and faculty members to appropriately design their admission, teaching and curriculum requirements. This section provides a review of the demand for doctorally qualified faculty members in tertiary education. While there are many means of assessing quality in a doctoral program such as dissertations and publication, the chapter focuses on Comprehensive Exams (Comp Exam). Based on an assessment of doctoral students' Comp exam results,[1] the section provides an example of quality assurance by studying the passing patterns of students on the Comp exams over an eight-year period. It further provides suggestions on how doctoral students can increase their probability of successfully passing their comprehensive examinations on the first attempt.

---

[1] This data was presented by Mujtaba and Abratt at the Applied Business Research Conference in Orlando, January 2005.

Adult Education in Academia, pages 143–166

The average scores of 968 doctoral students' (700 males and 268 females) Comp exams from an eight-year period are analyzed and discussed. Also discussed are the results of 85 alumni surveys and their level of satisfaction with the doctoral program. Recommendations are provided for the Doctoral Program faculty members and administrators to enhance their offerings as a result of the feedback from students. Initially, the chapter explores doctoral education along with the growing demand for terminally degreed educators in the United States. Then, the chapter transitions to comp examinations used for purposes of learning assessment and other such variables that impact the success rate of learners in higher education as presented by Mujtaba and Abratt (2005).

THE GROWING WORLD OF ADULT LEARNING IN ACADEMIA

There has been an increasing trend with schools using part-time (adjunct) faculty members to teach in their doctoral programs. One reason for this is lack of sufficient funding to hire full-time faculty members and another reason has to do with the fact that there is a shortage of qualified candidates available. As such the cost of recruiting the right individuals with the right credentials has dramatically increased. Nonetheless, while many schools are dealing with the current shortage of qualified doctorate faculty members others are taking advantage of this opportunity to offer new Ph.D. programs to fill this need. The Doctorate of Philosophy (Ph.D.) programs in business is a quality niche specialization that can generate new enrollment for both traditional and non-traditional schools of higher education. According to a report by the Association to Advance Collegiate Schools of Business (AACSB) in 2003, there is a need for more than 1,100 doctorates or Ph.D.s in Business within the next 5 years and more than 2,400 new doctorates or Ph.D.s within 10 years. As demonstrated from the survey of 85 doctorate alumni at the Nova Southeastern University's School of Business and Entrepreneurship in 2003, about 66% of the respondents stated that they started teaching at a college level after graduation from the doctoral program and that their NSU degree was a factor in receiving teaching opportunities. Many non-traditional schools tend to offer doctorate of business administration (DBA), doctorate of public administration (DPA), Doctorate of international business administration (DIBA), doctorate of management (DM), doctorate of organizational leadership (DOL), etc. simply because the Ph.D. title has traditionally been reserved for students who mostly attend school on a full-time basis to conduct research. However, according to many colleagues, the quality of many DBA, DIBA, DPA, DM, DOL, and other such programs are just as good as many traditional programs that offer a Ph.D. While the title of the degree may not make much of a difference in the outcomes achieved, the Ph.D. degree seems to be more popular because it has been around in more schools than other equivalent programs offered through distance education for working adult professionals. Based on personal interactions, discussions and visits with many non-traditional doctoral students at two different accredited universities in the United States, it is apparent that many of them have been asking for a Ph.D. Program that can be completed while they work full-time since they are willing to get more involved in research and teaching both during and after their corporate and government careers. This demand provides another great marketing opportunity for both traditional and non-traditional schools that can fill this need for working professionals. Business Week (March 2004), noted that "The business Ph.D. is an endangered species. In 2002, a mere 1,095 people earned the degree versus more than 6,600 Ph.D.s in social sciences and 5,300 in humanities. And, some 40% of all business PhDs head directly from B-school to Corporate America. That leaves only about 650 to fill faculty slots at B-schools. The schools have been coping but some 500 spots for doctorate-holding faculty went vacant in 2003—more than double the number two years earlier."

A doctor of philosophy program can be a quality research-oriented degree that can fill the need for more Ph.D.s, create new enrollment and enhance a school's brand. According to some projections, there will be a need for more than 1,100 Ph.D.s in Business within the next 5 years and more than 2,400 new Ph.D.s within the next 10 years to conduct research and teach. As such, non-traditional schools can use their existing model and unique delivery format to prepare Ph.D.s that will be able to fill the educational needs of twenty first century institutions. While the traditional schools are finding it very difficult to enroll and successfully graduate Ph.D. students due to the high cost associated with such programs and lack of sufficient public funding, a non-traditional school's unique delivery format enables it to deliver this program much more efficiently than the traditionally operated institutions. A Ph.D. Program can prepare students for positions such as researchers, faculty members, university administrators, and practitioners in government, not for profit institutions and for profit organizations. With the projected increasing demand for Ph.D. graduates, these professionals will be able to differentiate themselves through their specialized fields of expertise from other professionals. The graduate of a specialized Ph.D. Program should be able to compete globally with both research and teaching oriented institutions.

According to the information provided by The U.S. Education Information Center (2004), "Historically, the DBA provided a more general perspective on management, while the Ph.D. emphasized research in a specialized area of management. However, the difference between the two degrees is no longer so precise and varies from institution to institution. The PhD is the more commonly offered degree." According to the Association to Advance Collegiate Schools of Business (AACSB) Report titled "Overview of U.S. Business Schools 2002–2003," there were 5,598 doctoral students at the 99 schools that responded to their survey. So, the market has a huge potential for student enrollment at schools that have flexible delivery formats for doctoral courses and the overall program. Of the total numbers (5,598) of students enrolled in doctoral programs,

- 825 (14.7%) of students were enrolled in the finance specialization.
- 596 (10.6%) were enrolled in the management specialization. And
- 605 (10.8%) were enrolled in the marketing specialization.

The same report, by AACSB, concluded that about 63% of the enrolled doctoral students were males and 37% were females. Furthermore, it was concluded that 50.2% of the enrolled students were American citizens or permanent residents of the United States while 49.8% were Non-U.S. citizens without permanent visas. From the 50.2% (2,835 students) that were either U.S. citizens or permanent residents, 76% were white (non-Hispanic), 3.7% were Hispanic, 7.1% were Black (non-Hispanic), and 7.7% were Asians or Pacific Islander. Since NSU has an excellent record of recruiting minorities and international students, the Huizenga School Programs are very competitive as it attracts talented working professionals from across the nation and around the world.

According to Jain (1997), business units introduce multiple brands to a market for two major reasons: 1) to grow by offering varied products in different market segments, and 2) to avoid competitive threats to a single brand/product. Jain adds that, "multiple brands must be diligently positioned in the market." So, there may be many good reasons for schools to go forward with offering or adding more doctoral (DBA or Ph.D.) programs in the fields of business. The Communicator: Council of Graduate Schools (2004) stated that "With attrition from Ph. D. programs averaging 30% to 50%, the nation is losing an important resource of highly trained personnel" while the demand is rising. The article further mentioned that the attrition is much more severe for women and minorities since they tend to leave doctoral programs at a greater rate than the majority and international students. Furthermore, this is a concern because projections show that about 80% of the growth in college-age students will come from minorities. The Council of Graduate Schools statistics showed that 39,955 students graduated with doctorate degrees in 2002 and this number was the lowest total since 1993. Because many schools are cutting back their doctoral programs, fewer percentage of qualified students get the opportunity to enter and successfully complete doctoral degrees. In an article titled "Is There a Doctorate in the House" written by Tricia Bisoux at the March/April issue of BizEd (2003), the author stated that "replenishing the world's supply of doctorates in business has become imperative." While there is an increase in the demand for more terminally degreed educators (DBAs and Ph.D.s), many traditional schools have been downsizing their programs for cost-cutting purposes. As cost rises, "many Ph.D.-granting institutions are shrinking their doctoral programs in business, especially those in the U.S." (BizEd, 2003). As business schools reduce their Ph.D. Program enrollment, fewer qualified educators enter the pipeline. As the number of qualified candidates decreases in the doctoral programs, salaries will rise in the United States thereby attracting terminally degreed faculty members from other countries. As such, schools throughout the world will find themselves in a "salary war that many will likely lose" as stated by BizEd (2003). The non-traditional schools are in a good position to offer doctoral programs and to economically fulfill society's needs for more research-oriented graduates. With today's internet age and advanced technology, making such programs available with a great quality should be much easier than ever before.

The twenty first century is the first century of comprehensive worldwide cyberspace education through distance learning both academically and for workforce development. Higher education students in this new millennium can and should be selective in choosing a doctoral program (be it a Ph.D., a DBA or other non-traditional programs) for enrollment since a doctorate of business administration (DBA) program can monetarily cost anywhere from $30,000 to over $100,000 depending on the program and school offering the degree. Of course, then there is the four to five years of time that has its opportunity cost as well. The business of higher education has become very competitive as schools move far beyond their main campuses to offer programs nationally and internationally. Many of the schools involved in distance education also use cyberspace technology as their students complete the doctoral program while remaining employed full-time. Learners need not be concerned about the modality of the education programs from accredited schools since many of the same educators who facilitate in the traditional programs are also now teaching at distance education programs. As such, the quality and outcomes achieved are likely to be the same for all programs. All doctoral students are likely to complete some form of comprehensive exams as part of the requirement for graduation and the questions tend to be the same for local and distance education students. Therefore, the quality of the education is likely to be the same when students are achieving similar outcomes as a result of their degree and perform equally well on the exams. Furthermore, educators must make sure that their distance education programs produce equivalent outcomes as the traditional formats since the quality of one aspect of learning is likely to impact the others as per systems thinking mentality.

TAKING A SYSTEMS APPROACH IN EDUCATION

Higher education institutions are one of the longest lasting organizational systems that society has created for the purpose of developing experts, practitioners and researchers (Carr et al, 2004). The formal educational system, dating back to the thirteenth century, has changed dramatically from its beginnings to today. According to Jacques (1996), as late as the mid 1800's a degree obtained from Harvard University was primarily a recognition of attendance, and the suggestion to implement grading, structured curricula, and standardized testing was considered radical. Today, universities are "standard producers of knowledge" (p. 131). Nova Southeastern University's doctoral programs in business have been a pioneer in making higher education available to working adult students through innovative distance education mediums. They have been successful because they have a holistic view of education rather than limiting themselves to just doing what has always been done. Rather, they made education available through non-traditional methods by thinking holistically and seeing how working adults can impact the society if they are given quality opportunities to advance their education without having to quit their jobs and attend the traditional schools.

The "systems thinking" approach or mindset is concerned with the whole and its properties while holistically examining a specific problem, organization, situation, process, or principle and not in the reductionist manner of previous science (Checkland, 1999). Capra (1996) called this a new paradigm, "seeing the world as an integrated whole rather than a dissociated collection of parts" (p. 6). According to Checkland (1999), the unquestioned prime value of a systems approach is that continuous, never-ending learning is a good thing. Learning and relearning is valuable and critical for the long-term success of an organization and personal achievement. The metaphor of knowledge as a building block is being replaced by that of a network that has interconnected models that have no foundations (Capra, 1996). "Systems thinking" is one cornerstone of a learning organization, along with personal mastery, positive mental models as to how the world works, building a shared vision, and team learning (Senge, 1990).

Taking a systems approach to analyzing organizational problems addresses the great complexity of the universe (Carr et al, 2004). As is with an ecological community, systems are interdependent and interconnected in a vast network of relationships, which Capra (1996) referred to as the web of life. The ability to sustain long-term effectiveness requires a partnership or exchange of energy and resources in order to live inside one another and can be viewed as the hallmark of life. Levine (1995) posited that organizations in America are fixated with short-term profits in order to meet investor expectations and the result is less of an investment in human capital because investing in human capital has a long-term payoff. According to Daily and Bishop (2003), lack of training is the most frequently cited factor that restricts employee participation. Training that is focused on broadening employees' knowledge and skills, as opposed to focused only on improving their current role, result in more proficient teams, improved employee adaptability, and is positively related to teamwork. In order for people within an organization to build and grow the skills and competencies needed for increased employee participation, Hesselbein, Marshall, and Beckhard (1997) asserted that organizations need to create learning communities. Organizations of the future will need to shift the learning paradigm from learning as a *Tabula Rasa*, or blank slate, to a paradigm that knowledge transfer and creation is a more fluid, organic process. As such, the distribution and creation of knowledge does not have to be limited to the traditional formats which is why there is a rise in distance education programs today.

ASSESSMENT OF DISTANCE EDUCATION

Integrating a systematic testing and evaluation plan into the curriculum for student learning and learning assessment is a basic necessity in today's competitive world of education. Fortunately, many educators and administrators have successfully implemented effective testing and evaluation methods in their distance education programs. However, much more may need to be done to make this an ongoing process of continually enhancing the programs holistically. As such, administrators should focus on the development, assessment, and implementation of comprehensive testing and evaluation strategies in their curriculums (online, on-ground, and blended formats of distance as well as traditional offerings) while focusing on effectively achieving learning outcomes equally well in all modalities.

Public and private colleges are viewed as public property and this view reflects the centrality of the American institutions today, said Carol Christ who is the president of Smith College and a former provost of the University of California at Berkeley (Forum, 2004). She further stated that "If accountability is our end, then the means to that end lie in an ethic of greater transparency...we in colleges must be more open about our business practices and in our governance." Chronicles of Higher Education published a forum on its September 3rd issue titled "*How Can Colleges Prove They're Doing Their Jobs?*" which focused on accountability and assessment. The forum published thoughts and views from experts on accountability and assessment which included the following general topics: we need an honest conversation, no less than a cultural shift, a more systematic approach, focus on a larger context, the word 'public' is the key, and strive for openness (Forum, 2004). Charles Reed and Edward Rust Jr. suggested that "colleges should define goals for student learning and provide evidence that they have met them" (Forum, 2004). Material in the forum pointed out that "Private colleges aren't immune to calls for greater accountability…with tuitions continually rising, students, parents, and other constituencies are demanding proof that students are getting what they are paying for and learning what they need to know." So, some strategic planning, changes for the better, and documentation of improvement are needed in order for business schools to successfully move forward.

Gary Hamel, visiting professor of strategic and international management at the London Business School, states that "business schools can be notorious institutions of habit" which has served them well for over a century but it is not going to get them through the next decade if they do not bring about appropriate changes. Business strategists in academia offer many suggestions for modern business schools wishing to be successful in today's technology-driven environment including that they need to defy conventions, be innovative and try different strategies to get better results, not follow fads, create new competitive contexts, go beyond doing research by actually experimenting, globalize the curriculum and its focus, and form the future instead of just following it (Westerbeck, 2004). The modern business schools should be creating meaningful change if they are to survive and thrive in the world of demanding stakeholders. This change must be driven based on the assessment of what the school claimed to deliver as per their mission and its progress or intended application. Such assessment should be systematic, progressive, formal, and institution-wide if the organization is to receive a benefit from it. The role of learning assessment and evaluation to a university's future success is important for its survival. For example, for a teaching institution, the primary measure of learning would be the degree to which students actually learn the intended material. Administrators could ask relevant questions to determine the effectiveness of each program. Do students know what they should know? Can students do what they should be able to do? Have students developed knowledge and skills appropriate to their professions? Was the achievement of students' personal and professional goals enhanced by their experience at the university? Furthermore, faculty members should be asking such questions as: What did our students learn, and how well did they learn it? Do students simply acquire information, or do they learn to analyze, synthesize, and exercise critical judgment about the subject matter? Do they learn to write clear, grammatical, logical arguments? Do they learn tolerance for differing perspectives? Can they logically defend their own opinions in a rational way? Can they apply what they know to other areas of their work and life? Does their learning last beyond the end of the course and program? If a teaching university is able to demonstrate continuing accomplishment of such essential student-learning goals, the logical consequence will be their accomplishment of the other goals and purposes.

From an internal perspective, the integrity of the learning assessment and institutional evaluation processes are essential because the data generated provide the energy needed for continuous improvement of how things are processed. The data also provides the means through which the faculty and administration assess the degree to which goals related to student learning and achievement are being accomplished. In addition, they serve as a tool in identifying gaps and making improvements. Technology can greatly assist in teaching and learning when used effectively. However one could ask: Do cyberspace technologies make the teaching and learning processes more effective? Does technology help students learn the material more efficiently as shown by the results of a systematic assessment? Perhaps technology used in distance education can assist students to learn the intended outcomes differently and a different amount of it in a speedier manner. As proven by scientific management principles and Ford's assembly lines for producing Model-T cars in black color, machines can create efficiency. However, efficiency does not always translate into long-term stakeholder satisfaction and research shows that people learn differently but not always efficiently since each individual has his/her own learning style. While cyberspace technology can make learning efficient, educators must also focus on the need for effectiveness. In other words, through systematic assessments, educators should determine if the technology is delivering the right results or the intended outcomes as effectively as available alternative methods. Of course, an effective assessment program requires a strategic plan for each curriculum and each program. The plans for assessing students' academic achievement in each program must then be put into action and evaluation for continuous improvement. The elements necessary for supporting such a strategic process include the functions of planning, assessment delivery, analysis of the result, reflection, recommendations, and eventually continuous improvement in order to close the loop for effective deployment and documentation of assessment for each program.

Corporate management development trainers know that they need to assess learning in terms of the course's stated objectives (exit competencies) and be able to provide evidence that demonstrates the achievement of learning outcomes, in terms of application and better management, if they are to continue receiving funding for their workshops. The same principle of assessment also applies in the academic world regardless of whether one is teaching traditional adults students (full-time students) or non-traditional adult students (part-time students that are working professionals) completing their program through distance education modalities. Academicians know that taking the strategic plans for measuring and assessing student achievement, analyzing them for improvement purposes, and implementing the resulting analysis throughout the university can present opportunities and challenges for schools committed to a process improvement philosophy. Universities use a good variety of tools that support the model of planning, delivery, assessment, reflection, recommendation, and continuous improvement of student learning. However, none of the tools can take the place of a faculty member's key role in effective deployment, improvement, and documentation of student learning in each session of his/her course so the next session can be improved, if needed. For example, an experienced faculty member can adjust his/her lecture or facilitation while assessing the audience to see how much they know and how fast they are able to process the information. Continuous improvement comes from keeping one's finger on the pulse of the customer (students) to get the right data and information in a timely manner so the appropriate actions can be taken after its assessment.

Assessment can be seen as the process of establishing and/or understanding the learning outcomes that meet the learners' needs, assessing students to determine whether or not they have achieved the learning outcomes through factual evidence, documenting those results, and reflecting on how to continually improve the process of teaching, learning and learner assessment. The purpose of the assessment process is to continually improve and document or credential learning. A structured review of the assessment model can enhance the assessment process by providing a framework that supports thoughtful planning and communication to relevant stakeholders before and during the learning process, deployment of valid and reliable assessment strategies, informed reflection on the results, as well as improvement of teaching, learning and assessment in order to close the loop. When it comes to personal reflections for improvement, faculty members tend to have three formats for facilitation of learning: 1) the facilitation they plan to do; 2) the facilitation they actually do; and, 3) the facilitation they wish they had done. This type of reflection can certainly lead to improvement when the third format is put back into the loop thereby improving the next facilitation they plan to do. This closes the loop and improves the learning process for the students. It has been said that some universities have three curricula: The one that appears in the catalog, the one that professors teach, and one that students actually learn. Along with the administrators, it is also the faculty member's responsibility to find out the degree to which the curriculum asserted on paper or imagined by academic leaders accurately portrays what goes on in the minds of students. Making the curricula visible so its usefulness in terms of demonstrated learning and results through students' performance can be documented as evidence is the business of *assessment*, an activity practiced by each faculty member teaching the course.

While each faculty member should take responsibility for improving his/her teaching to enhance the outcomes achieved, it is the responsibility of program chairs, directors and other appropriate administrators to design assessment strategies for measuring learning across all courses at all locations for determining the effectiveness of distance education programs. The American Association of Higher Education (AAHE) offered the following "Principles of Good Practice for Assessing Student Learning" at the AAHE Assessment forum in December of 1992 for those who are involved in the assessment process:

1. The assessment of student learning begins with educational values. Assessment is not an end in itself but a vehicle for educational improvement.
2. Assessment is most effective when it reflects an understanding of learning as multidimensional, integrated, and revealed in performance over time.
3. Assessment works best when the programs it seeks to improve have clear, explicitly stated purposes. It entails comparing educational performance with educational purposes and expectations.
4. Assessment requires attention to outcomes but also and equally to the experiences that lead to those outcomes.
5. Assessment works best when it is ongoing, not episodic. This means tracking the performance of individual students or groups through various modalities.
6. Assessment fosters wider improvement when representatives from across the educational community are involved.
7. Assessment makes a difference when it begins with issues of use and illuminates questions that people really care about.
8. Assessment is most likely to lead to improvement when it is part of a larger set of conditions that promote change.
9. Through assessment, educators meet their responsibilities to students and to the public.

Educators have a responsibility to students and to the public that depend on them to provide accurate information on how students meet their goals and objectives. Of course, this responsibility extends beyond reporting to actually improving and enhancing the program in a purposeful manner. In order to meet their responsibilities and document student learning, program directors and chairs along with their faculty members often strategically create an outcomes assessment plan for their programs. These plans are usually comprehensive, systematic, structured, and goal-oriented. The purpose of a comprehensive assessment process is to contribute to the pursuit of an institution's vision by assisting faculty, staff, and administrators in identifying the needs of stakeholders and adapting courses, curricula, delivery methods, and services according to these needs. The following characteristics are often found in the student outcomes assessment process: (a) evidence is produced that measures student achievement of learning outcomes; (b) evidence is produced to show where course changes and improvements are needed; (c) faculty, administrators, students, and other stakeholders are involved in the assessment and planning processes; and (d) assessment is linked to the planning and budgeting process. The remaining sections of this document explore NSU's School of Business Entrepreneurship and how their doctoral students are doing in their comprehensive exams. The Comp exams, besides the dissertation and publication requirements for the program, provide evidence of students' success as to how well the program is achieving its intended outcomes.

DOCTORAL PROGRAM ASSESSMENT—AN EXAMPLE

Nova Southeastern University has been active in many countries including the United States, the Bahamas, Trinidad, China, Brazil, France, Germany, Dominican Republic, England, Greece, Panama, Venezuela, Jamaica, and many others to offer degrees in business, law, education, pharmacy, nursing, dentistry, medicine, optometry, conflict resolution, psychology, humanities, and many others. However, NSU's doctorate in business at the H. Wayne Huizenga School of Business and Entrepreneurship (Huizenga School) has traditionally been offered only throughout the United States and Jamaica, besides the main campus which is in Fort Lauderdale, Florida. NSU's Doctorate Programs in business (Doctorate of Business Administration, Doctorate of International Business Administration, Doctorate of Public Administration, and the available specialties) have been very successful and students continue to enjoy the flexibility of completing the classes on weekends through national clusters, and the practical application of their courses. In fact, the enrollment into the doctoral program mostly comes from "word-of-mouth" advertisement and testimonials of previous graduates and currently enrolled students. In the next section, we provide a history of the current Doctoral Program so the reader becomes familiar with the NSU's business programs to determine how it differs from the traditional formats.

The Doctor of Business Administration (DBA) program at the H. Wayne Huizenga School of Business and Entrepreneurship (Huizenga School) attempts to transform mature students into more effective global leaders. Doctoral candidates not only learn the most advanced decision-making techniques needed for success in the twenty first century, but also develop the research and writing skills that accompany high-level responsibility in the academic and business environments. The program encourages executives, educators, and consultants to use their professional backgrounds to explore, design, and manage large systems within the complex organizations of the increasingly multifaceted and multisectored economy. The start of the Doctoral Programs at the Huizenga School can be traced back to the late 1970s. In 1971, the Center for the Study of Administration was formed at NSU (renamed later in 1979 as the School of Business and Entrepreneurship and in 2001 as the H. Wayne Huizenga Graduate School of Business and Entrepreneurship). In 1973, the Center for Public Affairs and Administration (PAA) was established and Graduate Management Programs (GMP) was implemented. In 1978, Doctoral programs in business administration began within the Graduate Management Program. In 1979, GMP and PAA programs were combined forming the School of Business and Entrepreneurship (SBE). In 1999, the School of Business and Entrepreneurship was renamed the Wayne Huizenga Graduate School of Business and Entrepreneurship and the board of trustees approved the construction of a new building for the school on the Main Campus. In 2002, the Undergraduate Business Programs from the Farquhar College of Arts and Sciences merged with the graduate business school. As such, the name of the school was changed to H. Wayne Huizenga School of Business and Entrepreneurship.

Huizenga School's D.B.A. program consists of four components: (1) the common core; (2) specialty courses in the fields of accounting, finance, health services administration, human resource management, information technology management, international management, management, and marketing; (3) competencies in the area of the student's major as demonstrated through the successful completion of the comprehensive exam; and (4) research (dissertation-related units).

The D.B.A. program operates on a year-round basis. All course work, seminars, workshops, and the comprehensive examination can be completed within four years. Each student progresses at his or her own pace in researching and writing the dissertation; the total length of time in the program is normally about four years. Cluster classes meet monthly in a convenient weekend format at over ten locations throughout the United States and Jamaica. Students generally attend cluster courses at one location, but the option to schedule at different locations is available for those who move, or who wish to attend a course during a term other than when it is available at the home cluster. This flexibility in scheduling is unique to the NSU program.

Enrollment in the Doctorate of Business Administration (DBA) program at the NSU's School of Business and Entrepreneurship was 458 students in first term of 2004 (see Table 11). The enrollment has remained steady

Table 11. Doctoral Enrollment by Term at NSU's School of Business

Year	2004	2003			2002			2001			2000		
Terms	1	1	2	3	1	2	3	1	2	3	1	2	3
Total Student Enrollment	458	446	381	527	514	238	531	467	318	527	544	300	566
Number of Students Taking Comp Exam*	38	27	21	23	46	22	25	22	12	4	71*	38	51

Year	1999			1998			1997		
Terms	1	2	3	1	2	3	1	2	3
Total Student Enrollment	529	305	546	496	312	550	524	309	531
Number of Students Taking Comp Exam	50	71	73	49	50	58	50	53	53

* After the period of 2000, students took both Comps I and II together as one Comp Exam resulting in lower numbers.

over the years while staffing, advising, and the number of faculty members has increased to further enhance the program's diversity and quality for all students. This consistency is the result of the program's popularity in both domestic and foreign locations. The program has been particularly popular among corporate managers and consultants who wish to teach and conduct further research in their fields.

According to NSU's statistics on business doctorate students, the proportion of African Americans enrolled in the program nearly doubled from 13% in 1988 to 24% in 2002 over the 5-year period. The increase is due to the popularity of the program among students of diverse racial/ethnic backgrounds. According to the Black Issues in Higher Education (June 5, 2003—Volume 20(8)), NSU's Business School is ranked number 2 in the nation for the number of doctorate degrees in business awarded to all minorities. Additionally, although the marketing strategy for the program does not specifically target ethnic segments, a multicultural dimension is reflected in the promotional elements used in the recruitment process. Finally, about 29% of the students enrolled in the program are females. This number of female students entering the doctorate programs is expected to increase in the coming years as more females pursue advanced business education in Nova Southeastern University's convenient formats.

According to NSU's e-Bulletin (electronic, university-wide newsletter) on August 8, 2004, NSU leads the nation in the number of doctorates awarded to African Americans and Hispanics: "NSU is once again the number one producer of African American doctorates among both traditionally white institutions and historically Black colleges and universities, as well as the number one producer of Hispanic doctorates based on survey results published in the July 29, 2004 edition of *"Black Issues in Higher Education." The NSU e-Bulletin (2004) further stated that* NSU also ranked as the number one producer of:

- African-American doctorates in the discipline of education,
- Hispanic doctorates in the discipline of education,
- Hispanic doctorates in the discipline of business, management, marketing and related support services,
- Total minority doctorates in the discipline of education, and
- Total minority doctorates in the discipline of business, management, marketing and related support services.

Survey of Doctoral Alumni

A survey was conducted of students who graduated in the 1999 - 2002 academic years. Surveys were sent to all recent graduates whose current addresses were available in the program's database. Questions on the survey addressed: the students' pre and post-graduation status with respect to employment or pursuit of graduate or professional studies; collection of information concerning student satisfaction with the program, and how well it prepared them for employment, promotion, or advanced study; determination of program completion and it's effectiveness on students' career advancement, salary, and job performance; and alumni perceptions of strengths and weaknesses of the program, as well as their overall satisfaction level.

The survey was divided into four sections. Section I collected background and status information in a forced choice format with regard to program delivery and pursuit of doctoral study. Section II collected information related to professional development, employment status, and skills acquisition of the graduate. Section III collected information related to alumni satisfaction with quality indicators of the program. Section IV collected data related to overall satisfaction and job preparedness with the program in a forced choice format.

Out of 190 surveys sent to recent graduates of the doctoral program, 90 were completed and returned, but only 85 were usable since they had complete information. So, the overall return rate was 47%, which is very good. However, only 45% were usable due to incomplete information on five omitted surveys. The following are some of the general results from the 85 surveys collected:

1. About 41% of the 85 respondents were majoring in Doctorate of Business Administration (with Management specialty) and 8% of the respondents were DIBA and DPA majors.
2. About 66% of the respondents agreed that they started teaching at a college level after graduation and that their degree was a factor in receiving teaching opportunities at the college level.
3. Over 91% reported that their experience at the Huizenga School enhanced their employment opportunities either extremely, considerably, moderately, or somewhat.
4. Approximately 53% of the respondents reported that they received a promotion and/or a raise and believed that their degree from the Huizenga School was a factor. However, only 33% of the respondents changed jobs a result of their education at the Huizenga School and 64% of them received more income as a result of the job change.
5. With regard to the quality indicators for the majority of the questions in the Doctoral Programs, over 90% of the students consistently reported that they were satisfied, quite satisfied or extremely satisfied.
6. Over 90% of the respondents reported being satisfied, quite satisfied, or extremely satisfied with their program at Huizenga School. Over 69% were either quite satisfied or extremely satisfied.

While all of the respondents were employed at the time of survey, about 66% of the respondents agreed that they started teaching at a college level after graduation from Huizenga School and that their degrees were a factor in receiving teaching opportunities at the college level. Furthermore, over 91% reported that their experience at Huizenga School enhanced their employment opportunities extremely, considerably, moderately, or somewhat but only less than 9% said "not at all." So, the statement of expected results "At least 80% of graduates will be employed in appropriate positions after graduation" was met based on the reported results.

Approximately 53% of the respondents reported that they received a promotion and/or a raise and believed that their degree from Huizenga School was a factor. However, about 33% of the respondents changed jobs as a result of their education at Huizenga School and 64% of them received more income as a result of the job change. Overall, the statement of expected results "At least 80% of graduates will report the program had a significant positive effect on the advancement of their professional interests and career aspirations" were not confirmed. As reflected in many of the responses, the primary reason for joining the doctoral program is for entering academia at a future date. As such, doctoral faculty members are heavily involved with students in the areas of research, publishing, and dissertation development. In addition, core and specialty classes are designed to lead to the successful completion of these areas.

Anticipating and reacting to market demand, the Huizenga School used various methods to further support the students to increase the probability of success with the dissertation. Students are encouraged to begin their research courses during their first year so they can begin working on their concept paper for the dissertation. Students are also provided training programs for effectively using technology and the library for their literature review in the dissertation and course work. As stated in the mission statement, Nova Southeastern University offers academic programs at times convenient to students, employing innovative delivery systems and rich learning resources on campus and at distant sites. Survey results indicate that 60% of the respondents used and preferred to complete the majority of the program in the weekend format with classes conducted at a cluster (field-based) location. Given NSU's mission and responses from doctoral alumni, the Huizenga School continues to develop cluster sites meeting the educational needs of doctoral candidates throughout the United States as well as outside of the country.

The result of the assessment and surveys clearly indicate that the Doctoral Program prepares its students and graduates for success in their academic and professional endeavors. The results of the faculty evaluations at the end of course surveys also indicate that the faculty members are performing satisfactorily. Another success of the doctoral faculty is demonstrated by the high passing rates on the comprehensive exam which indicate that the doctoral students are adequately prepared to demonstrate mastery of the subject matter for their program.

Assessment of Comprehensive Exams

As mentioned earlier, enrollment in the Doctorate of Business Administration (DBA) program at the NSU's School of Business and Entrepreneurship was somewhat consistent over the years while at times fluctuating from term to term between 340–560 students. The summer terms seem to have the lowest enrollment each year possibly because people are taking their vacations at this time of the year (see Figure 3 for the overall trends). Only the first term of 2004 was recorded on the left side of Figure 3 in this study with an enrollment of 458 students. The last term on the figure is the first semester of 1997 with an enrollment of 537 students on the right side of Figure 3.

While enrollment stayed consistent over the eight-year period studied, so did the number of students completing their Comp exams. Prior to the year 2001, most doctoral students took the first comprehensive exam in their sec-

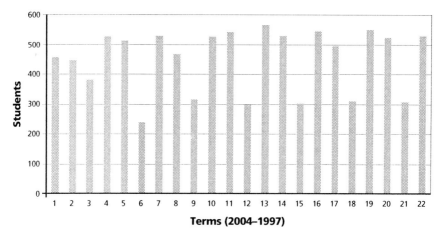

Figure 3. Enrollment trends

ond year while taking the second comprehensive exam toward the end of their program. So, they registered for the Comps in two separate sections. Starting with 2001, students were required to take both parts of the exam during the same time (one full day). This is why there is a lower number of students taking the Comp exam during 2001 and subsequent years.

Of the 968 students taking the Comp exam in the eight-year period, 88.74% successfully passed it in their first attempt; and 73% were males while 27% were females. As can be seen from Table 12, in the latter years there is a trend toward a higher percentage of students failing their comprehensive exams on their first attempt. For example in 1997, the passing rates for the three periods were 98%, 98% and 94% but in 2003 the percentages were 91%, 71% and 89% respectively. The trends from Table 12 seem to show that while the success rate in the Comp exam for men has decreased drastically by 31% during the eight years (from 84% in 1996 to 53% in 2004), the success rate for women has increased from 16% in 1996 to 47% in 2004 with a gain of 31%.

The high success rate for women is likely to be caused by the higher percentage of women entering the doctoral program and taking the Comp exam. On the other side, perhaps women are better than men at retaining the information learned in the classes or it could be because they were better prepared for the comprehensive exams. Another factor might be their test-taking ability such as being able to solve problems more accurately and writing clearer in the required format or manner thus influencing the evaluators to provide them with higher passing rates. While the reasons for their higher success rates in the Comp exam are not clear from this study,

Table 12. Comp Passing Rate Statistics

Year	Number of Students Taking the Comp Exam	Pass		Men		Women	
		#	%	#	%	#	%
2004	38	30	79%	16	53%	14	47%
2003	27	24	89%	12	50%	12	50%
	21	15	71%	9	60%	5	40%
2002	23	21	91%	13	62%	8	38%
	46	38	83%	31	82%	7	18%
	22	20	91%	15	75%	5	25%
2001	24	21	87.50%	14	67%	7	33%
	22	17	77%	11	65%	6	35%
	12	10	83%	5	50%	5	50%
2000	4	4	100%	3	75%	1	25%
	71	60	85%	48	80%	12	20%
	38	32	84%	22	69%	10	31%
1999	51	43	84%	31	72%	12	28%
	50	39	78%	24	62%	15	38%
	71	60	85%	52	87%	8	13%
1998	73	69	95%	46	66.6%	23	33.3%
	49	44	90%	29	66%	15	34%
	50	41	82%	30	73%	11	27%
1997	58	58	100.00%	43	74%	15	26%
	50	47	94%	38	81%	9	19%
	53	52	98%	42	81%	10	19%
	53	52	98%	41	79%	11	21%
1996	62	62	100%	52	84%	10	16%
Total	968	859	88.74%	627	73%	232	27%

it certainly merits a deeper analysis and perhaps a qualitative study to determine best practices for their success rates.

To see if there is a statistically significant difference in the average passing rates or percentages of students in the first four years and the later four years, the authors conducted a t-test of the average sample means of the passing rate percentages for the two populations. The two categories are 1996–1999 which covered ten Comp exam periods (population one) and 2000–2004 which covered thirteen Comp exam periods (population two). It is hypothesized that there is no statistically significant difference in the average passing rate percentages for the two populations.

**Table 13. *t*-Test for Differences in Two Means
of Comp Students Groups**

Data:	
Hypothesized Difference	0
Level of Significance	0.05
Population 1 Sample:	
Sample Size: 1996–1999—Ten Periods of Comp	10
Sample Mean	92
Sample Standard Deviation	0.079
Population 2 Sample:	
Sample Size: 2000–2004—Thirteen Periods of Comp	13
Sample Mean	84
Sample Standard Deviation	0.072
Intermediate Calculations:	
Population 1 Sample Degrees of Freedom	9
Population 2 Sample Degrees of Freedom	12
Total Degrees of Freedom	21
Pooled Variance	0.005637
Difference in Sample Means	7
t-Test Statistic	221.6571683
Two-Tailed Test:	
Lower Critical Value	–2.079614205
Upper Critical Value	2.079614205
p-Value	7.20748E-37
Reject the null hypothesis	

The results are tabulated for the two categories of populations that include a total of 968 students who took the comprehensive examinations. Using a 0.05 level of significance, the null hypothesis (Ho) is rejected because $t = 221.657$ is larger than the critical value of +2.0796 (see Table 13). Also, because the p-value of 0.0000 is less than alpha (α) = 0.05, there is sufficient evidence to reject the null hypothesis. Based on these results, the students in the first category (1996–1999) seem to have Comp scores (92% on the average) that are statistically different than the students' in the second category (2000–2004) Comp scores (84% on the average). As such, one can conclude that the first category (1996–1999) Comp scores' are significantly higher than the second category (2000–2004) Comp scores.

So, according to the statistical analysis, students seem to be doing worse in their comprehensive exams during the last four years. There are many possibilities for this downward trend:

1. The expectations have increased and, therefore, more students are not passing the comp exam on their first attempt.
2. The answers are being evaluated with stricter guidelines.
3. Maybe the questions and answers have changed but the right content is not being comprehensively covered in each course.
4. The students in the first category (1996–1999) completed only one part of the Comp exam during a given time. As such, they only had to prepare for one Comp exam which might be a factor in their higher success rates.
5. Most of the students in the last four years took both Comps I and II together as one Comp exam which takes all day and can be stressful. This might be a cause for their lower percentage of passing rates. Furthermore, these students had to read more material as a review to prepare for answering more questions since all the questions were in one Comp.
6. Students today are not doing their work in each course as well as they used to in previous decades. Maybe faculty members are not expecting the same level of learning as they used to in the previous decades.
7. Today's students are not preparing as well as they should for the comprehensive exams.
8. The quality of students entering the program has decreased in the last four years.

Table 14. Pass Rates for Doctoral Comp Exam (2000–2004)

Year	Total Taking Exam	Pass		Fail	
		Number	*Percent*	*Number*	*Percent*
2000	160	135	84.38%	25	15.63%
2001	38	31	81.58%	7	18.42%
2002	92	79	85.87%	13	14.13%
2003	71	60	84.51%	11	15.49%
2004	38	30	79.00%	8	21.00%
Total	399	335	84.00%	14	16.00%

While there might be many other possibilities, besides the ones listed above, for the lower passing rates in the Comp exam in the last four years the most likely reason could be that Comp I and Comp II exams are now being taken at one time. So, there is more pressure and more questions to prepare for and complete all the questions on the same day. Perhaps another sample of students in the next fours years (2005-2008) can be compared with the last four years to see if the average percentages of scores are significantly different.

While there seems to be a downward trend in the success rates of students in the last four years on Comp exams with an average passing rate of 84% for the years 2000 through the first term of 2004 (as can be seen from Table 14), the average overall passing rates for the past eight years is still 88.74%, showing good evidence of student learning. So, a great majority of students are able to successfully complete their exams on the first attempt. However, in the spirit of continuous improvement, the school can and should provide more resources and suggestions on how more students can perform better in their first attempt in the comprehensive examinations. Some of the basic suggestions for students to do better in their individual comprehensive examinations are to take good notes in the individual classes, make sure they understand the objectives of each class and be able to meet them at the outset of the class, take the Comp exams shortly after completing the relevant courses, review all course material and projects completed in the classes the month before the Comp exam, review relevant literature and textbooks prior to the exam, take some time off work the week before the exam to reduce the pressure, and get plenty of sleep the night before the exam.

As another option, consideration could be given to changing the Comp exam to test the students` ability to apply knowledge to specific real world problems and dilemmas. At present, many of the exam questions seem to be subject content exams that are similar to summative questions used when the subject is examined at the end of the each course. This may place at least some students at a disadvantage as they may have attended that particular course 3 years prior to taking the comps. What is needed is a set of questions that can test the students` ability to deal with current issues that influence modern business. Typical comp questions could be: 1-What are the issues and consequences of privatizing social security? 2-What are the ethical components of advertising directed at children? These types of questions will test the student's ability to debate issues of importance to business as well as society while integrating as well as referencing relevant theories and current literature. This will also test whether they understand how to apply the theory that is covered in the core and specialty courses. It is also suggested that students should be given a choice of questions so they can select those that are more relevant to their area of specialization or expertise.

Overall, the world of distance and higher education, using blended formats of distance learning delivery, has achieved a special market in the adult environment by offering quality educational programs both nationally and internationally at times convenient to working adults. Through professional faculty members committed to student learning and their ability to combine academic theory with successful practical tools as well as their ability to effectively adjust to the changing educational needs of working professionals, doctoral educators have and can offer great value to their students and the community at large.

SUMMARY

The H. Wayne Huizenga School of Business and Entrepreneurship (SBE) of Nova Southeastern University (NSU) has been offering graduate programs in the fields of business administration through various distance delivery modes for the past thirty years. They have been able to do this partially because they take a holistic view and understand how working adult students do not always have the option of attending classes in a traditional format as that would negatively impact many other parts of their lives. Table 15 pro-

Table 15. Huizenga School's Mission and Selected Objectives

"Advance the personal growth and professional development of individuals in business, government, and nonprofit organizations by providing readily accessible and convenient educational opportunities of superior value."

Objectives and Activities	*Evidence of Achieving the Mission*
Advance the personal growth of students.	Alumni survey showed that 66% of doctoral graduates began teaching at a college level as a result of their degree with Nova Southeastern University's School of Business and Entrepreneurship.
Provide high-quality educational business programs of distinction.	Huizenga School faculty members and chairs attend academic and professional workshops each year to glean the best content for their classes and curriculums.
Prepare students for lifelong learning and leadership roles in business and their selected professions.	Huizenga School offers a variety of programs and services to meet the needs of its students and alumni. Alumni survey showed that about 53% of graduates received promotions and/or raises because of the education at NSU.
Offer academic programs at times convenient to students while uniting them with competent faculty.	Classes have been made available to students on many locations outside of the Main Campus within the United States as well as abroad to meet the demand. Huizenga School continually recruits practitioner faculty so they can share current best practices from the corporate, government and nonprofit arenas with students.
Be consistent in achieving the required curriculum and course outcomes as a result of successfully completing each course and session regardless of location, modality or faculty.	Through institutional effectiveness review of all programs every four years, the outcomes assessment plan as well as the ad hoc studies and reports of learning achievement, Huizenga School has demonstrated that students are achieving similar outcomes regardless of educational delivery modality or location. Full-time faculty members who teach at the Main Campus also teach at the clusters to make sure there is consistency in all programs.

vides an overview of activities and results on how the H. Wayne Huizenga School of Business and Entrepreneurship achieves its mission and vision by providing qualitative and convenient educational opportunities to its current and prospective students.

Systems thinking is applicable to researchers for seeing the whole not just the parts, interrelationships rather than things, for identifying patterns rather than taking a static picture of the events. "Systems thinking" is the cornerstone of a learning organization and is designed to integrate the various disparate parts of a problem or issue (Senge, 1990). While there is no *perfect* organization, higher education programs should have an infrastructure in place that ensures learning happens at a high-level consistently. There should be an emphasis on the development of high-level curricula that blends pragmatic and theoretical knowledge. The systems infrastructure and student support services should be in place for continued growth. These systemic processes enable students, who may not have had the opportunity to achieve a doctorate in the traditional system of education, the prospect to go to school and continue to work full-time. This innovative approach to advanced studies brings added value and a rich vision of education to the process of institutional learning.

Today, cyberspace technologies offer many possibilities in the twenty first century but such possibilities cannot be realized without breaking the outdated industry rules of the past. Breaking industry rules requires effective training of both faculty members and administrative staff so they can jointly be more flexible in hearing their students' learning needs and so they can be empowered to be innovative in integrating student feedback in the education process while trying new learning strategies. This section presented the results of alumni survey and their level of satisfaction as a result of completing their degrees. The chapter further explored the success rates of doctoral students in their comprehensive exam for the past eight years. Trends were analyzed and suggestions were offered for the program office to further explore and examine.

CHAPTER 8

ETHICS AND DIVERSITY ISSUES IN HIGHER EDUCATION

In today's school environment there has been an influx of reports and news concerning student cheating and dishonesty. Having an environment where cheating is perceived as a necessity is not a good form of conditioning and preparing students for the real world. Young students eventually end up running schools, governments and corporations where cheating is not productive for the society. As such, innovative and new measures must be taken to reduce cheating among students by showing them a better way and by removing their need for resorting to such tactics. Fortunately, there are dedicated faculty members that attempt to reduce dishonesty and cheating in the classroom by being innovative. Innovative techniques are important and emphasized because there are no "cookie cutter" approaches to stop all practices of cheating. This chapter informs the reader on some means of affectively changing the venue of learning today, by applying participatory facilitation skills to increase interest and retention with today's students. This was espoused by Benjamin Bloom, through his work "Bloom's Taxonomy of Learning."

Effective education to all students is a moral imperative in today's diverse environment of adult learning. Educators are obligated to avoid all issues that present a conflict of interest in order to create a healthy learning en-

Adult Education in Academia, pages 167–197
Copyright © 2006 by Information Age Publishing
All rights of reproduction in any form reserved.

vironment for all students. This latter part of the chapter provides a review of diversity related issues such as sexual harassment, self-fulfilling prophecy in relation to the diverse environment of education, diversity management concerns in learning, and adult teaching practices geared toward new adult educators of diverse student populations. Initial portions of this material on ethical challenges were prepared by Mujtaba and Kennedy (2005) and presented at the College Teaching and Learning Conference in Orlando, FL.

ETHICAL CHALLENGES

On April 29th 2004, ABC's (American Broadcasting Corporation) *Prime Time* had a segment on cheating in the education system by students. They tackled the issue of cheating in colleges and high schools. They found that 75% of students admitted to cheating on an exam or paper. This *Prime Time* segment titled "Caught Cheating in School" was a six month study of college and high school students about cheating practices and the reasons why students cheat. The research, claiming that cheating is at an all time high, was facilitated and narrated by Charlie Gibson.

Of the 12,000 college students, 75% admitted that they have cheated on an exam or term project. These students said that they know cheating is wrong but they do it in order to be better prepared for real life in the business world where cheating and manipulating the system to get ahead seems to be the norm. Students are using calculators, cell phones, computers, and other devices to store and/or download relevant information to complete the exam. Many schools have wireless access to the internet and students are fully able to use this system to download the answers and cheat very easily. One student was timed by Charlie Gibson to see how long it took her to get the answer for one of the questions from another student using her cell phone's text messaging function. It took her less than 30 seconds, using one hand under table while the other hand seemed to be attempting to take the test, to ask the question and receive the answer. Furthermore, ABC's poll concluded that 36% of high school students admitted that they had cheated. Furthermore, 7 out of 10 students say that their friends have cheated.

Researchers on the show stated that business administration students are the top cheaters in self reported surveys. They tend to rank first or second amongst the highest cheaters. Some students feel that they need to cheat since their counterparts are doing it. Others feel that they need to cheat as the school system is simply a "dress rehearsal" for the "cut throat" world of business. Many students feel that if senior business officers or religious leaders cheat, and politicians including governors and presidents lie, then they too have the right to cheat and get ahead using tactics available to them.

They tend to see the school system as their laboratory for experimentation of tactics used in the real world as senior managers and leaders attempt to manipulate employees, colleagues and other stakeholders for their own personal gain.

Michael Josephson, ethics consultant, stated that students feel as though it is OK to cheat since professors allow it. There is nothing wrong with the students since they simply think they will get behind if they don't do what they are allowed to do in order to have high performance. In a survey of 4,000 American and Canadian school educators, about 50% stated they have ignored obvious cases of cheating. As such, adults must be aware of cheating methods, stop cheating, teach students that cheating is wrong, and tell them that cheaters will be punished. In one case, a college professor found that about a half dozen of his students had cheated from an online site where information was prepared and presented by fifth grade students. It is sad to see that college students do not have time to prepare their own material but rather are plagiarizing from fifth graders. They feel that they have to keep up their grade point average (GPA) since college recruiters tend to hire those with high GPAs. Some students feel they must cheat since there is too much work for them to complete in such a short period of time. However, others thought it is the fault of the teachers for not punishing those who cheat.

During one experiment, students were caught cheating by checking their papers in the Turnitin.com website to see how many of the submitted papers were plagiarized. Turnitin.com is one tool that many educators use to catch cheaters. It can scan about 15,000 papers submitted by educators every day. Turnitin.com tells the faculty what is copied from other sources and what percentage of each paper is directly copied from these sources. The software marks all copied items in red and underlines them for the faculty. All this can be done in a matter of minutes based on the personal experiences of these authors and many colleagues that regularly use it.

Some students cheat because they don't think that they have the time to do a quality job in order to get a good grade. One student said that the "general student body" feels that cheating is OK in some cases, especially when one has several assignments that are due on the same day which leaves little to no time to complete them all qualitatively. One of the teachers in the experiment asked her class "How many of them would cheat if they knew that they would not get caught?" Practically all of the students raised their hands. These students were given an assignment after this discussion and about 67% (two third) of the class had copied much of the material from other sources as their own without proper citation and referencing. In some cases, students had only copied a few phrases as their own while others had copied as much as 80% of the material despite the fact that these students had seen the Robinson's Honor Code posted everywhere in their school and had a discussion on cheating during the same week. Subsequent discussions with these students showed that they felt cheating on academic assignments was a necessity for high performance and college entry. One high school student who had copied 80% of the material said he started the paper early in the evening, then ate dinner and finally helped his mother with the dishes before returning to complete the paper. At this time, it was 11:00 PM and he cheated because he did not want to stay up until 3:00 AM to complete the assignment. Another student who had also copied 80% of the assignment said he did it because he did not care much about this class and chose to spend most of his time studying for other more important subjects since he had several other exams and assignments due on the same day. Such forms of cheating are not limited to high schools or two year community colleges. Research shows that even top universities have had high rates of self-reported cheating. Michael Josephson said the higher the status of the school (such as Ivy League Schools), the more competitive the environment, the more pressure to earn higher grades, then the higher the rates of cheating will be in such environments. This is also true of the real world where the biggest bankers get caught cheating at the highest rates since the competition is very tough for them to do well.

Some students hire a professional writer to write their papers at a cost of approximately $25 each. One writer, named Andy, said that he has written over 500 papers thus far for his "clients" who come to him mainly through word-of-mouth advertising. Andy, who sees himself as a business person and an entrepreneur, stated that for a fee he sometimes takes tests for students in classes or for entry exams. For papers, Andy downloads the needed material for his "client's" topic and re-writes each sentence in order to beat "Turnitin.com" and other such software. He feels as though he is helping students earn better grades while earning a regular income for expenditure in society. So, based on Andy's thinking, this is a win-win situation for all involved. Andy also writes applications and essays for students who are trying to get into medical and law schools which tend to have higher enrollment standards than most other schools. In terms of goals Andy, who is currently a student, wants to become a medical doctor. Other students in this discussion also stated that they are going to school to become lawyers, doctors, and senior business officers. However, Charlie Gibson stated that none of them mentioned that they are going to school to get an education.

It has now become easier to cheat in college with the availability of carry-on technologies such as calculators, IPAQs, cell phones, and two way pagers. It was extremely easy for the students to cheat through these mediums. One of the students said that, "Cheating in college prepares you for the cut-throat business practices of the real world." They consider it a "dress rehearsal for life." Of-course, many educators are stunned to hear this mindset with America's youth. It is not like these are just one in a million. These students figure if they are getting a lower grade when they study, they might as well cheat. They have lost the integrity of actually studying to learn regardless of how much time it takes to understand the concepts. The high school students and college students had the same attitude. The only difference was their motivation: the high school students needed acceptable or competitive grades to get into college and, for many of these students, it didn't matter how they got the grades.

It appalls most educators, to say the least, to know that higher-level students would actually steal words from fifth-graders. That doesn't say too much for the educational system, does it? There is another site on the web (www. cheathouse.com) that houses term papers, essays, and book reports for high school and college students. There are several more sites that students seem to come across in assisting them to prepare papers. These sites are such that one can easily buy an essay or report whenever needed. Furthermore, some sites even promise that they have not been plagiarized! It is just a sad state of the world when students place no faith in themselves to do their own research and write their own papers, or they are just too lazy to do it. Perhaps, it just goes to show that many individuals with these upper-level careers do not even belong there if they got ahead using such tactics.

It causes one to wonder what ethics is all about. People are reading about business ethics to discover the differences in today's population's values. There seems to be a segment of the population (students or senior officers of large corporations) that will take the low road in every case regardless of the cost or the means. Cheating seems to be similar to a computer virus and worms that mess up programs and hinder productivity. Obviously we are working from a deficit in leaders with character and integrity. How can we change our leaders, too?

Back in the old days when most of today's educators went to college there were papers for sale. Some of the campus groups maintained a file for the members to use for various classes. There were people that wrote papers for a price. Yes, there may always be individuals in the population that will try a short cut in every case but their numbers seem to be increasing with the wide usage and availability of cyberspace technology. Technology and the internet can be a good thing and a bad thing in terms of their usage when people do not think about their actions and morals. People have to hold on to their morals and think about that when they are faced with such temptations since these urges for short cuts do not end during one's commencement or graduation. Michael Josephson, founder of the Josephson Institute, was asked about cheating in schools and he said these kids know that it is wrong, but they also think it is the norm. Mr. Josephson has been involved in character education in schools for most of his life and he passionately spoke about these issues in California (Long Beach) as a keynote speaker at the Eighth National Conference on Applied Ethics (sponsored by California State University) where Dr. Bahaudin Mujtaba also presented a paper on ethics in 1997, and where Dr. Joseph W. Kennedy conducted his dissertation research on ethical business practices, utilizing James Rest's Defining Issues Test of Kohlberg's maturity levels. Mr. Josephson was right on target at that time and the problem has only become much more widespread in the past decade. Certainly, educators have to respond to this dilemma and challenge. Almost all schools have some type of a guide that states a "zero tolerance" policy for cheating which basically equates to or is analogous to a corporation's "open door" policy - not having much of an impact. So, more action has to be taken and policies have to be enforced to effectively assess learning and to focus on learning through various means.

While, cheating goes on and is becoming part of the norm for some students, there is another dilemma or trend where some students who have great potential are not even going to class or doing homework. Teachers, at times, are not making the necessary inquiries and the students are suffering. The students know right from wrong and have often taken responsibility for their actions...to a point. However, it is the adult's responsibility to point out to these students their shortcomings. One educator, let's call him Sam, mentioned that "One student that fits this mold is labeled a "troublemaker" by everyone but me. I recognize he has behavior issues in class which seems to be due to the fact he has limited reading skills (this was assessed privately) and he or she is acting out. What a mess and it is getting worse." So, how do schools turn this cheating phenomenon that is becoming a huge problem around before it gets out of hand? Turning this around must start with adults and senior business role models by not cheating stockholders and investors out of their hard earned incomes. These senior officers and political role models must become model citizens by having fair accounting practices and by promoting integrity and honor which are not separate entities from the practice of doing business and getting ahead. Furthermore, as Mahatma Gandhi once stated, "these role models in society must become the change they would like to see in others."

Most people tend to agree with the solution of the "zero tolerance" policy, while modeling expected behaviors and believing that it can work. However, many also believe that it is unlikely to happen on the scale necessary to make a major impact on reducing the level of cheating in schools any time soon. The reasoning stems from witnessing an adult population in schools which has become complacent and let students do almost anything but fight one another in their vicinity. It is as if the attitude is "they are not trying to kill me or each other, so their behavior is ok, and besides I don't need any more hassles." The adults have let the atmosphere deteriorate into this state. So, it is going to be very difficult to rely on them to revive the culture to a new and improved state. Many individuals know we do not have many choices but to rely on adults to lead and children to comply; which might be the best alternative to the current challenge. Administrators, faculty and staff have the power to create and cultivate any atmosphere they "collectively" choose to implement. In some districts, leaders are looked upon with skepticism and distrust where people do not always trust one another wholeheartedly. There is the widespread "us vs. them" mentality reinforcing the dichotomy where people relieve themselves of the responsibility to fix the problem. There are still racial issues and concerns about unfair treatment of minorities and females that educators and employers must overcome as well. There is no "quick fix," no panaceas or easy answers for such complex challenges facing the community. However, most people agree and believe that the adults are just as responsible for the attitudes and behaviors as the students themselves. Once everyone recognizes this responsibility, then there may be hope for all educators, administrators and students on internalizing a commitment for change.

There are hidden issues for some kids that must be considered as the reality of today's life. There are more children today being raised by single parents that have a limited amount of time. Also, today more children and students do not have the benefit of having their extended family members nearby to socialize and interact with them. There is substance abuse on the part of many parents, and students. The children of many substance abusers come to school with limited potential. We have an aging population along with a shortage of qualified teachers entering the profession which leaves the industry with some teachers that are not mentally or physically fit for any level of confrontation. The population is increasing and technology is becoming sophisticated very rapidly where students can keep themselves busy in cyberspace using stimulating games instead of having to listen to monotone lectures about subjects they consider boring. Increased competition, lack of strong values and personal ethics have brought the society to this point where cheating is widespread. The industry is not ready for mass retirements that are going to take place in the next ten years. So, where is the education industry headed in the next few years? Most people claim that education by legislation has not been good for improving the system. Therefore, what is the ethical approach to education?

According to Bloom's research "95% of test questions students encounter require them to think only at the lowest possible level to recall the information," which is a common practice in courses today. Perhaps, educators need to start using affective facilitation skills to increase learning and decrease cheating. Affective learning today requires instructors to have their students function within an environment that is respectful of their major. A student who is majoring in Business Administration should be expected to operate within a cross-functional team environment, exhibit affective communication skills, teamwork, and the ability to adapt to a variety of diverse issues within the business world (Colbeck, Campbell, & Bjorklund 2000).

A study by Shaohua and Gnyawali, 2003, Synergistic Knowledge Development (SKD) concluded that the use of team based collaborative learning in the classroom increases student performance by embracing practitioner based approaches; however, instructors must be able to apply an efficient system in order to manage student conflict, in order to effectively manage student work teams, and to help students be successful with their team-based assignments. According to Bolton (1999), students are not satisfied with team assignments. The authors receive the same reaction from some students; however, they also understand that it is a necessity in order to maximize learning and retention with today's adult students in the classroom. The requirement of diverse assignments and interactions with other team members are not always looked upon positively by students because it requires them to be more involved in the learning process in order to develop higher-order knowledge while improving interaction skills. Utilizing affective teaching practices in the classroom brings forth holistic learning for the student, which predicates the students' ability to think critically, to evaluate substantive problems, and reflect in ways that integrate the required facets of the students' ability and role within Bloom's Taxonomy of Learning (1956) which develops a persons' knowledge and skills at higher levels through affective instruction of analysis, synthesis, and evaluation (Lang & Dittrich 1982).

AFFECTIVE FACILITATION AND TEACHING

The basis of affective facilitation and teaching philosophy presumes a continuous, working relationship between the professor and student. The authors use a variety of teaching strategies in all classes, including small group problem solving techniques, group discussions, case analyses, and team assignments to provide a significant insight for the course. Furthermore, the authors use technology as a catalyst to bridge the business philosophies as an instrument in the learning process, and to provide students with a three-tier system of learning.

The three-tier system of learning (refer to Figure 4) provides students' with a repetitive learning environment, which culminates the students' interests by their participation (Bloom's Taxonomy, 2004).

1. *Lecture Process:* Lecturing involves developing theoretical constructs and frameworks for the students. For example, the philosophy and theories of Adam Smith, Frederick W. Taylor and Abraham Maslow would be discussed in the Principles of Management course. Thus, providing students with a foundation of historical and modern theory in management.

2. *Visual Aid Technology*: Electronic computer based software, such as, Microsoft Office: MS PowerPoint, MS Word, Internet and E-mail to assist students with their academic pursuits. As the student receives the lecture content, he/she will visually review the material using technology to enhance their learning and retention.

3. *Class Discussion*: The classroom discussion phase with the students concerns the topics of the course lecture material to bridge the theoretical to the applied aspects for the course. The other areas for class discussion are assignments, research paper assignments and mechanics, and any other topic relevant for the course. The classroom discussion phase is one of the most important aspects of adult education.

The ultimate goal of an affective teaching philosophy is to provide students with an effective learning environment. One way of doing this is to place significant emphasis on the theory to business practitioner relevancy. Education of adults should continually seek and acknowledge the wealth of experience from students; which is conducted during the discussion phase of classes. All students are treated with respect and are encouraged to discuss their views in class. As professors, the authors encourage students to develop their leadership roles within the classes by conducting presentations, leading classroom discussions, being effective team players, and by having an active role in the topics for the course. Basically, there are four critical elements of learning that must be addressed to ensure that students learn.

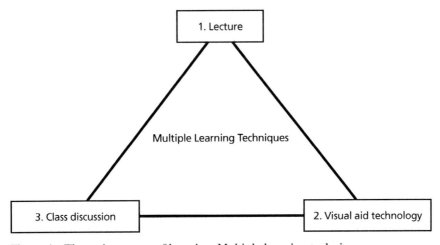

Figure 4 Three tier system of learning: Multiple learning techniques.

1. *Facilitation of Learning*: Setting an appropriate level of teaching with a relevant level of difficulty for each group of students.
2. *Reinforcement*: The use of positive and negative reinforcements.
3. *Retention*: Students must be able to interpret and apply different theories and practical business applications.
4. *Transference*: The ability of the student to apply what they learned in the course to specific business situations.

Such forms of facilitation should increase learning for students thereby decreasing their desire to cheat on the exams and term projects. Extraordinary educators should focus on student learning, reinforcement of learning, retention of concepts, and the transference of these concepts to the work environment.

EVALUATION OF PERFORMANCE IN HIGHER EDUCATION

As previously mentioned, grading inflation is a problem in higher education today and faculty members must jointly work toward reducing or eliminating this phenomenon in their programs. The following content on grade inflation are summarized from a speech by Brad P. Wilson (1998) and elaborated upon to reduce grade inflation in higher education. This topic was presented by Bradford P. Wilson (Wilson, 1998), who was an Executive Director at the National Association of Scholars, at the meeting of Virginia Association of Scholars, Radford University, on October 24 of 1998. Grade inflation in higher education has been reference to as "upward grade homogenization?" Yes, it exists in higher education throughout many institutions. Wilson (1998) states that, "there is substantial and credible information that grades have been inflating over a thirty-year period at American campuses."

Data shows that the percentage of "Cs" and "As" students received over a 24 year period from early 1969 to 1993 seems to have reversed itself. Wilson states that in 1969, 7 percent of all students received grades of A⁻ or higher. However, in 1993, this proportion (7%) had risen to 26 percent. In contrast, grades of C or less changed from the 25% figure in 1969 to 9% in 1993. When researchers look at their own individual institutions for grading patterns over the past 25 or 30 years, they are likely to find grade inflation, regardless of institutional type (Wilson, 1998). He sites how at Princeton University, the median grade point average (GPA) for the class of 1973 was 3.078. However, the median GPA for the class of 1997 went up to 3.422. Similarly, a Dartmouth University, the average GPA had risen from 3.06 to 3.23 from 1968 to 1994. At Harvard University, 46 percent of the undergraduate grades given during the 1996–97 year were A⁻s and As, more than double the figure for 1966, which was 22 percent. The percentage of C+s and below has fallen from 28 percent in 1966–67 to 9 percent in 1991–92.

Does It Matter? Yes, it does. Wilson states that "The highest purpose served by the grading system, it seems to me, is that of making distinctions, distinctions between excellence and competence, and between competence and incompetence." Grades should be the main criteria for honest discriminations among individual student performance, not just effort but actual results. Some see grade inflation as a corrupting process of the young minds that will be going to the real world with similar expectations.

What can be done about grade inflation? One approach used at some institutions is "to include on student transcripts not only the grade for the class, but also the average grade for *all* students enrolled in the class so prospective employers and graduate admissions committees could then get a better idea of whether that A⁻ is to be admired or ignored. The students would then be less prone to shop for easy grades" (Wilson, 1998). Wilson state that another option is to require "schools and departments to review their grading practices with a view of bringing consistency and rigor to the process." Other suggestions offered by Wilson (1998) and faculty members might include the following:

- With the faculty, tighten up the curriculum, both the general education curriculum and that of the majors, with a view to ridding it of options that allow students to select academically inferior courses and programs.
- Radically revise the existing system of student evaluations of faculty so that any evaluation focuses exclusively on the academic content of the course and the teacher's academic seriousness.
- Greet student complaints about low grades with the contempt they deserve, and stop putting tough graders in the dock.
- Dispense academic honors to only the very top students, say the top 10 percent, rather than, for example, the current 82 percent that now receive honors at Harvard.
- Continue to show you care for your students by taking a critical eye to their work. Tell them that you are tough with them because you want them to grow as quickly as possible into great students.

Understanding and reducing plagiarism. Plagiarism (derived from the Latin word for "kidnapper") is commonly defined as the presentation of someone else's ideas, thoughts, or words as one's own. Whether deliberate or accidental, plagiarism is cheating and it is a serious unethical and punishable offense. So, plagiarism is basically taking another person's ideas and using them as one's own. Some examples of plagiarism include:

- Turning in another student's work.
- Paraphrasing work from a source without documenting the source.
- Quoting work from a source without documenting the source (Quotes from *all* sources should be documented including books, articles, newspapers, CD-ROMs, responses from Internet discussion groups, Internet web sites, etc.).
- Turning in a paper that has been downloaded from a term paper site such as www.cheathouse.com.

Generally, universities trust each student to maintain high standards of honesty and ethical behavior. All assignments submitted in fulfillment of course requirements are required to be the students' own work. All assignments except those designed as "group work" are meant to be individual efforts. Teamwork is defined to mean the equal efforts by all group members. It is assumed that students will perform professionally in preparing work required for this and all other classes.

Plagiarism is cheating and is not acceptable, so care must be taken to credit any sources used in preparing term papers, thesis, or other program projects. Additionally, the submission of written assignments and papers for one course, originally submitted and receiving a grade for another course is cheating and is unacceptable. Faculty members can encourage students to study the *APA Style Manual*; it explains how to credit sources. Collaboration on examinations or assignments that are expected to be individual work is another form of cheating and is unacceptable conduct. Also unacceptable is behavior that is flagrantly disruptive to the effective conduct of the program; behavior that is clearly unprofessional, unethical, or that reflects adversely on the university or the professional community; or behavior that violates the general understanding of proper conduct for students. Violations may result in suspension or dismissal from the university. Students and faculty members are encouraged to review their code of conduct and adhere to/enforce them in each course.

Anti-plagiarism strategies for research papers. The widespread availability of textual material in electronic format through the cyberspace has made plagiarism easier than ever. Copying and pasting of paragraphs or even entire essays (as is the case in the following material dealing with anti-plagiarism awareness, prevention and detection) can be performed with just a few mouse clicks. The strategies discussed by Robert Harris (2001) can be used to combat what some believe is an increasing amount of plagiarism on research papers. By employing these strategies, you can help encourage students to value the assignment and to do their own work. Harris (2001) offers the following strategies and information for awareness, prevention, and detection of plagiarism:

1. *Understand why students cheat.* By understanding some of the reasons students are tempted to cheat on papers, you can take steps to prevent cheating by attacking the causes.
2. *Educate yourself about plagiarism.* Plagiarism on research papers takes many forms.
3. *Educate students about plagiarism.* Do not assume that students know what plagiarism is, even if they nod their heads when you ask them. Provide an explicit definition for them. For example, "Plagiarism is using another person's words or ideas without giving credit to the other person. When you use someone else's words, you must put quotation marks around them and give the writer or speaker credit by revealing the source in a citation. Even if you revise or paraphrase the words of someone else or just use their ideas, you still must give the author credit in a note. Not giving due credit to the creator of an idea or writing is very much like lying." In addition to a definition, though, it is good discuss with students the difference between appropriate, referenced use of ideas or quotations and inappropriate use. You might show them an example of a permissible paraphrase (with its citation) and an impermissible paraphrase (containing some paraphrasing and some copying), and discuss the difference. Discuss also quoting a passage and using quotation marks and a citation as opposed to quoting a passage with neither (in other words, merely copying without attribution). Such a discussion should educate those who truly do not understand citation issues ("But I put it in my own words, so I didn't think I had to cite it") and it will also warn the truly dishonest that you are watching. Discussing with students why plagiarism is wrong may be helpful also. Clarifying for them that plagiarism is a combination of stealing (another's words) and lying (claiming implicitly that the words are the student's own) should be mentioned at some point, but should not be the whole emphasis or you risk setting up a challenge for the rebels (those who like to break the rules just for fun). Many statements on plagiarism also remind students that such cheating shows contempt for the professor, other students, and the entire academic enterprise. Plagiarizers by their actions declare that they are not at the university to gain an education, but only to pretend to do so, and that they therefore intend to gain by fraud the credentials (the degree) of an educated person. Perhaps the most effective discussion will ask the students to think about who is really being cheated when someone plagiarizes. Copying papers or even parts of papers short circuits a number of learning experiences and opportunities for the development of skills: actually doing the work of the research paper rather than counterfeiting it gives the student not only knowledge of the sub-

ject and insights into the world of information and controversy, but improves research skills, thinking and analyzing, organizing, writing, planning and time management, and even meticulousness (those picky citation styles actually help improve one's attention to detail). All this is missed when the paper is faked, and it is these missed skills which will be of high value in the working world. A degree will help students get a first job, but performance—using the skills developed by doing just such assignments as research papers—will be required for promotion.

4. *Discuss the benefits of citing sources.* Many students do not seem to realize that whenever they cite a source, they are strengthening their writing. Citing a source, whether paraphrased or quoted, reveals that they have performed research work and synthesized the findings into their own argument. Using sources shows that the student engaged in "the great conversation," the world of ideas, and that the student is aware of other thinkers' positions on the topic. By quoting (and citing) writers who support the student's position, the student adds strength to the position. By responding reasonably to those who oppose the position, the student shows that there are valid counter arguments. In a nutshell, citing helps make the essay stronger and sounder and will probably result in a better grade.

Appropriate quoting and citing also evidences the student's respect for the creators of ideas and arguments—honoring thinkers and their intellectual property. Most college graduates will become knowledge workers themselves, earning at least part of their living creating information products. They therefore have an interest in maintaining a respect for intellectual property and the proper attribution of ideas and words.

5. *Make the penalties clear.* If an institutional policy exists, quote it in your syllabus. If you have your own policy, specify the penalties involved. For example, "Cheating on a paper will result in an F on that paper with no possibility of a makeup. A second act of cheating will result in an F in the course regardless of the student's grade otherwise." If you teach at a university where the penalty for plagiarism is dismissal from the university or being reported to the Academic Dean or Dean of Students, you should make that clear as well. Even the penalties can be presented in a positive light. Penalties exist to reassure honest students that their efforts are respected and valued, so much so that those who would escape the work by fakery will be punished substantially.

The overall goal of these specific strategies is to make the assignment and requirements unique enough that an off-the-shelf paper or a paper written for another class or a friend's paper will not fulfill the requirements. Only a newly written paper will:

1. Make the assignment clear.
2. Provide a list of specific topics and require students to choose one of them.
3. Require specific components in the paper.
4. Require process steps for the paper.
5. Require oral reports of student papers.
6. Have students include an annotated bibliography.
7. Require most references to be up-to-date.
8. Require a meta-learning essay.

One can look for the clues to detect plagiarism. As you read the papers, look for internal evidence that may indicate plagiarism. Among the clues are the following:

- *Mixed citation styles.* If some paragraphs are cited in MLA style, while other references are in APA, and perhaps one or two are in CBE or Chicago, you are probably looking at a paste-up.
- *Lack of references or quotations.* Lengthy, well written sections without documentation may have been taken from general knowledge sources, such as encyclopedias, popular magazines, or Web sites.
- *Unusual formatting.* Strange margins, skewed tables, lines broken in half, mixed subhead styles and other formatting anomalies may indicate a hasty copy and paste job.
- *Off topic.* If the paper does not develop one of the assigned topics or even the topic it announces, it may have been borrowed at the last minute or downloaded. Similarly, if parts of the paper do develop the subject, but other parts seem oddly off, the product may be a cut and paste.
- *Signs of datedness.* If there are no references after some well past date (e.g., 1985), or if a data table offers a company's sales from 1989 to 1994, either the student is using very old material or the paper itself is rather old.
- *Anachronisms.* If the paper refers to long-past events as current ("Only after the Gulf War is over will we see lower oil prices" or "Why isn't the Carter administration acting on this?"), you almost certainly have a recycled paper on your hands.
- *Anomalies of diction.* Many undergraduates do not understand the concept of levels of diction. They think all words are equally welcome in every paper. As a result, when those who plagiarize with the cut-and-paste method perform their deeds, they often mix

paragraphs of varying levels together—the sophisticated scholar's paragraph precedes the breezy journalist's commentary, which may be followed by the student's own highly colloquial addition. Similarly, you may come upon some suspiciously elevated vocabulary usages. "Thesaurusitis" is one source of this, to be sure, but a common source of such vocabulary is another writer, who should have been quoted rather than simply copied. "What do you mean by 'ineffable'?" can sometimes provide you with inexpressible information. Lastly, if you find that the paper uses several archaic terms, or words no longer used in the way the paper uses them, you may be looking at some very old text.

- *Anomalies of style.* Is the prose style remarkable? Are there two-page paragraphs that remind you of a nineteenth-century encyclopedia? Is there ornate rhetorical structure? Does the introduction get in its own way and stumble around, only to give way to glowing, flowing discourse? Is there a mixture of British and American punctuation or spelling, with consistent usage within large sections?
- *Smoking guns.* This category might be called "blunders of the clueless," since it includes obvious indicators of copying. Reported in the past have been labels left at the end of papers ("Thank you for using TermPaperMania"), title pages stapled to Web printouts (complete with dates and URL in the corners), title pages claiming the paper is by Tom Jones when subsequent pages say "Smith, page 2," and papers with whiteout over the previous author's name.

Few of these clues will provide courtroom proof of plagiarism, of course, but their presence should alert you to investigate the paper. Even if you do not find the source of the paper, you may be able to use these clues profitably in a discussion with the student in your office.

CLASSROOM DIVERSITY AND EXPECTATIONS

Today's workforce population is more diverse than ever before and the student population has been changing rapidly along with it. Such diverse students need teachers and facilitators who are cultural competent and can manage diversity in the classroom. Becoming an effective educator and learning to remain as such is a moral imperative in adult education. Being an effective educator in a diverse environment of adult education requires expecting the same standards from all students regardless of their race, gender, language, and general background. Educators/teachers should not grade students differently because of their gender, nationality, or language since such differences have a negative consequence as a result of self-fulfilling prophecy. All students must *earn* their grades based on their actual performance in the course according to the evaluation criteria communicated. Faculty members of higher education are obligated to treat each student fairly and expect high standards from them regardless of gender, ethnicity/nationality, primary language, age, experience, disability, and other such variables.

Furthermore, teachers should and must avoid all issues that present a conflict of interest in their faculty-student relationship. For example, students must not be put in *"quid pro quo"* positions of doing things for faculty members as this could very well lead to cases of sexual harassment. Whether "quid pro quo" cases are intentional or unintentional, they must be avoided since they put students in a challenging position when their course grade depends on the faculty member's perception. This section discusses the basics of sexual harassment, implications of the self-fulfilling prophecy concept as it is applied in the diverse environment of adult education, diversity management concerns in education, and best teaching practices while offering suggestions and effective practices for new adult educators of diverse student populations. One purpose of this section with regard to effective practices is similar to Professor Robert Preziosi's business management philosophy, which is "to find out what we're doing well and get the whole organization to do it well." As such, what works for one educator may also be helpful for other educators, provided that many of the situational variables are similar. The suggestions offer ideas so adult educators can be successful in achieving their learning outcomes based on adult learning practices that can produce positive results through application in academia. Many of the suggestions have been used both academically and in the corporate arena by trainers, managers, faculty members, and administrators of both undergraduate and graduate business programs.

DIVERSITY MANAGEMENT AND ADULT EDUCATION

The student population of nearly all institutions has drastically changed from what it was twenty and thirty years ago. Some institutions have predominantly traditional students of 18 to 23 years of age attending college on a full-time basis while other institutions might have all working adult students and/or a mixture of the two. It is apparent that both student populations are much more diverse in terms of their gender, ethnicity/nationality, age, disability, and beliefs than they were twenty years ago. Therefore, these student populations need diverse teaching skills, different experiences, and more facilitation abilities in order for them to learn best as per their learning styles. One of the needed skills would be to acknowledge their differences and actively incorporate their experiences into the learning objectives of each session. Recognizing and understanding these differences are neither easy, nor automatic since they require conscious focus and a good level of comfort on the part of the faculty with cultural diversity issues. In order for educators and students to be successful, they need to become culturally competent. *"Cultural competency"* for all practical purposes refers to the continuous learning process that enables both educators and students to function effectively in the context of cultural differences both in academia and in the workforce.

Nearly all organizations and academic institutions have various forms of formal or mandatory training for their associates, faculty and/or staff during their initial hiring process and as an ongoing process annually. Much of this training is formally required to make sure employees of these institutions are aware that the organization expects them to treat everyone fairly. However, in many academic as well as corporate settings, much of the training on ethics and sexual harassment topics are not reinforced. Oftentimes, employees are provided a handbook or a website to read the material for themselves and to sign a document that they have read the material. Furthermore, some organizations that do offer a formal face-to-face training session on such important topics tend to brush through the content to make sure the legal side is covered without making sure that the material is received, understood, fully comprehended, and the specific behaviors can be successfully applied by those who attended the session. Nonetheless, many of such topics are professionally presented by experienced educators and a review of them seems relevant for adult educators.

"Sexual harassment" is often times seen as behavior that is *un-welcomed* (the recipient does not want it), *unsolicited* (the recipient did not ask for it), and *repeated* (the behavior is not one isolated incident). A behavior can be considered sexual harassment when submission to such conduct is made a condition of the individual's employment; when submission to, or rejection of, such conduct by an individual is used as the basis for employment decisions (such as salary increases, promotions, etc.) affecting the individual; and when such conduct has the purpose or effect of interfering with the individual's work performance or of creating an unfriendly or offensive work environment. As referred to in the introductory paragraph, quid pro quo is a condition created by the harasser in which the harassed submits to unwanted sexual and physical advances to either obtain a reward (such as a good grade without earning it through objective performance in the course) or to avoid a consequence. An actual act is not required to establish quid pro quo. Such situations must be avoided by using professional, consistent and fair treatment strategies for all students in the class. Also, adult educators should be aware and eliminate the presence of a "hostile learning environment" in their classroom. A *"hostile learning environment"* can be described

as a situation where inappropriate remarks consistently take place and it is not corrected by the teacher/faculty member. This is a situation where insensitive and inappropriate remarks should be addressed publicly by the faculty members so everyone in the class understands the ground rules and the fact that inappropriate/insensitive comments are not appreciated nor tolerated. Educators must also avoid and eliminate the presence of sexual harassment from taking place in the classroom while maintaining a faculty-student relationship. Tangible consequences such as a lowered grade do not have to occur to substantiate the existence of sexual harassment. If a student's emotional and psychological abilities are substantially affected, there may be enough proof that sexual harassment occurred.

Today, we have a very diverse student population in terms of their background, abilities, age, language, body size, geographic location, culture, desires, learning styles, cultural conditioning, etc. Diversity describes the many unique characteristics and qualities that make a person (or student in this case) similar to or different from others. Some of these characteristics might be apparent such as skin color, hair color, body size, and general appearance. While other characteristics such as ethnicity, disability, religion, financial status, age, value, cultural background and many others may not be apparent based on first impressions. It is imperative that we do not judge students based on assumptions and must treat everyone fairly and equitably.

Diversity also encompasses the multitude of experiences, aptitudes and attitudes available in today's workforce. Diversity initiatives encourage leaders and educators to empower their associates and students as well as to tap into their wealth of differences in order to achieve synergistic results. In return, these students and associates will be ready to satisfy, excite and delight their diverse customers and achieve organizational effectiveness by delivering superior customer value as a result of diversity initiatives modeled in the classroom by the educators. Robert Reich, Secretary of Labor during Clinton's Administration, said, "No longer are Americans rising and falling together as if in one large national boat. We are, increasingly, in different smaller boats." So, our classroom students, customers, organizations, and societies will become progressively more diverse and we as educators need to tolerate differences, respect them, understand their nature, and educate our students about them so they can successfully work with their diverse organizations and customers. Eventually, this may lead to student's personal and professional success and they can be as successful as they so desire to be. What is success and who defines it? According to Sophocles, "success is dependent on effort" and not necessarily physical characteristics or limitations. According to Brian Tracy, Author and Speaker, "One of the most important rules for success is this: Every great success is the result of hundreds and thousands of small efforts and accomplishments that no one ever sees or appreciates." In the summer issue of Nova Southeastern

University's *Foresight* publication (2001), Dr. Randolph Pohlman, Dean of the Graduate School of Business and Entrepreneurship, wrote, "In this final issue…we strive to get at the core of what is success. By sharing with you the thoughts of various leaders, educators, and entrepreneurs, we hope to help our readers define for themselves what is success." The same is true for students; therefore, success should be defined by students based on their desires, abilities, goals and efforts. At his primary school, Malcolm X (African American leader) was told by one of his (white) teachers that he should not dream of becoming a lawyer since he could not be very successful in that job and should pursue something that requires the use of his hands. Unfortunately, due to strong biases and stereotypes such incompetency may still exist in the American Education System and we need to do everything possible to ensure it does not happen in our schools or to our students. It is not the place of the faculty member to determine how successful a student can or should be based on his/her first impression of the student or based on the student's physical/personality characteristics. Ralph Waldo Emerson said, "What is success? To laugh often and much; to win the respect of intelligent people and the affection of children; to earn the appreciation of honest critics and endure the betrayal of false friends; to appreciate beauty; to find the best in others; to leave the world a bit better, whether by a healthy child, a garden patch, or a redeemed social condition; to know even one life has breathed easier because you have lived." Simply put, success can be practicing what you preach, progressively realizing predetermined goals/ideals, and doing one's best to make worthwhile contributions to society. It is our moral imperative and obligation as educators and faculty members to (assume and) proceed as though limits to our students' abilities do not exist, unless objective evidence tells otherwise.

Recognize and Respect Diversity in the Classroom

Educators need to encourage students to think critically, add value to the class by participating, and to synergize as teams or as a whole class. Appreciating, understanding and valuing personal differences in each individual student can eliminate groupthink both in the classroom as well as in the boardroom. *Groupthink* is a pattern of faulty and biased decision making that occurs in groups whose members strive for agreement, among themselves, at the expense of accurately assessing information relevant to a decision. Groupthink is not a desirable objective in today's diverse and very sophisticated world of intermingled competition. This usually happens in homogeneous teams and groups because everyone's societal values tend to be similar. Research has shown that homogeneous teams are neither as creative nor as productive as heterogeneous teams when dealing with or solving complex problems. Diverse teams can achieve synergistic results if they appreciate, understand and value their differences effectively. *Synergy* is where the whole is greater than the sum of its parts. Ultimately, synergy is performance gains that result when individuals, teams and departments co-ordinate their actions toward the same goals. Synergistic teams, colleagues, peers and departments tend to function more cooperatively and produc-tively than if they were operating in isolation.

Synergy happens when two or more individuals working together pro-duce more than their combined efforts individually. For example, a team of four students should produce a final project (product) that is much better than the combined results of each of the four students' work that is pro-duced individually. Diversity awareness can help teams function harmoni-ously in the context of cultural differences and produces synergistic results. On the other hand, lack of diversity awareness and lack of respect for di-versity can lead to negative synergy. Negative synergy is when two or more people working together produce less than what they could produce indi-vidually. According Stephen R. Covey, author of " *The Seven Habits of Highly Effective People,*" negative synergy takes place when people do not respect and appreciate each other's differences.

Differences may exist in how male and female students relate to and understand material presented in the classroom. Using sports analogies to make a point in the classroom may not clarify the concepts or objectives to those who are not familiar with the rules of a specific game. This can apply to both males and females in the same way. Faculty members need to be aware of their audience and create an "inclusive learning environ-ment." An *"inclusive learning environment"* is where all of the students and participants are actively involved in the learning process and can fully relate to the concepts being presented. In 1991, the Kinney Shoe Corporation realized that, gender differences (in orientation, communication, and be-havior) seem subtle, yet they represent great dissimilarities in the ways that men and women function on a daily basis. Simply put, the differences can translate into an institutionalized tendency to work only within one's comfort zone, men working only with men and women working with women unless this tendency is consciously acknowledged and avoided. Many firms have established gender-sensitivity training in order to create awareness and to eventually produce synergistic results among teams. During the training at The Kinney Shoe Corporation, the participants learned that females, in general, view work as a process while males usually focus on the end result and desire specific action plans and these results were further validated in 1995 by a study of over 700 male and female managers in the Central Flor-ida area (Mujtaba, 1997) with managers. Researchers have concluded that many of the males were raised with a competitive nature, where power was the key. Furthermore, males have been found to have more of a succinct speaking style, similar to military speech, whereas, females communicated in a storytelling style. While many females prefer a circular style of group discussion so everyone can be heard, seen and acknowledged; males tend to prefer the lecture style where the group is directed and the meeting can be brought to a closure in a timely manner. Females tend to put more focus on the process (how we get there) while males may focus more on the results (where are we going and when will we get there). Such differences may exist in the classroom as well and adult educators need to recognize and capitalize on such differences appropriately as per their course learning outcomes. Understanding and respecting such differences can create an "*inclusive learning environment*" where *groupthink* is avoided and *synergistic* results flow infinitely as learners think for themselves and stretch their abilities beyond their existing boundaries.

Pygmalion Effect: Self-Fulfilling Prophecy in "A Class Divided" with Jane Elliot

A video titled "*The Eye of the Storm*" was released in 1970 of an actual classroom setting in Riceville, Iowa. The children were actual third grade students and not actors. Jane Elliot, their teacher, conducted an activity that allowed her students to experience the effects of conditioning and discrimination. This video also appeared on Frontline, which was conducted as a follow-up documentary by Judy Woodruff through Public Broadcasting Systems (PBS) titled "*A Class Divided*." The video titled "*A Class Divided*" is actually a follow up of the first experiment, after fifteen years, with Jane Elliot and most of her third grade students involved in the original documentary. Jane Elliot and the students discuss the impact of the experiment on all the students involved. It appears to have had positive results on her students' lives.

The actual experiment demonstrates how discrimination and stereotypes can be created rapidly in a very short period of time. On the first day of the experiment, she gives special privileges to children with blue eyes (things like second lunches, taking longer breaks, going to lunch first, etc.) and explains to the class that blue eyed people are better than brown eyed people since she along with many other intelligent people have blue eyes. Furthermore, she required the children on the bottom (brown-eyed children) to wear large collars that distinguished them from the smart kids. Jane Elliot kept reinforcing statements like "blue-eyed children are smarter than brown-eyed kids", "blue-eyed children learn faster than brown-eyed children", and "brown-eyed children are wasteful, forgetful and lazy." Pretty soon, the students started calling each other malicious names (brown-eyed, etc.) in a condescending and offensive way while treating the brown-eyed students as inferior, stupid and dumb. The superior group (actually about ninety percent of them) seemed very willing and helpful when it came to finding ways of punishing the inferior group if they got out of line and didn't follow the rules.

However, on the second day Jane Elliot told the class that she was wrong about the blue-eyed people being smarter. It was actually the opposite. So, the special privileges were taken away from the blue-eyed children and given to the brown-eyed children and they were continuously reinforced to be the smarter group. The blue-eyed children wore the large collars and had to sit in the back of the class since they were the inferior group on this day. It was not long before the "brown-eyed" kids started treating the blue-eyed children as inferior and started acting more confidently as they knew everything. The overall results showed that children responded to how they were treated and became what they were expected to become. The children on top (smart and privileged) consistently did better on the exams and exercises than when they were on the bottom or inferior. When the children were wearing collars, the results were very negative.

- *Loss of self-esteem and/or self-confidence.* They lost confidence in themselves in about fifteen minutes of consistent conditioning by the teacher. Bryan, one of the third graders in class, had his head down on the desk and some children were actually crying since they were labeled as inferior. The facial expressions and body language exhibited by some of the children were very negative.
- *Loss of performance.* The children were not able to fully concentrate on schoolwork because they were unhappy about being inferior.
- *Conflict among them.* Fighting, acting-out, name-calling, and hitting each other were a few of the obvious results because they were labeled as inferior. Revenge, finger-pointing, blame, and anti-social behavior were some of the common responses by all the students who were in the inferior group.

These children had previously formed some stereotypes or "mental tapes" about people who were different from them and Jane Elliot was hoping that she could help them form new and more accurate pictures of people who didn't look like them. Jane Elliot said she learned more from the children when they were "on top" (considered superior). She learned that the superior group sought hierarchy, wanted revenge and were delighted to be superior.

- The superior group wanted revenge. It was survival of the fittest.
- The superior group liked superiority; was "delighted" to place the collars on the inferior group. Even the second day, when they knew how it felt to be treated badly, it was time to get even.

- The superior group sought hierarchy. "I am better than you because…" and "you are less than us because…" mentality existed. They even looked for ways to reinforce the hierarchy by locating the yardstick and asking the teacher to use it if the "inferior" kids get out of hand. They were also encouraging Mrs. Elliot to alert the cafeteria staff to help enforce the "rules" for the inferior group since some of them may have two or more lunches/servings.

Jane Elliot, the teacher who is considered to be one of the best facilitators of adult education, has now been facilitating her brown eyes/blue eyes exercise for over 30 years. In 1999, during a morning discussion with her in Washington DC at the National Multicultural Institute Conference (NMCI), she told Dr. Bahaudin Mujtaba that racial injustice is very much prevalent throughout our society and we have much work to do in order to eliminate this conditioning from the minds of our children, our students and our workforce. As a conclusion to the video and a summation of what she has learned, she offers the following comment as a concluding remark that emphasized the critical role of the educator / faculty member: "It's not how "*they*" are…it is how *anybody* will become when treated in this manner." What educators expect from their students is likely to be produced by those students. Therefore, expecting less from minorities or foreign students (whose primary language is not English) and evaluating them based on different standards would be unethical and unfair due to the concept of self-fulfilling prophecy. According to professor Dr. Dan Austin, professor of health administration and accounting, a teacher "has to be careful about making judgments and must work with students to help them find the pleasure of learning regardless of their level of passion." It is also a teacher's responsibility to help students find the pleasure of learning regardless of their nationality, race, gender or language. Because of the teacher's influence over students and/or because of the level of students respect for the teacher, it is expected that students will either live up to or down to the teacher's expectations. So, educators should avoid expecting less or even expressing the perception that they expect less from students based on preconceived notions and stereotypes associated with their gender, disabilities, place of birth, race, skin color, body size, sexual orientation, hair color, eye color, etc. The educator should expect great commitment and high quality from all students.

Stereotyping, prejudice, or biases impact the society in many ways. One way is that human beings, as individuals, may not treat some people very well because of societal conditioning and autobiographical perceptions. Many people experience unpleasant and unjust incidents daily solely due to some readily apparent physical characteristics. These incidents are referred to as daily indignities. Educators must make sure that such unpleasant and unjust incidents do not exist in their classrooms or work environments.

Understand and Effectively Manage Differences

Understanding diversity and effectively managing it is imperative in to-day's rapidly changing global environment. It has been said that about two thirds of the world's immigration is coming into the United States of America which also brings much global competition for the skills of our students. Immigration trends have greatly shifted during the past one hundred years. In the early 1900's, the majority of immigrants were from Europe; today, the majority of immigrants come from Central and South America, Asia, Africa, and the Middle East. Today, approximately one out of three American workers are African-American, Hispanic, or Asian; 6 out of 7 working age women are at work, and 1 out of 10 workers has some form of legally recognized disability. There are over 50 different forms of legally recognized disabilities and many of them are not apparent to the naked eye. English is expected to be a second language for the majority of Californians as well as those living in Miami, Florida.

In the mid 1980's, the Department of Labor commissioned the Hudson Institute to conduct a study on the demographic, sociological, economic, and political trends in America from post-World War II to the year 2000. The results, published in 1987 in a document titled "Work Force 2000: Work and Workers for the 21st Century," indicated the following trends:

- The pool of younger workers is decreasing and the average age of workers is rising.
- More women are visible on the job and overall minorities comprise 1/3 of new workers. More immigrants are in the workforce and this trend is likely to continue.
- Service and information jobs are increasing and higher skill levels are required to compete effectively in today's global world of business.

As one can see, the challenge for businesses will be immense. Educational institutions, governments, corporations, and communities are now recognizing the necessity of valuing diversity to remain competitive in today's complex global world of business. Since the current workforce is indeed demographically diverse, leadership and management techniques of inclusion are imperative. Creating an inclusive environment (and eliminating the exclusive world of bias and stereotypes) is necessary for an effective learning environment with all learners. As a faculty member or teacher of current and future leaders and managers, a professor must create an inclusive learning environment and educate all learners in this direction as well. The classroom is the laboratory for learning such interactions with diverse colleagues and eventually co-workers.

All educators need to understand that valuing diversity requires the creation of an open, supportive, and responsive environment where differences are accepted, valued, and managed effectively toward organizational synergy. Creating such an open atmosphere in the classroom is the responsibility of the teacher. Valuing diversity means the management of a group of people with differences so that all individuals perform at their maximum potential for the achievement of organizational goals by using their unique skills, competencies, and talents. Each educator or faculty member can ask the following question and apply the appropriate answers into his/her classroom sessions: "In what specific ways, can I recognize and effectively manage diversity in the classroom to ensure a productive learning environment as well as to provide a "superior educational value for students?" The teacher along with his/her colleagues or students can brainstorm and mention specific strategies that are aligned with their vision, mission, and guiding principles that would benefit every one of the students.

Adult Learners Require Respect and Involvement

Successful and prepared faculty members and educators understand how adults learn best and accommodate individual needs of diverse learners. Compared to young students, some adult learners have different needs and requirements that must be accommodated in order for them to learn best. Adults have different motivations than their young counterparts that energize them to learn. Adults are not "pushed or forced" into the school's classrooms as is the case with many young children until they become conditioned. Adults choose to attend school and class voluntarily and have different expectations than elementary, middle school and high school children. Unlike children and teenagers, adults have many responsibilities besides learning. Because of these responsibilities that keep them away from learning at times, adults have *barriers against participating in learning.* Some of these barriers include lack of time, money, confidence, or interest, lack of information about opportunities to learn, scheduling problems, "red tape," and other challenges facing all adults. So, adults have a strong need to balance their learning with their critical roles at work, community and families. On the other hand, we know that adults are willing to engage in learning experiences before, after, or even during life changing events. Once convinced that change is a certainty, adults will engage in any learning that promises to help them cope with the transition and/or accelerate their progress toward worthwhile and predetermined goals. Adults who are motivated to seek out a learning experience do so primarily because they have use for the knowledge or skill being sought. Learning is a means to an end, not an end in itself. Increasing or maintaining one's sense of self-esteem and pleasure are strong secondary motivators for engaging in learning experiences.

According to researchers, learning results from stimulation of the various senses. In some people, one sense is used more than others to learn or recall information. Educators must present materials that stimulate as many of the senses as possible in order to increase learning and long-term retention. In the past, many faculty members used to provide a mid-term and a final exam to assess and evaluate the understanding of their students. The first mistake with this strategy is that the faculty is not assessing the learning on a continual basis but continues to lecture with the assumption that students are learning. The second mistake is that the students are not involved in the application of the material but rather are studying to pass the exam in the course. The third mistake is that students wait to see what is likely to be on the exam and study those concepts to increase their chances of success. The fourth mistake with this strategy is that this method encourages students to study the week before the test so the material is fresh in their minds for the test. Often this leads to the traditional cramming session before the exam, which takes away from the real learning and long-term retention of the material. Unfortunately, there are many faculty members that still use such traditional methods of assessment that used to be widespread in the educational arena. Luckily, there are many informed adult educators that use a good variety of assessment tools to actively involve adult students in the learning process so the material can be retained and reinforced for both immediate and long-term application.

Educators need to remember that students must retain the information in their memory for more than just a 24-hour period in order to benefit from the learning in the work environment. The educator's job is not finished until they have assisted the learner in retaining the information for long-term application. Long-term retention can come from being actively involved in the learning process. Retention is directly affected by the amount of thinking, application and practice that takes place during the learning process. As previously discussed, many informed adult educators use a good variety of ways to involve and assess students' learning for long-term retention and application. For example, many faculty members use different forms of quizzes to assess current knowledge and to see if the students are reading the assignments. While objective quizzes and tests assess the understanding, they can also be used to reinforce learning. Other means of involving students and assessing their understanding can come from having students present specific topics orally, assigning them a team project, having students debate each side of a situation, completing case studies, preparing and conducting role-plays, having mid-term and final exams, asking students to prepare a term project, etc. Having students complete a number of different projects (besides exams) takes time to grade and assess their learning but it can also lead to involving them in meaningful projects that can raise their interest and result in better learning, better retention of the learning, and long-term transference of the learning. *Transference* of learning is the desired result of education—it is the ability to use the information taught in a new setting. This is the overall objective of each educator and can happen when students are offered many exposures and assessment tools to understand and reinforce the material in their minds.

Become a TRUE Educator

Working and teaching in a diverse environment requires understanding and accommodating the various learning styles of students as well as the effective use of differences. One can become a TRUE cross-cultural educator who would be able to work effectively in the context of cultural differences both nationally and internationally with diverse populations. Becoming a *TRUE* global educator requires:

- **T**olerating differences,
- **R**especting differences,
- **U**nderstanding differences, and
- **E**xamining differences for the purpose of **E**ducating students.

The first step is usually the most difficult but a very important step in the process of becoming a TRUE educator. For example, tolerance is a personal decision and it comes from an attitude that is learned. Every human being needs to embrace the belief that each person on earth is a treasure who must be treated with respect. Everyone has the power to change his/her attitude to overcome ignorance as well as to influence his/her students, offspring, peers, and colleagues positively. It begins with a personal commitment to consciously choose one's speech and thought patterns based on intrinsically chosen values. It starts with the fact that many individuals should and can stop labeling others simply as "rednecks," "thieves," "sissies," "terrorists," or other oppressive terms based on misinformation, first impressions and/or physical appearances. As such, managers, employees and faculty members must prevent inappropriate or offensive jokes (such as Polish or gay related one-liners) from taking place in the classroom or outside of the classroom in order to create an inclusive and healthy learning environment and to become a TRUE educator. Becoming a TRUE educator will enable a person to provide a supportive and inclusive learning atmosphere/environment for students. This will result in fairness, equality, and a talented diverse workforce that can successfully function in today's global competitive marketplace. Some of the common benefits of incorporating diversity initiatives into the classroom can be satisfied students which will eventually benefit the society by having a talented diverse workforce with satisfied customers, high morale and commitment, low employee recruitment and retention cost, better teamwork and increased productivity, and an inclusive as well as a supportive work environment. So, be a TRUE educator, take "The Educator's Challenge" and you will make a difference.

THE EDUCATOR'S CHALLENGE

Our challenge is to say something good about the people we see
  And to never ever let them settle for less than what they can be.
The challenge is not to shout "Raa Raa Ree, kick'em in the knee"
  But to believe in them and say "Let learning be, so we can all be free."
Imagine learning flowing harmoniously as the world and sea
  For that which is intrinsically imagined can most definitely be.
Personal success is a process hidden inside the educator in "me"
  It can be best achieved by serving others and contributing to "we."
Our challenge is to say something good about the people we see
  And to never ever let them settle for less than what they can be.

SUMMARY

In order for instructors to expect ethical behavior from their students, the instructor must be persistent in facilitating a classroom environment which focuses on student discussion, team based assignments, and critical thinking skills. Furthermore, the instructor must expect students to apply what they study in order to master the concepts of the course. The instructor to student relationship is the primary means of learning today, which culminates the students' entire process of understanding the course material by applying Bloom's Taxonomy of Learning of analysis, synthesis, and evaluation in the classroom. Involving students in the learning process might be the best way to increase their interest and learning while hopefully reducing the need for cheating.

Diversity exists in both the student and workforce population today and will continue to increase. There is a moral responsibility for each faculty member to become a cultural ally and a TRUE educator with regard to today's diverse students and workforce. Valuing diversity and becoming a TRUE educator requires each person to tolerate differences, respect differences, understand differences, and to educate others about those differences in order to maximize the productivity of students in the workforce so they can remain competitive.

Valuing diversity is not just an idea that sounds good and promotes positive publicity for the institution. Valuing diversity and the educator's genuine commitment to its thorough implementation are critical to one's success as an individual educator and to his/her student's survival in the real world. In order for educators and students to be successful, they should become culturally competent. Cultural competency refers to the continuous learning process that enables individuals (faculty and students) to function effectively in the context of cultural differences both in school and in the work environment.

Dr. Martin Luther King, Jr. dreamed that someday people would be judged by the content of their character and not by the color of their skin, not by their gender, not by their ethnic backgrounds, and not by their disabilities. He also dreamed that all individuals would sit down together at the table of brotherhood and sisterhood. Those tables are in the classrooms, conference rooms, boardrooms, cafeterias, restaurants, and manufacturing floors. The responsibility and challenge for educators are to not only take their seats at the heads of these tables but to sit there with an open mind and unclenched fists so they can be the role models for students.

Being ethical and acting as such consistently toward students and colleagues is a must for all educators and faculty members. Being ethical means expecting the same standards from each student regardless of the individual make-up of the student's background. Teachers should not grade students differently because of their race, nationality, or language. Students must *earn* their grades based on their performance in the course. Faculty members of higher education are required and obligated to treat each student fairly and expect high standards from each student regardless of his/her ethnicity/nationality, primary language, age, experience, disability, and other such variables. Shelby Steele, author of *The Content of Our Character* published in 1990, said "What is needed now is a new spirit of pragmatism in racial matters where 'disadvantaged minorities' are seen simply as American citizens who deserve complete fairness and in some cases developmental assistance, but in no case special entitlements based on "minority status." The only individuals that should be given special accommodations in the classroom, as directed by the university officials, are students with legally recognized disabilities whose needs are communicated to educators by the university officials prior to the start of the class.

Furthermore, teachers should and must avoid all issues that present a conflict of interest in their faculty–student relationship. For example, just as faculty members must not use student information for marketing or promotional purposes they must not put students in *"quid pro quo"* positions

that are often linked to cases of sexual harassment. Many of the (students')
"employers are concerned with proper employee behavior and code of conduct compliance in relation to their industries and related organizations
(Mujtaba, 2003). As such, educators have the responsibility of being and
becoming role models for students as these future leaders/managers are
likely to mimic the actions of their teachers. Overall, this section has pointed out the moral/ethical implications of adult education and self-fulfilling
prophecy to the educator in the diverse environment. It offered suggestions for adult educators and discussed suggestions for incoming college
faculty members.

CHAPTER 9

UNDERSTANDING VARIOUS GENERATIONS OF LEARNERS AND EMPLOYEES

This chapter focuses on learning about the various generations of the workforce and techniques that employers can utilize to organize collaborative teams in today's multigenerational and multicultural workplaces. Trainers and teachers can use this material to provide effective skills for managers that deal with multi-generations of employees. Furthermore, educators can use appropriate teaching techniques with different generations of students since teachers of working adults are likely to have diverse generations of learners in their classes. There are at least four different generations in today's workforce that are categorized as traditionalists (Veterans), baby boomers, generation X, and generation Y individuals. Managers should be aware of the personality characteristics of individuals in all generations as well as their cultural backgrounds, and act accordingly. The section further discusses how decision-making, for managers of any generation, is a very critical and time-consuming procedure, and how managerial decisions do affect the company's processes dramatically. Managers should always make certain, regardless of their personal interests, likes and dislikes, that their decisions are appropriate for each generation of employees and their organizations. And so should trainers and professors.

Adult Education in Academia, pages 199–223
Copyright © 2006 by Information Age Publishing

199

Organizational learning, from a systems perspective, is discussed as an effective method of understanding the processes and strategies suitable for an organization. In order to create a learning organization, managers need to emphasize teamwork and practice group activities that effectively involve people of all generations in the decision making processes. Following the eight facets of Value Driven Management can guide and focus everyone's energies toward the common vision set forth by the company. Besides dealing with a multi-generation of employees, international managers face an even more complex task since they also deal with various cultures. Hence, a multi-cultural manager should acquire appropriate cultural knowledge regarding the local norms, mores and customs to effectively work with individuals of different generations throughout the world. And so should trainers and higher education faculty members. Some of the material in the following pages was prepared by Mujtaba and Thomas (2004) and presented at the International Teaching Methods and Styles conference at Reno, Nevada.

IMPACT OF DIVERSE GENERATIONS
IN A LEARNING ORGANIZATION

The systems thinking, or a holistic, paradigm allows all senses to work synergistically in the creation of a learning environment through their interactions with the external environment. Perhaps the effectiveness of the five senses working together can result in the awakening of the sixth sense due to the ability to see beyond time and space. The twenty first century organization is much more complex and the best way to effectively address this complexity is to see the interconnectedness of the parts through the five senses from the detail to general as well as from internal to external variables while predicting the future. Instead of managing through a critical eye or micro managing, managers need to unleash their potential to see other systems beyond their limits to lead disparate generations in the twenty first century workforce. Also, as the organizations become more complex, managers will need to teach employees to think from a holistic and systemic perspective in order to discover new methods of leading the diverse generations. They need to help employees see how their jobs affect the next step in the chain process and how their functions positively impact the environment. The skills and systems thinking process can be learned to support diverse generations. According to Gazzaniga (1988), the human brain and mindset or paradigm can adapt according to the needs of each generation. Capra (1997) stated that the human mind is powerful enough to facilitate the conceptualization of system thinking including chaotic (complexity) theory and non-lineal mathematical models. The twenty first century manager cannot rely just on the past to effectively move forward and lead diverse generations into the future. As effective leaders and intellectuals, these managers should realize that their self-imposed ideologies of reality must evolve with nature, science, and time in order to foster new strategies for leading today's diverse workforce. These managers must learn to embrace the diversity of various generations in the workforce through the creation of a learning environment throughout the organization.

In the twenty first century's fast pace global environment, organizations need to embrace change as a constant motivating force that provides both opportunities as well as challenges. Throughout the past century, many academic and practitioners have contributed to various schools of organizational theory. These learning organizational theories are commonly categorized into different schools of thought including Classical, Human Resources, Neo-Classical, Systems, Agency, Power, and Sense-Making. The major thoughts of organization theory can change over time and through the ages because of new paradigms and new knowledge. As with any discipline that evolves, organizational theory has been built upon the ideas and paradigms that have been in place prior to the discovery of a new paradigm or a new shift in thinking. An understanding of organizational theory should include, but not be limited to, the historical contexts of the discipline, the cultural nuances of the discipline, and the metaphorical background of the discipline that have given precedence to the established body of knowledge. Having a strong foundation of the basics, as well as, the main authors and contributors to the organizational learning literature are critical for twenty first century managers and academic scholars. More importantly, it is imperative that managers study their employees and the impact of having a multi-generation workforce in the organization. The concepts presented in Senge's (1990) book titled *The Fifth Discipline: the Art and Practice of the Learning Organization* assists individuals in overcoming the illusion that the world is created of separate or unrelated forces (p. 3). It is the letting go of such an illusion that makes a learning organization a possibility. Learning organizations, according to Senge, are "organizations where people continually expand their capacity to create the results they truly desire, where new and expansive patterns of thinking are nurtured, where collective aspiration is set free, and where people are continually learning how to learn together."

Decision making is one of the most interesting and pervasive concepts in all organizations because people of all generations make decisions concerning various concepts such as leadership style, motivation, productivity, conflict management, human resources management, and so on. As a matter-of-fact, Senge states that the ability to learn faster than one's competitors for making effective decisions might be the only true competitive advantage for twenty first century managers and organizations. One can always think and reflect upon the importance of decision making and the consequences of making both good and bad decisions. One can also evaluate some of the major decisions and think of how leaders could have approached them differently from a holistic perspective. In the past ten years, every twenty first century leader probably has heard of the merger of Hewlett-Packard and Compaq, Microsoft fighting monopoly allegations, many organizations including Levi Strauss shutting down their factories in the United States and moving overseas which has resulted in layoffs, allowing China to join the World Trade Organization (WTO) despite its questionable human rights record, sending air power to Afghanistan to assist in the removal of the Taliban from power, and American and British soldiers occupying Iraq while removing Saddam Hussein from government. So, there have been many examples of major decisions made by corporate and world leaders in hopes of either making the society a better place to live or their organizations more competitive in their industries. As can be seen through the media, there have also been crisis in corporate governance due to unethical decisions, short-term focus on quick profits, excessive senior leadership pay, weak vision for direction, corrupt analysts, complacent boards, and questionable accounting practices in some of the largest organizations. With the controversies surrounding Enron, Arthur Andersen, WorldCom and a host of other large organizations that have admitted to, at the very least, having used "poor" judgment in managing stocks and acquisitions, the public trust will have to be restored in the credibility of business. In order to remedy such problems in the business environment and improve the level of trust among the stakeholders, perhaps the senior leaders can set the company's moral tone, ban stock sales by directors for the duration of their terms, send some CFOs and CEOs to jail, and a host of other suggestions might be appropriate as well. However, none of these suggestions will be complete when the focus is on short-term profitability with no consideration on how one aspect impacts all the other elements both inside and outside of the organization. The leaders must see the impact of their decision from a system's perspective as they attempt to create a learning organization.

In a learning organization, leaders and managers can increase everyone's ability to make non-programmed decisions, those that allow them to adapt, modify, and alter their tasks by creating an effective and inclusive learning environment (Mujtaba & Mujtaba, 2004). A *learning organization* is one in which leaders and managers do everything possible to maximize the potential for organizational learning to take place. *Organizational learning* is the *process* through which managers seek to improve understanding and meeting employees' desires and their ability to understand and manage the organization (Jones et al, 2003). This type of environment allows a free flow of ideas from decisions to dealing with their consequences and further creativity. *Creativity* can be defined as the ability of a decision maker to discover original and novel ideas that lead to feasible alternative courses of action. *Brainstorming* is an idea-generating and a problem-solving technique in which managers meet face-to-face to discuss and debate a wide variety of alternatives from which to make a decision (Jones & George, 2003). Companies such as 3M, Microsoft and Newell Rubbermaid have been well known for their creative cultures. In such organizational cultures, generally one person describes the problem in broad outline. Then, group members share their ideas and generate courses of action without criticizing each alternative until all suggestions have been heard. Then, group members are encouraged to be innovative and "piggy back" on the ideas they have heard. When all alternatives have been generated, the group members debate the pros and cons and develop a list of the best alternatives. In order to create a learning organization, senior leaders and managers must integrate such creativity and brainstorming in the organization and allow every person in the organization to develop a sense of personal mastery (Senge, 1990). Senge goes on to say that such organizations also need to encourage employees of all generations to develop and use complex mental models. Leaders and managers must do everything they can to promote group creativity and team learning. Leaders and managers must emphasize the importance of building a shared vision. Faculty, trainers and managers must model and encourage systems thinking because building a learning organization requires leaders and managers to radically change their assumptions. Incorporating systems thinking into the organizational structure provides a vehicle to effectively deal with change at the planning phase as well as the problem analysis phase. The "systems thinking" paradigm provides an avenue for organizations to continuously improve their processes and embrace change using new perspectives and new methods of thinking. Today's organizations can no longer operate in silos or closed systems and expect to be competitive with other national or international firms that effectively operate using all of the resources available to them in the open environment. As such, these organizations must embrace change as well as new ways of seeing and doing things as per a systems thinking mentality. Systems thinking is basically a multidiscipline approach that involves the wholeness of an organization. While basic analysis through any means can result in knowledge, systems thinking results in understanding as well as lasting changes. In the application of systems thinking, the entire organization and its subsystems can be investigated to understand each segment of the operation. Understanding the interdependence and interconnections of systems in operation and employees can provide a more holistic environment that embraces change. "Systems thinking" is basically a method of analyzing organizational problems of modern technology, society and organizations from a new weltanschauung, or a new perspective.

Organizations come in all sizes and as such they have differing but distinctive boundaries, rules, roles, communication channels, and views of authority and human stature based on their culture. Consequently there is a high degree of fit between organizational models (metaphors) and how they operate. To some degree all organizational leaders use their mental models in seeking to achieve the goals of the organization, albeit in many cases with externalities or social consequences that impact the effectiveness and productivity of the organization. Most organizational leaders understand that their firms need to stay efficient, effective and sensitive to their environments in order to remain successful and socially responsible. This applies equally to both for-profit and non-for-profit organizations. The degree to which an organization is described as bureaucratic is probably directly correlated to the degree to which it is "unfit for future action." Contributing to fitness for future action is the need for organizational leaders to keep their members aware and focused on the collective vision of the organization in order to attain the unity of action required for success. They can best complete this responsibility by clearly communicating this reality and then helping people see and achieve the vision. All of this is directly related to the agility with which organizations are able to change internally in meeting the challenge of the turbulence in their environment.

Because of cultural and technological changes, organizations are required to make internal changes periodically in order to continue to be sustainable. These internal changes are a result of the organization's ability to effectively use their human assets which can be inclusive of different generations. The degree to which organizations are successful in these change efforts is in part a function of the degree to which they keep members of different generations in mind and are aware of specific required changes and the general need for continual change. Systemic change without considering the culture or the needs of each generation of the workforce in which they are contained is doomed to failure. For this reason, organizational leaders need to understand the needs, desires and work habits of the various generations in the workforce before planning or implementing major changes.

UNDERSTANDING THE FOUR GENERATIONS

Currently, American corporate leaders and faculty in the United States are dealing with a multi-generational workforce as they have four distinct generations working simultaneously. As can be seen from Table 16, the four generations currently in the United States workforce are known as the traditionalists (or veterans), baby boomers, Gen X, and Gen Y individuals. Members of each generation tend to share certain experiences, events and history that help shape their "generational personality" during their socialization in the society.

Table 16. Various Generations in the United States

Generation Category	Birth Years	Population in the USA	Common Characteristics
Traditionalists	1900–1945	75 million	Stability and security
Baby Boomers	1946–1964	80 million	Teamwork and human rights
Generation X	1965–1976	46 million	Empowerment and social responsibility
Generation Y	1977–1994	70 million	Technology and personal growth
Cyberspace Generation	1995–present	20 million	Globalization and internet
Total		290 million	

The characteristics discussed are generalities and they do not necessarily all apply to each person and some of the characteristics described for one generation may very well apply to individuals of other generations as well. However, the characteristics described are likely to apply more often to individuals of the specified generation. As such, managers must be cautious and not stereotype specific individuals when it comes to hiring and evaluation solely based on these categories since each person is unique and may not necessarily fit the mold for the specified generation based on his or her place of birth. Nonetheless, understanding the various generational personalities can help managers and leaders build bridges in the work environment to create collaborative teams in today's learning organizations. Furthermore, this understanding may assist them to effectively recruit and retain diverse individuals by meeting the majority of their intrinsic needs in order to keep them loyal and committed to the organization. As one reads about the different generations, it is best to look for potential implications on one's own organizational systems and environments. As learning and wisdom increases, one can then appropriately use human systems (on an individual and organizational basis) to gain a true competitive advantage in the twenty first century work environment. Current leaders, like past leaders, can reap bottom-line benefits from using "big picture" systems thinking to create user friendly cultures that accommodate the needs of a diverse generation of workers (Lancaster *et al*, 2002). According to Lancaster *et al* (2002), with the existence of four diverse generations of employees in the work system, misunderstandings might become a common everyday occurrence if teamwork and team learning is not encouraged. When generational collisions occur in the workplace, the results can reduce profitability, present hiring challenges, increase turnover rates, and decrease morale among all generations of employees in the department. Understanding the various generational personalities is essential in building bridges and creating new learning and development opportunities in the work environment. The four generations are identified below and since each generation is somewhat different, note the various suggested rewards and retention methods.

Traditionalists (veterans) were born between the turn of the last century and the end of World War II (1900–1945) and they make up about 75 million individuals in the United States. Traditionalists, because of their experience, have learned to do without much participation, and the management style they learned came from the military (Lancaster *et al*, 2002). They were cautious, did not take much risk, spoke only when spoken to, and have been obedient to societal rules. They expect career security of life-long employment and do not appreciate job-hopping or downsizing jobs. Currently, there are many Traditionalists working in large numbers at fast food locations and retail outlets such as various department stores, McDonalds, Wal-Mart, Home Depot, and many top Fortune 500 organizations. This generation prefers a learning environment that offers predictability, stability, and security.

The *baby boomers*, born between 1946–1964, number about 80 million individuals in the United States (Lancaster *et al*, 2002). They grew up in suburbs, had educational opportunities above their parents, and saw lots of consumer products hit the marketplace (calculators, appliances). The television had a significant impact on their views of the world regarding equal opportunity and other human rights. Many members of this generation served in the military throughout the United States and around the globe. They enjoy perks that allow them to have more free time like errand-running service, car washes, food service, etc. The preferred learning environment of the Boomers is interactive and team activities.

Generation X, making up about 46 million individuals in the United States, born from 1965 through 1976, transitioned into the work environment during the 1990s. They had plenty of choices in choosing their professions and jobs (Lancaster *et al*, 2002). The technological advancements exacerbated their successors as they are techno savvy unlike some of their Boomer counterparts. Rather than 'paying their dues for a number of years' as previous generations did, they were able to demand that organizations adapt to their way of doing things, creating disbelief from the previous generations. This generation was raised in the fast lane with one or both parents working. They detest micro-management in the work environment and want constant feedback on how they are performing. They are the job-hopping generation and are attracted to work projects instead of jobs. They are making a difference in society by expecting firms to be socially responsible (i.e. Green peace, recycling, bettering the environment). For this group, freedom and autonomy are considered the ultimate rewards as this generation grew up being independent (Mujtaba & Karadayi, 2004). This generation believes as long as the job gets done, it is not important where or when it occurs. They have been raised in 'fun environments' and like for their training to be fun and interactive with immediate feedback.

Generation Y individuals, mostly born between 1977–1994, make up about 70 million individuals (Mujtaba & Karadayi, 2004) who are techno-savvy, multi-tasking and have had access to cell phones, personal pagers, computers, and concern for personal safety most of their lives. It is predicted that this generation will be more loyal than the Gen Xers provided they are stimulated and have learning opportunities. They are likely to challenge 'why' systems function the way they do and how things operate, and futurists feel this generation will make the greatest contributions (Lancaster *et al*, 2002). According to Eisner (2004) and Spence (2001), Gen Y individuals will be more likely to deal with finding facts quickly and to find more of such data as they will have a short "shelf life." So, today's college age students must learn to think on their feet, make decisions based on new knowledge, create new knowledge through inductive and deductive reasoning, experience different methods and cultures, and learn faster than previous generations because information is changing faster than ever and continuous learning is becoming the norm. The global world of training and education will spend about $2 trillion annually and around $740 billion just in the United States (Eisner, 2004) to make sure their employees are well educated, flexible and are able to think at a fast pace while adjusting to the changing needs of their clients. So, in terms of learning style, Generation Y, students expect education to be about application and doing of things that relate to their current interests. Also, they learn best when the learning process and facilitation involves them in a fun and humorous manner. This generation strongly resists the traditional style of lecturing by academicians and "know-it-all" experts since they prefer to be involved in the process. As a matter of fact, Spence (2001) mentioned that Gen Y students are likely to "treat traditional assignments like the throwaway instructions you get with a new computer." Perhaps, this mindset is why the formats of case analysis, debates, teamwork, presentations, and jointly working on real world exercises seem to be most suitable and more enjoyable in many of today's educational settings.

Understanding Generation X

The *Generation X* population has had plenty of choices in choosing their professions and jobs in their entry to the workforce. Kupperschmidt (2000) summarized the typical characteristics of GenX employees as follows: They are self-reliant, they want a balance, they do not like to commit, they are skeptical, and they embrace diversity in the culture. GenX employees have been labeled as slackers who lack strong work ethics since many are supposedly focused on their wants and needs (Harken, 2000). The have also been described as job hoppers who are rebellious; workers changing jobs about every 3 years (Cordeniz, 2002). According to Rodriguez *et al* (2003), a survey found that 55% of one organization's employees had planned or had the thought of leaving before hitting the three-year mark with the organization. GenX employees are said to be the "work to live" generation, whereas the baby boomers are considered to be the "live to work" population (Rodriguez *et al*, 2003).

Researchers and workforce leaders know that the baby boomers are on their way to retirement and the workforce shortage will become tighter. As such, recruiting and retaining qualified workers becomes an important aspect of any large organization's task. Harken (2000) said that GenX prefers "naked management," which requires managers and leaders to create a positive work culture where a trusting and genuine relationship can be built with GenX employees. According to Harken (2000), the components of the naked model are freedom, interaction and involvement, recognition, empathy strengthening the working relationship between managers and GenX workers, and effective communication on a regular basis. Tulgan (1996), a researcher on this generation, interviewed 85 diverse groups of GenX individuals by asking them "how are you being managed and how is that management style affecting your work?" A majority of the responses found that they are not motivated by long term rewards or the use of fear. Furthermore, GenX workers do not want to be micromanaged and don't want managers to waste their time with lectures and boring meetings. Tulgan (1996) summarized the GenX expectations into various categories as this generation of workers expect managers to:

1. Invest in their employees.
2. Be able and willing to provide effective feedback.
3. Understand work issues and be able to respond to their needs and concerns (in other words they do not like being ignored). And
4. Possess and have the power to access information and resources.

Some researchers claim that the GenX employees have a lower expectation of what institutions and society have to offer them (O'Neill, 2002). One reason for understanding the expectations of workers is to effectively maximize recruiting and retention efforts of qualified employees in the competitive economic times. As such, this generation of employees expects some leeway and control over the work environment, reward and recognition, and interaction with managers. Overall, one can summarize that GenX employees do not care much about long-term loyalty because they want to be regarded as free agents. They prefer being trained, developed and ready for more responsibilities and opportunities. At the same time, they want flexibility and choose jobs that offer them the most immediate joy and exploration of opportunities.

Understanding Generation Y Workers

In the Generation Y (Gen Y) segment of the American market, consumers have needs and preferences that are very different than any other generation due to their upbringing and socialization factors. Organizational leaders must pay attention to Gen Y-ers as they make up about 70 million Americans born from 1977 through 1994. Their shared experiences have included invasion of Iraq, the removal of Taliban in Afghanistan, the attacks on New York's Twin Towers during September 11th 2001, the widespread profiling of individuals associated with terrorism, the impeachment trials of President Clinton over sex allegation statements, the Columbine high school shootings, several cult members of different groups committing suicide, the fuss over the Y2K challenges which did not cause the expected problems, the wave of electronic shopping/banking, and the Dot. Com bust among many others (Mujtaba & Karadayi, 2004). They also seem to prefer video games, internet and DVD compared to mass media television and movies.

Generation Y individuals are more technologically savvy and more interactive than any other generation prior to them. It is estimated that those who are currently between the ages of 18-24 years of age tend to spend about ten hours online each week while watching television about ten hours as well. Jason Ritter, a television actor, falls in this age category and, during an interview on October 15th 2004 with the hosts of *The View* on the American Broadcasting Corporation (ABC), admitted that he is hooked on video games. Jason, son of the late actor John Ritter, mentioned how he is actually addicted to video games since he often plays by himself while ignoring friends, family members and important chores. He mentioned that he knows he is addicted to video games because he read that these are the same exact symptoms shown by those who are addicted to alcohol. So, some Generation Y members tend to heavily engage in video games and instant messaging through their computers while listening to the latest diverse music online. Researchers conclude that organizations can best reach this group via word-of-mouth advertisement which can reach millions of individuals instantly through the connectivity of technology savvy individuals. Generation Y-ers tend not to take too much risk as they have seen the Dot.Com bust and the downfall of large organizations such Enron and WorldCom where people either invested heavily in them for quick returns or their leaders lied to their stakeholders. They also distrust the media because they know politicians and governments tend to use media to sway perceptions. They feel as though they are living in a very uncertain world where much animosity exists between individuals in different countries due to their personal beliefs which may be very different than that of Americans. A good percentage of the Generation Y-ers are worried about crimes, wars, and terrorism attacks. Research has shown that while concerns about possible terrorist attacks on the United States either were reduced or stayed the same for many individuals, Generation Y individuals' level of concern about such attacks actually increased from 51% in 2002 to 61% in the year 2003 (Mujtaba & Karadayi, 2004). This two digits or eleven percent increase in the level of concern could be due to the widespread mistrust of the American government, by outsiders, which is seen as an imperialist trying to exercise aspects of colonialism in developing countries.

Generation Y individuals tend to be open to diversity of ideas, cultures, music, and points of views. They are able to adapt quickly to new lifestyles and cultures compared to their parents. They are not hard core "my way or the highway" or dichotomous individuals as they believe in contrasting points of views. Their values include diversity, dignity, fairness, and equality for people in all respects. They also like to challenge the status quo and extreme paradigms as they want proof in order to believe and trust others (they may say "*Show me the money*" as seen in the movie Jerry Maguire with Tom Cruise as the lead actor). They do not like telemarketers nor do they like those who are involved in hard sell. This generation is best reached by friends, colleagues and technology that is fun, exciting and in touch with their values. They tend to like reality shows because they seem to be more natural than the regular television shows.

Generation Y employees tend to be very interactive and they value learning, flexibility and mutual trust. They follow the rules of their organizations and professions and they tend to be good team players with challenging assignments. They are confident, time-impoverished, can multi-task better than previous generations, and are willing to work hard for good causes. They are also willing to leave organizations for others that are more fair, socially responsive and loyal to their people. The same is true for their choices in buying products, services and vacations.

This generation has been called the "digital natives" who are connected at all times through their laptops and state of the art wired telephones. They seem to be immersed in a "fun focused" world and heavily involved with fun technology. They value entertainment, humor, fun, excitement, and unique cultural experiences which seem to drive their buying patterns and behaviors. Values theory states that what people value drives their behaviors (Pohlman and Gardiner, 2000) and this is certainly the case with individuals of this generation. They don't watch regular television shows or big Hollywood movies which attracted previous generations because their values are different. As such, they are considered to be immune to traditional marketing and advertising strategies which organizations use in their conquest for more revenues. Generation Y-ers tend to trust real time information coming from their friends, family members, colleagues, and those in the online community that tend to speak honestly from their hearts about movies, television shows, and best products. They value reality which is why many of them are watching "reality shows" on television. They are the "just-in-time" (JIT) generation of individuals and get information on a JIT basis for product buying choices. They want information that is of use to them in their current situation which is why they rely so much on instant information available on the internet for instant customization. So, "word of mouth" and "story telling" form of advertisement seem to be the best strategy with the Generation Y group of individuals. Overall, with regards to absorbing new information, Generation Y learners expect their education to be about current application and very relevant to their immediate interests. Educators must remember that Gen Y learners learn best when the learning is fun and when the facilitation process involves them since the traditional style of lecturing is not their preferred mode of learning.

MAKING EFFECTIVE CONNECTIONS
WITH ALL GENERATIONS

Lancaster (2002) offers some ideas that organizational systems might use to make generational connections and prevent possible problems. The following are some of Lancaster's suggestions for making effective connections with various generations in the workforce.

1. Organizations should have generational-specific tactics for feedback strategies and to recruit, retain, and train each of the four generations.
2. Recruiting—one-size fits all approach—will not work as we move forward. Two keys here involve knowing the audience the organization wants to attract and understanding their values.
3. An orientation program is a crucial retention tool. This is the first opportunity that an employee can 'connect' to the organization. If the orientation program does not ignite that spark, employees will soon leave. Orientation designers must focus on the history, culture, and mission of the organization.
4. Mentoring programs should link new and experienced workers. Mentoring shortens the learning curve and helps build effective bridges between generations.

5. In a learning organization, information should flow in all directions and every employee should be heard.
6. Benefits, the number of work hours required, and places of employment (home/office) have different meanings to the various generations of workers today. Repackaging benefits and allowing benefit package choices are starting to emerge attracting the four generations needed to fill job vacancies.
7. Equalize rewards with each generation by linking rewards to performance.
8. Exit interviews should take place and be documented as they can serve as a feedback loop to gain insight on why specific generations are leaving.

 Making connections at the right times with the right individuals and by the right means is a critical element of making any system or culture successful. While it is important to make productive connections with employees and customers of various generations, one must remember that there are other relevant stakeholders impacting the success of each organization as well. Other stakeholders and customers can include the community, unions, suppliers, vendors, etc. that are an important part of keeping the system functioning smoothly. Checkland used the acronym "CATWOE" to demonstrate one aspect of systems thinking application (1999, page 18) by pointing out the various elements in the acronym "CATWOE" which stands for customers, actors, transformation, weltanschauung (paradigm or perspective), owners, and environmental constraints. Similarly, Pohlman and Gardiner (2000) provided a decision making framework that considers the values of all stakeholders which are critical to the success of the system in order to maximize the organization's value in the long-term.

 A valuable resource for all managers and leaders is the textbook written by Pohlman and Gardiner (2000) which offers a comprehensive introduction to *Value Driven Management* (VDM) and the holistic approach to decisions. VDM provides a decision-making framework that can be used in a variety of situations with each generation of the workforce. VDM is based upon Values Theory which claims that what people truly value drives their actions and behaviors. The underlying theme is to make decisions that maximize value over time for all relevant stakeholders in the long-term. Value Driven Management is a practical model that managers can use in their daily work life in a variety of decision-making scenarios. VDM enlarges upon the concept of value over time and explains that the two key elements of using VDM in decision-making are: one, understanding the values of the organization and its employees; and two, knowing the appropriate time horizon for decision making. The authors explore the underlying assumptions of VDM including (1) what is valued drives action; (2) the creation of knowledge and its appropriate use leads to value creation; (3) there are value adders and value destroy-ers; (4) values can compete or be complementary; and, last but certainly not least, (5) all employees are employees—emphasizing that everyone's input and actions are critically important to the success of the organization!

The basic purpose of Value Driven Management (VDM) is to motivate managers and employees, when contemplating making decisions or tak-ing actions, to consider the impact of these decisions and actions on the value of the organization over time (Cavico and Mujtaba, 2005). This de-termination can be accomplished only by an examination of the sets of values held by the relevant constituents (or "stakeholder" groups) of the organization. These encompass world, national, societal cultures and sub-cultures, organizational culture, the values of employees, suppliers, custom-ers, competitors, and third parties (such as unions and government regula-tors), and most importantly, but not exclusively, the values of the "owners" of the organization. The subjectivity and diversity of value, the long-term view, and the necessity of foreseeing consequences make VDM decisions quite complex; and thus will require the VDM decision-maker to engage in careful determinations, accurate predictions, equitable balancing and weighing in order to use wise judgment. There are people, processes, and systems within organizations that add and destroy value. There are, for ex-ample, employees within organizations who destroy more value than they create, perhaps as a result of being in the wrong position with the wrong types of skills and abilities, or perhaps they are totally incompatible with their organization's means or ends. It is every employee's responsibility to seek out a role that adds value and ensures success; and the organization's responsibility to eliminate value destroyers by placing people in the proper jobs and instituting proper processes and systems.

The VDM model and method is a philosophical as well as a practical ap-proach, which is simple to state and discuss, but laborious to implement. Implementation is difficult because organizations and people are complex, values are diverse and subjective, values of constituent groups are hard to comprehend, and calculating consequences and their long-range impact on value maximization are very challenging tasks. Nonetheless, if VDM is learned well and administered thoughtfully and consistently with today's multi-generational workforce, then the ultimate goals of achieving, creat-ing, and sustaining long-term growth, surplus, wealth, and value maximiza-tion can be attained in any national or international organization.

Cultural Variables and Considerations

The combination of the eight facets of Value Driven Management and its successful implementation are an appropriate guide for business success in today's multi-generational workforce. Conducting business internationally can be more complex than conducting business locally since companies are often dealing with several countries and different cultures. According to Nelson (1999), the climate of international business is created of eight key elements which are relationships, language, religion, values and attributes, laws and the legal government, education, technology, and social organizations. International companies need to ensure that they consider these elements in their decisions along with the implementation of the eight value drivers of VDM in order to make appropriate choices regarding each generation of the workers and customers. Within each culture outside of the United States, there might be different practices and mentalities based on the various generations. In order to be successful in different cultures, international managers have to commit extra time and effort to ensure their business practices are suitable for both the culture and the diverse generations. They need to become fully aware of the foreign culture's basic mores and norms before starting as managers.

International managers should be cautious and not always follow the culture of their native country; they should try to practice and accommodate the norms and customs of the host country where business is held. According to Mendenhall, Kuhlmann & Stahl (2001), an effective method for international managers to acquire knowledge regarding a foreign culture before starting the managerial position is through spending time in the foreign country while practicing their day-to-day lifestyle. This approach will provide managers the opportunity to understand the local lifestyle, their needs, their desires, and other cultural practices through personal experience as opposed to reading a book. Once managers have adequate knowledge of the local culture, they will be able to work effectively with the various generations of the workforce. Maintaining a relationship with employees is also an essential part of working cooperatively and achieving team success. Periodic evaluation of business practices is a great tool for managers to determine the positives and negatives of their business. This data might allow improvement of business practices, as well as employee satisfaction.

Employee satisfaction and motivation concepts are very important in successful international management. In some cultures rewards and recognition can be appropriate strategies to motivate employees and in other cultures bonuses are the main motivational device. Motivational strategies can differ based on different generations of employees in each culture. Collectivistic countries treasure group accomplishments and individualistic countries value individual achievements. For example, India is a collectivistic country; therefore, Indians may enjoy group success. On the other hand, the United States is an individualistic country; hence, Americans may enjoy individual success. When international managers decide to appreciate their employees' efforts with rewards and recognition; they need to make sure that the appreciation will motivate employees and that they reinforce good performance. For some individuals, such as those who are young and financially unstable, money can be a very effective tool for motivation; therefore, managers need to act accordingly.

The western influence has changed India dramatically in many areas including following the trends established in other countries. Generations X and Y in particular seem to follow many western trends that they see in television and on the internet. India's western influence is increasing as international businesses are increasing their presence there in an attempt to capture the market share of nearly one billion prospective consumers. Rapid growth of outsourcing is an example of the international business growth in India. The Indian workforce appreciates appropriate benefits from their employers and these employees of international corporations require various types of benefits suitable to their generation and culture. For example, many of the Indian companies do not offer appropriate medical insurance and workers' compensation to their employees. Therefore, providing adequate medical insurance and workers' compensation might attract potential employees while motivating current employees. International managers should always ensure the safety of their subsidiaries in foreign nations to prevent disasters like the Bhopal tragedy. The Bhopal tragedy occurred on December 3rd, 1984 at a chemical plant called Union Carbide in Bhopal, India. Union Carbide, India was a subsidiary of an American company. The disaster killed and injured thousands of people and such tragedies are disliked by all generations. The disaster mainly occurred due to insufficient safety mechanisms in the company. Even though it was reported that all of the deficiencies were corrected; it was not enough to prevent the disaster from happening (Cavico & Mujtaba, 2004). Managers need to ensure that employees of subsidiaries are treated the same as employees in the parent company. If disasters like the Bhopal tragedy occur, then not only will employees mistrust their managers but companies will also lose a vast amount of money since they will have to compensate all the victims.

Corporate training programs are one of the main methods to bring international employees together to share knowledge and best practices, and to gain the requisite knowledge regarding the company. In training programs, it is beneficial for employees from all generations to attend and voice their concerns. This will provide an opportunity for employees and employers to understand each other regardless of cultural and generational differences. Ethical training programs, in the international environment, are another excellent avenue to ensure people are treated fairly and many companies offer such interaction opportunities and workshops in order to hear the concerns of the local people. According to Mitchell (2003), "The aim of an ethics training program is to reinforce existing personal values and tie them into 'the big picture' values of the company." Effective ethics training programs will allow employer and employees to understand various ethical standards. When companies conduct ethical training programs, they need to ensure that the content of the training is appropriate for a specific culture as well as for other cultures (Mitchell, 2003). Basically, managers should act according to the norms and customs of the country and local culture in order to win the hearts and minds of its citizens regardless of their generational differences.

MENTORING AND PEER REVIEW

In today's 21st century global business environment, effective mentoring of staff and faculty members enhances internal business relationships, perceived career success, organizational commitment, overall performance, and the reduction of turnover (Mujtaba & Kennedy, 2005). When an organization invests monetarily in a person, it is best to establish a relationship with that person to ensure that he/she is receiving the best support possible. This is even more important for international assignments, diverse groups, and for those who deal with faculty and students in multinational environments. Many businesses have paid the high price of losing key personnel due to the lack of an effective mentoring and socialization program regarding the culture of the organization and the countries involved. One main goal of mentoring is to support the new employee through effective socialization and indoctrination practices. This section discusses best practices in mentoring new employees through effective socialization and indoctrination programs and provides an example of online faculty peer review process which can be utilized in national and international environments.

At a general level, the term mentor applies to a person who helps another become familiarized with an organization's culture, people and tasks in order to function effectively, and/or progressively move upward on the ladder of success, as defined by the internal culture. Depending on the assigned mentor and his/her influence in the organization, mentoring relationships can greatly enhance a person's growth and advancement opportunities. Mentoring can be formal and or informal. Informal mentorship programs are natural connections that bond two or more individuals together based on some similarity, liking for each other, or common goals. On the other side, formal mentoring programs are developed purposefully by managers or the organization to partner a new employee with a veteran employee in the organization. Some common forms of mentorship include peer mentorship, supervisor/subordinate mentorship, and third party mentorship where the new employee is assigned an outside coach. Regardless of format or level of formality, mentoring programs tend to focus

on familiarizing the new employee with the organization, career development opportunities, psychological well-being while learning the ropes and
politics of the culture, and role modeling.

Businesses also invest considerable monetary resources to hire people
with the same attributable cultural values as the institution. People seek
normalcy which aspires to specific affective, cognitive, and behavioral patterns of people based on their level of cognitive dissonance. For example,
as new employees enter a company, they seek to have commonality within
their environment, which will reduce the level of self efficacy or anxiety
within the new organization. If new employees' perceive they have the same
values with the company they are entering, the level of cognitive dissonance
will be lower (Mujtaba & Kennedy, 2005). Of course, people with the same
nuances will benefit the organization because of similarities in values, beliefs and work behaviors which can lead to higher productivity and better
teamwork. The socialization process within an organization is a very important function which establishes the foundation of affective job satisfaction
and organizational commitment for the new employee. The employee must
be able to adapt to his/her new work environment by assessing the organization's internal capabilities and to derive one's full capacity within this
new environment. Successful socialization processes allow new employees
to effectively understand their place within this environment. An effective
socialization process creates value for the organization by escalating the
process of a new hire to become proficient on the job more quickly, thus
increasing overall effectiveness for the organization.

Mentors as Coaches to Enhance Performance

Great mentors can use the skills of great coaches to lead associates to
better performance before, during and after the socialization process. As
such mentors should acquire the skills needed to coach employees for good
performance, bad performance, and for no performance. Effective coaching is a continuous process of conversational collaborations and interactions aimed at assisting new and veteran employees to unlock and realize
their full potential one task or one skill at a time, and at a pace appropriate
for the person being coached. The essence of coaching is unlocking an
employee's potential, through stimulating questions, so they can maximize
their own performance. Effective coaches keep in mind that imposing their
way of accomplishing tasks is not their objective because that is not part of
coaching but rather dictating. Effective coaches accept the challenge knowing that the growth and development journey is a continuous process, and
that learning how to learn and develop are the real goals for both individu-

als (coach and the coached). Effective coaches, as originally recommended by Plum International, FOCUS on being:

- *Fair.* Coaches earn respect by being just and equitable to all of their associates.
- *Objective.* Successful coaching requires measurable criteria for observation and thoughtful analysis. They observe, analyze and discuss relevant issues with their associates for development purposes.
- *Collaborative.* Effective coaches acknowledge that the responsibility for improving performance and increased knowledge rests with the individual where the coach only offers assistance and guidance to the right direction. They lead, support, encourage, and synergize together with the individual.
- *Useful.* Impactful coaching produces value-added action plans that are doable given the time frames as well as the individual's level of competence and skills. The execution makes a difference.
- *Sincere.* Coaches must genuinely believe that employees and associates are the most important asset of the organization. They speak and act from heart.

Effective coaches play the roles of communicators (encourage, inform, praise, raise awareness, and collaborate), performance leaders (set clear expectations, serve as role models, empower, help, and challenge), and catalysts (vehicles for change, remove barriers, and enable others to reach their full potential). Coaching is not an innate skill but rather it is learned. It occurs through one's life personally and professionally. Effective coaching is the process of letting people know that what they do matters to you and to the organization. Furthermore, it is about letting them know that the mentors are there to help them be the best they can be as their success is important. It is also about being sincere, specific and to the point about both good and poor performance so they can take personal responsibility for their achievements. From this perspective, coaching is and it can be one of the most important functions managers perform because it communicates performance levels, expectations, importance of the tasks and responsibilities, and it communicates a caring attitude.

There are five specific steps in the coaching process as managers oversee the work done through their associates. These five key steps will help managers become more effective in getting the work done with and/or through associates. As such, effective coaching requires the steps of planning, supporting associates for good performance, communicating and/or setting a time to increase performance, leading associates to higher performance, and following up and confirming effective achievement of objectives and expectations. The following list summarizes some of the main elements involved in coaching direct reports.

1. Before beginning the coaching session, be sure to plan exactly what you want to achieve, and the potential benefits for the other person.
2. Start on a positive note and establish a common ground by having a supportive environment.
3. Communicate clearly, listen effectively, show that you care, and do not "beat around the bush." Clearly and caringly state the challenge, opportunity, and/or expectations.
4. Be respectful of the other person's feelings, honor and dignity. Create a non-threatening environment for the interaction, dialogue and discussion.
5. Be culturally sensitive by getting to know the other person's background, culture, values, and anticipate his/her reactions.
6. Avoid value judgments, stereotyping and labeling the behavior of others.
7. Use empathic listening skills to clarify your understanding and the other person's perspective.
8. Stay with the point and do not get side tracked with other issues. Restate the purpose of the session and ask what specific things can be done to increase or improve performance. You can offer assistance but avoid providing solutions—let the individual come up with the solutions. Your job is to lead them in the right direction.
9. Document and clarify the specific plan suggested by the employee, the expected level of performance and how the plan will improve performance. Seek agreement and summarize the conversation.
10. End on a positive note and thank the person for coming up with the specific plan.

Good coaches will always give support to associates, but when associates are not performing up to the standard for the job, it is necessary to provide effective coaching by asking leading questions to assist them in the thinking and solution generation process. When working with associates, coaches can help them solve problems they are having with the tasks they have been assigned. Every associate is likely to have difficulties with some task at one time or another. That is why the coach's support is so vital. A good coach will be able to spot an associate who is having trouble and coach them to a solution for the problem by asking good questions. When supporting and leading associates, it is important to focus on the work results and not on the person. If the results are not what were expected, ask the following questions: What happened? Why did it happen? What can be done to prevent it from happening again? These questions can be effective with new and veteran employees as it encourages them to think for themselves.

Online Faculty Mentoring through Peer Review: Exploring a Model

As we all know, timely and constructive feedback benefits the faculty, students and the institution itself; in that regard, a formal mentoring program in the form of a peer review can be one of the most positive features of the Online teaching experience. This type of cyberspace mentoring and review program for national and international faculty members should be designed to provide online faculty members with personalized feedback, based on performance, as observed by experienced online faculty leaders/reviewers (Mujtaba, 2004). The feedback should be designed to help faculty members in their continued development and to enhance their online skills in order to provide the finest educational experience for students. Let us discuss one example that has been applied at some insinuations such as the University of Phoenix (U of P), where each new online faculty member can expect to have an assigned mentor for his or her first course, and they can expect to be formally reviewed after the fourth course, followed by annual reviews on the anniversary of the first review. The first author, as an academic director, has used this process with two institutions and a similar version of this format with management development specialists in the corporate arena. Since the first author was responsible for the hiring and development of faculty members at the Main Campus (which has thousand of traditional students attending classes full time), online modalities, and for offsite locations throughout the United States, the Bahamas, as well as in Jamaica, the author used this mentoring and peer review process to ensure good facilitation and enhance the quality of learning for all students. Each time a new faculty is hired to teach classes at the undergraduate or graduate level, a mentor is formally assigned to this new faculty so s/he can be successful in first teaching experience with the institution. This process also ensures that learning outcomes are effectively being achieved since the mentor can intervene and guide the new faculty in the right direction. The initial mentoring is formal and the mentor is known. Once the new faculty successfully teaches his or her first course, then a formal "blind" peer review process begins which helps the new faculty to continuously enhance his or her facilitation skills. In this review process, the reviewers (or mentors) are not known and the process is scheduled randomly by the program office. For a review of the peer review model suggested toward effective mentoring, see the formal review processes discussed in chapter two (Faculty Peer Review Process). Based on the success of the Peer Review program, it is hoped that every faculty will continue to welcome and embrace quality education.

As stated before, such a Peer Review model seems to work very effectively as it provides timely feedback for educators and shares best practices with them to enhance their repertoire of teaching skills. One faculty member had stated that

> This type of comprehensive report, suggestions and coaching is most helpful. I find it to be highly valuable as it gives me incentive to enhance my approach which will bring added excellence to my materials and facilitation. This will positively influence my future classes.

The comments from faculty members that have gone through the process are very positive and they appreciate having such a standardized process for personal development and improvement. Integrated with effective development programs should be appropriate policies regarding teaching loads and compensation methods for online educators. Most traditional schools that are teaching oriented (as opposed to research orientation) tend to have about 20–30 students in the masters programs for on-ground courses. A teaching load of four courses per term seems normal when no other expectations are placed upon the faculty. However, many traditional schools have graduate assistants that help faculty members in course preparation, teaching, and examinations. However, because online education requires continuous and daily asynchronous interaction through bulletin board, chat sessions, assignment feedback, lectures, etc. with faculty (and not graduate students) it may be extremely challenging to teach four courses effectively for first time online faculty members when there are 30 students in each section. This may even be more challenging for the first couple of years when an institution is just beginning to offer and teach online courses. In such cases, institutions should reduce teaching loads because there is a huge learning curve for both faculty members and technical administrators in resolving day-to-day operational challenges while attempting to ensure learning of students is not hindered. Overall, institutions should limit the size of their courses with regard to enrollment based on such variables as the experience of the faculty, the number of technical administrators who can help students and faculty, the comfort level of beginning online students, the daily or weekly requirements for online interaction, the software availability for exams and quizzes, and other relevant considerations. More importantly, institutions should have a formal process to assign experienced mentors with new faculty members so they can successfully adjust and enhance their facilitation skills while effectively using cyberspace technologies.

Mentoring is a growing strategy used today for developing the talent of employees in professional positions. The aforementioned material focused on mentoring practices through the socialization process for the retention and developmental aspect of new employees. Mentoring programs in large organizations tend to be formal while allowing a great deal of flexibility and informality in the interpersonal relationships. Effective mentoring programs benefit the mentee, the mentor and the organization. A mentoring program can develop the leadership, management and coaching skills of managers to create a productive culture. Effective mentoring in the twenty first century organization requires the skills of management, leadership, and coaching which are critical to the new employee's development.

SUMMARY

Today's managers, trainers and higher education faculty members are likely to face a diverse audience, made up of different generations. Decision-making with regard to dealing with diverse learners and employees is one of the critical tasks today; therefore, managers, trainers and faculty members need to ensure that their decisions are appropriate for the business while considering the personal interests and desires of each person. Organizational learning is an appropriate method for employees to expand their knowledge regarding the organization, and teamwork is an excellent method for employees to work together effectively. Due to late retirements and early employment, the number of different generations in the workforce is increasing and it is important that managers understand the various generations' desires in order to effectively work with them as a team. This understanding can further help them target their recruitment efforts to each segment of the workforce in order to have a diverse pool of qualified applicants for job postings. The knowledge about the various generations can also assist managers to be effective coaches and mentors to new employees and "rising stars" as they make their way up the leadership ladder in the organization. Value Driven Management is one application of the system thinking paradigm where decisions are analyzed in terms of its total impact from a holistic approach. Understanding systems and applying systems thinking in a format such as the VDM concept is a critical leadership and organizational skill necessary in the 21st century's multi-generational workforce. As the environment becomes increasingly complex, and as organizational leaders search for means to deal with this complexity, it will become natural for them to turn to the foundations and practices of systems theory, to see the impact of each generation on the success of the firm, in order to effectively maneuver through this changing landscape. In the 21st century, international business is dramatically increasing; therefore, the corporate world has more international managers than previous years. International managers should not practice ethnocentricity (imposing one's cultural values on others) but rather they should attempt to consider their actions with regard to the local customs and practices. Managers should work and use appropriate practices based on the culture of the country where the business is being conducted. Dealing with various cultures and generations is a critical task for twenty first century managers of learning organizations. Therefore, managers should have the requisite knowledge of various cultures in their workforce along with an understanding of the desires of various generations to be successful as leaders both with employees and consumers. Furthermore, academic and corporate educators should appropriately inform and equip their learners about the differences in the workforce and consumer populations so they can make the right decisions while functioning effectively in the context of generational and cultural differences in the twenty first century organization.

This section discussed the needs of various generations of learner and employees. All learners (students and employees) prepare themselves to eventually apply their knowledge into the workplace and, as such, must be inculcated appropriately. Therefore, this section further explored mentoring programs as new employees are being socialized and indoctrinated into the culture. Furthermore, it discussed the skills of coaching which can be used to lead coaches in the right direction toward high performance while developing them to think for themselves. Such mentoring relationships are helpful for most new employees and they are especially helpful for employees working in different cities and cultures. One best way to reduce the impact of culture can be to have one or more formal or informal mentors.

CHAPTER 10

COMPARISON OF LEARNING OUTCOMES ACROSS DIFFERENT LOCATIONS

This chapter discusses documentation of learning and student performance through objective tests with graduate students in Kingston-Jamaica and compares the final exam results with students taking the same course, the same test, with the same instructor at different sites throughout the United States and in Nassau, Bahamas. The scores are further compared with students who completed this course and final exam in the online format. The groups of Jamaican, Bahamian and students in Tampa completing this course received traditional, face-to-face instruction in a classroom setting, with classes delivered in a weekend format with 32 face-to-face contact hours during the semester.

As expected, findings revealed that there was a statistically significant difference in the mean test scores of the pre-test and post-test for this group of students enrolled at the Kingston, Jamaica cluster. Furthermore, the results of final exam comparison with similar groups in the United States and Bahamas showed no significant differences. The comparison of student performance in Kingston, Jamaica with online students is also discussed. Some of this material was co-presented by Bahaudin Mujtaba and Rosemarie Hinds during November 2004 in Ocho Rios, Jamaica, at the Caribbean Area Network for Quality Assurance in Tertiary Education (CANQATE)

Adult Education in Academia, pages 225–238
Copyright © 2006 by Information Age Publishing

Conference. Overall, it is concluded that many of the learning outcomes designed to be achieved as a result of the course activities, specifically the final exam, were achieved consistently for students taking this course with the assigned faculty member in Jamaica, the United States and Bahamas.

LEARNING EFFECTIVENESS AND DISTANCE EDUCATION IN JAMAICA

Many international schools and universities have extended their offerings beyond their main campus and some have started clusters in the Caribbean countries. Jamaica is one of the countries that many such institutions are attracted to because of the ever-increasing demand for higher education. For example, since 1984, Nova Southeastern University (NSU) has been offering classes in Jamaica, starting with the Ocho Rios cluster and later expanding to Kingston and Montego Bay. Students travel from across the island to attend classes at these cluster sites. Today NSU has close to 800 active students in these cities. Interestingly, Jamaica with its small population had the highest enrollment in 2004, although NSU has been active in many countries including Bahamas, Trinidad, China, Brazil, France, Germany, Dominican Republic, England, Greece, Panama, and Venezuela. Some of the other international Universities facilitating distance education in Jamaica include Florida International University (US), Manchester Business College (England) and University of Dalhousie (Canada). Jamaicans are attracting diverse educational institutions because they want to be globally competitive and economically prosperous.

Jamaica is one of the many islands in the Caribbean with strong historical and cultural ties to both West Africa and Great Britain (Mujtaba, Hinds and Oskal, 2004). The population, almost three million, is a diverse blend of many different races with the majority being of African descent. The Jamaican culture is expressed through local stories, songs, dances, the use of herbs and bush medicine, local beliefs, the preparation of indigenous foods and through religious practices. Jamaicans perform folk songs and dance mainly during festivals and independence celebrations. During celebrations it is customary to wear their national costumes, called the Bandana. Jamaica's folk culture began mainly in the rural and mountainous villages. The main contributors to the Jamaican culture are the groups of people who made Jamaica their home. These contributors are the Africans, the English, the Spaniards, and the Indians. Jamaica, an island country, is the third largest island of the Greater Antilles of the West Indies and is situated south of Cuba. With its picturesque mountains and beautiful beaches, the island is known for its serene natural surroundings and is a popular tourist destination for many individuals throughout the world. Jamaica became a

British colony in 1670. During the 18th century, planters began importing African slaves to work on the sugar plantations. Today the island's culture and customs blend its British and African roots. Jamaica gained its independence from Britain in 1962 and maintains a two-party political system. The island is named after the Native American word *Xaymaca*, meaning "isle of springs."

Over the centuries, there has been a variety of marriages of both different races and cultures, inevitably resulting in a fair tolerance of diversity. The advent of the information age, aided by the Worldwide Web and Cable Television, has exposed Jamaicans to various other cultures. One could assume that with the majority of Jamaicans being of African descent, as well as the British influence on their culture, Jamaicans would have very distinct ideas on social issues and education systems. And, they do, but in reality Jamaicans seem to take their cues from the outside world and no single culture has impacted the Jamaican people as much as that of North America. Jamaican attitudes tend to mirror American norms, beliefs and values more as the years progress (Mujtaba et al, 2004). It is expected that the education programs offered by American schools also mirror that of the United States' infrastructure. However, the differences between the British system, which has greatly impacted Jamaicans, and the United States educational systems cannot be disregarded. One major difference, with regard to the teaching faculty, that should be kept in mind is that the British tend to go deep into a few topics, while the United States educators tend to touch briefly on many topics. This difference in style may create some confusion for students, as students can overestimate the requirements of the course. This research attempts to study the learning outcomes achieved by Jamaican students, in Kingston, completing a graduate course with performance results of students in the United States and the Grand Bahamas.

Global trends toward the removal of cultural, geographic, social, and economic boundaries are providing education options and opportunities to individuals worldwide. The field of academia is fast catching up in this regard using cyberspace technology. Various forms of distance education, including the phenomenon of the virtual classroom and offsite campuses, are now being explored and developed. New challenges are presented by these developments, both for educational institutions and their stakeholders. As a developing country, Jamaica is challenged by various resource constraints. However, as global boundaries disappear, the country is still expected to compete against larger countries with greater resources. Therefore, innovative and cost effective methods have to be employed in the development of the country's human development. Nonetheless, distance education provides one opportunity for Jamaicans to compete effectively in the global marketplace. However, the quality of distance education courses must be equivalent as traditional courses if the graduates are to be successful on a global basis. Participants in this new era of distance education have many factors to consider including cross cultural challenges; the availability of the various infrastructural support systems; and hiring, training, compensating, and retaining the human resources needed to facilitate this development. Additionally, the needs of students, as well as the organizations that will be purchasing their skills must be considered in the development and facilitation of a business curriculum. Furthermore, the learning outcomes of students finishing their courses through distance education should be documented with students completing these courses in traditional formats.

Trends in delivery of today's graduate business programs include distance education, electronic-based instruction, as well as traditional ground-based classes offered in weekend, daytime, and evening formats. Preziosi *et al.* (2000) state that "Today considerable attention is being paid to distance education...and much of the interest in distance education is due to the increasing use of Internet-based instruction." Distance education has been the reality of life for many institutions and adult learners in the past few decades and it is becoming more widespread. There have been many evolutionary changes in distance education mainly brought on by technology and these changes have raised questions pertaining to learning effectiveness across various teaching formats. Researchers agree that much attention has been directed at the number of distance education offerings and delivery mechanisms among institutions as well as to questions of learning equivalency between course and program offerings through various sites and formats. Similarly, accrediting bodies have raised questions of equivalency that range from the resources provided to students in all modalities to the outcomes of student learning. As distance education both nationally and internationally increases in importance, continuous and documented evaluation will continue to be a critical component of process improvement. Of course, the schools offering distance education programs are held accountable for achieving the same level of effectiveness as traditional approaches available to students. Such accountability requires that institutions understand their stakeholders and their needs on a proactive basis in order to deliver superior value to them in today's new and demanding economy. One element of delivering superior value for educational institutions is to assess the achievement of learning outcomes among their students at various sites and to use such results for continuous improvement in order to always have a healthy learning environment for everyone (Mujtaba and Mujtaba, 2004).

The H. Wayne Huizenga School of Business and Entrepreneurship (Huizenga School) of Nova Southeastern University (NSU) has been offering undergraduate and graduate programs in the fields of business administration through various distance delivery modes for the past thirty years. One mode of distance delivery of education to adult students has been face-to-face instructor/student interaction in a classroom setting on four or five weekends in a given quarter while regularly exchanging assignments and feedback between faculty and students using electronic avenues. There are at least four different delivery methods (non-traditional offsite locations, traditional, online, and evening), and each format is expected to achieve the same outcomes. The Huizenga School has been testing each of its program's outcomes to ensure all programs demonstrate educational competencies that are comparable to those of traditional campus-based courses in Fort Lauderdale.

During the April–June 2004 quarter, Huizenga School's Masters Program offered "*GMP5017—Delivering Superior Customer Value*" course through traditional, face-to-face instruction at the main campus for full-time as well as part-time students; at off-campus locations on alternating weekends for working students; and, through online formats. This one section of the course under study offered in Kingston through the on-ground format was taught by an experienced instructor who has been regularly teaching this course in various formats. The faculty used a pre-test to assess everyone's current knowledge during the first session of the class and eventually used the same questions on the post-test to see how much improvement can be seen as a result of the learning activities during the semester. Classes met four different weekends during the term at hotels in Kingston, Jamaica. The class met about every three weeks during the term on Saturdays and Sundays from about 1:00–5:00 PM for four hours each day. The classes started one hour later on Saturdays and accordingly ended one hour later to accommodate students that were traveling from outside of Kingston. Students met many other times at various locations to complete their group assignments. The average time spent face-to-face outside of the class for group activities was reported to be nine hours. Some groups met more often in the face-to-face format while others were able to use technology to reduce face-to-face interactions since students lived at various sites throughout the Island.

There were a total of 38 students enrolled in "*GMP5017—Delivering Superior Customer Value.*" While a few of the students were about to finish the masters program, about 90% of them were totally new to the graduate program and this was their first semester. With regards to gender distribution, there were 8 males (21% of the class) and 30 females (79%) in the class. In the Islands, such low ratios of male to female student distribution in the graduate program are not unusual. As a matter of fact, some classes of 20 or more students taught by the author have included no male students. The average age, based on faculty observation and estimation, was about 27 years for this group. All of the students were working adults, some being school teachers while others were working as administrators or employees in the banking industry, government, private or pubic sector tourism-related jobs. This group showed great interest in the topics of this class as they all understood the importance of delivering value to customers in today's competitive global world of business.

COURSE DESCRIPTION AND LEARNING OBJECTIVES

This course stressed the service aspects of an organization, especially customer service, marketing and organizational responsiveness, and how to create superior customer value. With an integrated marketing and operations perspective and the use of case analysis, students understand how to blend the delivery of service and quality, together with pricing strategies (as well as image, innovation, and intangibles) to maximize the value proposition. Strategies for optimizing and communicating customer value, measuring customer orientation, and relationship/retention marketing were also examined.

As stated in the course syllabus, students were expected to meet the exit competencies at the end of the courses based on the completion of the required readings and activities as determined by the Chairs and lead faculty members. Upon completion of this course, the student is expected to be able to:

1. Explain what is meant by customer orientation and responsiveness,
2. Understand the concept of customer value and how it impacts business decision-making.
3. Discuss how the various components of customer value (quality, service, pricing, and image) interact to build customer satisfaction.
4. Use operations and logistics processes to improve the delivery, monitoring, and measurement of customer services.
5. Consider the impact of quality on the value of an organization's offering and how quality can be improved.
6. Understand how pricing contributes to perceived customer value.
7. Examine how the relationship marketing paradigm creates long-term customer value.
8. Demonstrate a mature level of communication skills, especially the ability to present and defend positions; which is predicated on a sound value/values-based, customer-driven decision-making framework which responds to the business challenges of complex, competitive, and changing global markets.

The book used for the class was titled "Designing & Delivering Superior Customer Value: Concepts, Cases & Applications" authored by Dr. Art Weinstein and Dr. Bill Johnson in 1999. Students thought the textbook was very timely and very relevant in terms of applicability for their places of employment. They seemed to enjoy the exercises, case studies and the application of the "*Customer Value Action Items*" to their current departments and customer base. Additional material was also distributed in class by the faculty. To keep up with current material on the topic, students were encouraged to review at least one relevant website each week and at least one newspaper or journal article to see how firms are delivering value to their customers.

COURSE ASSIGNMENTS AND LEARNING OUTCOMES

The students were required to read the textbook, current event articles brought to the class by the faculty or students, and to conduct research for their individual and team projects. Oral parts of assignments required students to prepare a detailed presentation for the class. This was purposely designed this way so their colleagues can benefit from their thoughts and individual research. The following table (Table 17) represents a summary of the activities required for this course.

There was a total of four weekends during the term that the class formally met face-to-face for four hours each of the eight sessions. The assignments were distributed evenly throughout the term so the learning outcomes of the course are achieved progressively and reinforced many times over the semester for long-term retention. Even the final exam was used to reinforce learning one last time. Students were required to complete their final exam by marking the right choices and recording their answers on separate answer sheets. They were required to write their names on both the exam and the answer sheet. Once students completed their final exam

Table 17. Course Assignments for Submission

Assignments Topics	Points	Delivery Method	Due Date	Achieves Learning Objectives Number
Chapter Application (in-class)		Group	Session 1	1, 2, 3, 4, 5, 6, 7, and 8
Value Propositions and Quality (in-class discussion)		Group	Session 2	1, 2, 3, and 8
Customer Value Action Items— select a chapter (individual)	10%	Written	Session 3	1, 2, 3, 4, 5, 6, 7, and 8
First Case Analysis (group)	20%	Written and Oral	Session 4	3, 4, 5, and 8
Second Case Analysis (individual)	10%	Written	Session 6	3, 4, 5, and 8
Applied Customer Value Term Project (group) • Customer Service Philosophy Booklet (group)	35%	Mixed	Session 7 and 8	1, 2, 3, 4, 5, 6, 7, and 8
Final Exam (individual)	10%	Written	Session 8	1, 2, 3, 4, 5, 6, 7, and 8
Participation*—Includes answers to all the "Customer Value Application" exercises and other topics.	15%	* Two Quizzes offered as part of the participation points.		
Total	100%			

and recorded all of their answers on the answer sheet, the answer sheets were collected for confidential grading by the faculty. Then, the students and faculty member as a class went over the questions and answers so the students could clarify their understanding if they did not get the answers right thus, hopefully, leading to better learning and long-term retention as a result of the reinforcement. In the mean time, students could actually see their own exam results right after its completion. The actual final exams were also collected from students as to keep it out of the hands of prospective students taking the class.

METHODOLOGY AND RESULTS

The purposes of this study were to document learning and to determine the significance of the results for objective pre-test and post-test exams when the group received traditional, face-to-face instruction in a classroom setting, with classes delivered in a weekend format. The faculty used a pre-test to assess everyone's current knowledge during the first session of the class and eventually used the same questions on the post-test to see how much improvement could be seen as a result of the activities taking place during the semester. Another intention for the study was to compare the learning with students in other locations and sites. The instrument used to measure student performance was an examination consisting of a combination of standardized "multiple-choice" essay and true/false questions, for which a total of 100 points were available. Specifically, the examination included 16 multiple-choice items, 24 true and false questions and two essay questions. It was assumed that the objective questions were equal in their level of difficulty. Also, students were allotted one hour to complete their exams.

Research Questions: Hypothesis

The research question for this study was as follows: Is there a statistically significant difference in the performance of students in the pre-test and post-test examination and their final examination scores compared to students in other sites in the course titled "Delivering Superior Customer Value"?

Null Hypothesis (Ho) I: *Pre-test and post-test exam scores for Kingston students in GMP5017 will be similar.*

Null Hypothesis (Ho) II: *Final exam (post-test) scores for Kingston students in GMP5017 will be similar to the final exam scores of students in Florida and Bahamas.*

Results and Statistical Comparisons

The pre-test was administered on the first session of the class and students were told that they can earn up to four bonus points on this pre-assessment test for a score of 90 or above, three bonus points for a score of 80 or above, two bonus points for a score of 70 or above, and one bonus point for a score of 60 or more points. The bonus points encouraged students to take the pre-assessment test seriously and they were able to complete it in less than 40 minutes. Many of the students were able to earn bonus points which were used as part of their final course grade. So, if a student had a total average of 89% (B plus) by the end of the semester and had earned two bonus points on the pre-test, then this student's final course grade would be an "A minus" according to the scale provided on the syllabus. There were a total of 37 usable data points for comparison of the pre- and post-tests. The pre-test results show that the mean score for the group's pre-test was 73.4 out of 100 and the group's post-test score mean was 86.73 out of 100 possible points.

Students were allotted one hour for the post-test (final exam) and they were able to complete it during the allotted time. As can be seen from Table 18, the *t*-test statistics follows a t distribution with 36 (37–1) degrees of freedom. The test is done at a = 0.05 level of significance and as such the rejection area is divided into the two tails for this two tail test, i.e. two equal parts of 0.025 each. The critical values for this two-tail test are +2.02809133 and –2.02809133. As such, one would be able to reject the first null hypothesis if *t* with 36 degrees of freedom is greater than +2.02809133 or smaller than –2.02809133. The gain from pre-test to post-test score was 13 points which according to the analysis of paired *t*-test is statistically significant.

Table 18. *t*-Test: Paired Two Sample for Means or Pre- and Post-Tests

	Pre-Test	*Post-Test*
Mean	73.40540541	86.72972973
Variance	83.52552553	35.48048048
Observations	37	37
Pearson Correlation	0.409257628	
Hypothesized Mean Difference	0	
df	36	
t Stat	–9.393363987	
P (T <= t) one-tail	1.6089E-11	
t Critical one-tail	1.688297289	
P(T <= t) two-tail	3.2178E-11	
t Critical two-tail	2.02809133	

Using a 0.05 level of significance, the null hypothesis (Ho) is rejected because $t = -9.393363987$ is smaller than the critical value of -2.02809133. Also, because the p-value is less than alpha (α) = 0.05, there is sufficient evidence to reject the null hypothesis. Therefore, Null Hypothesis I (Ho) cannot be accepted since the scores are not similar. One can conclude that the post-test scores are different from the pre-test score. Based on these results, the pre-test exam scores appear to be significantly lower than the post-test (final) exam scores. So, one can summarize that many of the learning outcomes designed to be achieved as a result of the course activities for GMP5017 in Kingston during the summer 2004 term were achieved due to the significant gain on the post-test examination.

The post-test scores of students in Kingston, Jamaica were compared with the post scores of students who took this class with the same faculty using the same final exam in Nassau, Bahamas in 2003 (as presented in Table 19). Comparing the results of students in Kingston with students in Nassau does not pro-

Table 19: t-Test for Differences in Two Means for Final Exam: Kingston versus Bahamas

Data	
Hypothesized Difference	0
Level of Significance	0.05
Population 1 Sample—*Kingston*	
Sample Size	38
Sample Mean	86.73
Sample Standard Deviation	5.96
Population 2 Sample—*Bahamas*	
Sample Size	18
Sample Mean	87.11
Sample Standard Deviation	6.41
Intermediate Calculations	
Population 1 Sample Degrees of Freedom	37
Population 2 Sample Degrees of Freedom	17
Total Degrees of Freedom	54
Pooled Variance	37.27401667
Difference in Sample Means	−0.38
t-Test Statistic	−0.217527684
Two-Tailed Test	
Lower Critical Value	−2.004881026
Upper Critical Value	2.004881026
p-Value	0.828616996
Do not reject the null hypothesis	

duce any statistically significant results because the p-value is greater than alpha (α) = 0.05 and the *t*-test value of 0.217527684 falls within the critical values of +2.004881026 and –2.004881026. As such, Null Hypothesis II cannot be rejected which means that the post-test scores for Kingston students in GMP5017 are similar to the post-test scores of students in the Bahamas.

The post-test scores of students in Kingston, Jamaica were further compared with the post-test of students who took this class with the same faculty using the same post-test in Tampa, Florida, in 2002 (as presented in Table 20). Comparing the results of students in Kingston with students in Tampa does not produce any statistically significant results because the *p*-value (0.270888514) is greater than alpha (α) = 0.05 and the *t*-test value of –1.112001875 falls within the critical values of +2.003239388 and –2.003239388. As such, once again, Null Hypothesis II cannot be rejected which means that the post-test scores for Kingston students in GMP5017 are similar to the post-test scores of students in Tampa.

Table 20. *t*-Test for Differences in Two Means for Final Exam: Kingston versus Tampa

Data	
Hypothesized Difference	0
Level of Significance	0.05
Population 1 Sample—*Kingston*	
Sample Size	37
Sample Mean	86.73
Sample Standard Deviation	5.96
Population 2 Sample—*Tampa*	
Sample Size	21
Sample Mean	88.68
Sample Standard Deviation	7.17
Intermediate Calculations	
Population 1 Sample Degrees of Freedom	36
Population 2 Sample Degrees of Freedom	20
Total Degrees of Freedom	56
Pooled Variance	41.19563571
Difference in Sample Means	–1.95
t-Test Statistic	–1.112001875
Two-Tailed Test	
Lower Critical Value	–2.003239388
Upper Critical Value	2.003239388
p-Value	0.270888514
Do not reject the null hypothesis	

Last but not least, the post-test scores of students in Kingston-Jamaica were also compared with the post-test scores of students who took this class with the same faculty using the same post-test in the Online format using e-University platform in 2003 (as shown in Table 21). Similar to the results of the Bahamian and the group Tampa, comparing the results of students in Kingston with students in Online modality did not produce any statistically significant results because the p-value (0.07718) is greater than alpha (α) = 0.05 and the t-test value of 1.8017 falls within the critical values of +2.00488 and –2.00488. As such, once again, Null Hypothesis II cannot be rejected because the post-test scores for Kingston students in GMP5017 are similar to the post-test scores of students who completed this class in the online format.

Based on the data from the pre- and post-test scores, there appears to be sufficient data to state that there was a significant learning gain for students

Table 21. t-Test for Differences in Two Means: Kingston versus Online

Data	
Hypothesized Difference	0
Level of Significance	0.05
Population 1—Kingston	
Sample Size	38
Sample Mean	86.73
Sample Standard Deviation	5.96
Population 2—Online	
Sample Size	18
Sample Mean	83.43
Sample Standard Deviation	7.27
Intermediate Calculations	
Population 1 Sample Degrees of Freedom	37
Population 2 Sample Degrees of Freedom	17
Total Degrees of Freedom	54
Pooled Variance	40.97775
Difference in Sample Means	3.3
t-Test Statistic	1.801664507
Two-Tailed Test	
Lower Critical Value	–2.004881026
Upper Critical Value	2.004881026
p-Value	0.077181851
Do not reject the null hypothesis	

taking GMP5017 in Kingston during the summer 2004 term. Furthermore, the post-test scores of students in Kingston, Jamaica compared to the scores of students who took this class with the same faculty at the Nassau (2003) and Tampa (2002) clusters were similar. Furthermore, results show that Kingston students performed just as well as students who completed this class in the online format during 2003. This supports the second hypothesis that the post-test scores (student performance) for Kingston students in GMP5017 are similar to the post-test scores (student performance) of students in other locations, such as Tampa and Nassau, when the class is taught by the same faculty member.

Like many other studies, this research had limitations and assumptions that were taken into consideration. It was assumed that the scores represented interval data. In addition, the assumptions were made that the instrument was valid and that there were no significant, systematic differences between the tests results (other than actual increased learning as a result of completing the activities and assignments during the term) to which study results may be attributed. The small sample size in Nassau and Tampa is a limitation impacting inferences that may be drawn from results of the study. Applicability of the result of this study is anticipated to be limited for groups included in this research to documentation of learning for some of the course objectives in the sections taught by this faculty member.

SUMMARY

The increasing interest and pressure by various educational stakeholders in the quality of education has fostered concern among accrediting bodies, as well as the institutions they accredit, in schools demonstrating comparable learning outcomes on the competencies acquired by graduates. The study discussed in this chapter attempted to demonstrate outcome equivalency in one section of this course while comparing the results to students who took this course with the same faculty in Tampa and Nassau clusters as well as those who completed it in the online format. The faculty member teaching this course, author of the study, has taught adults in Jamaica, Bahamas, Brazil, and the United States for nearly a decade and is multicultural since he was born in Afghanistan and temporarily lived in Pakistan as well. Since all the sections of this course, for comparison purposes in this study, were taught by one faculty using the same content and exams, one can assume with a high level of certainty that all other variables were controlled and the only thing different was the cultural environment of students. So, the results provide a fair assessment of learning comparison across different groups and locations. Furthermore, the students in Tampa and Nassau were all working adults similar to students in Kingston and this provides another commonality among them.

It is concluded that students enrolled in the masters course GMP5017, offered at the Kingston cluster of Nova Southeastern University during the summer 2004 term, did show significant progress in student performance as measured by scores on the pre-test and post-test. Furthermore, their performance as measured by objective post-test scores seems to be very similar to the performance of students online as well as those in Nassau and Tampa who completed their classes in 2003 and 2002 respectively. It is possible that the results of this study may be applicable to future offerings of the same course and/or to additional master's courses; however, specific inferences drawn from data generated from this study should be limited only to similar situations in which faculty members and students jointly work on gaining knowledge related to course learning objectives.

The Huizenga School continues to expand its distance education offerings, in particular, those that are offered through face-to-face format at off-site locations. It is recommended that the Huizenga School build on the results of this study by pursuing additional studies to assess comparative student performance under circumstances in which courses are offered through different sites and delivery modes. Furthermore, it is recommended that the Huizenga School administer standardized tests for courses at different sites in Jamaica, Nassau and throughout the various sites in the United States that are taught by different faculty members to see how consistently students are achieving the stated course outcomes.

CHAPTER 11

ASSESSMENT OF HYBRID EDUCATION

The purpose of this section is to show how to document student learning in hybrid programs as compared to the traditional formats. Specifically, the section provides an example of how learning was gained in three different master of business administration courses (six sections) and compare student performance through common evaluation forms via the hybrid and on-ground (traditional face-to-face) formats. The groups being compared were completing their classes during the winter term of 2004 using two different education delivery modalities with the same instructor expecting the same outcomes. Student performance was defined as the score on the final examination and term project. The courses were taught by the same faculty using the same syllabus, course material, the same assignments, and expecting the same outcomes (high quality master level work). This data, originally prepared by Mujtaba, Cavico and Weinstein, were presented at the Academy of Business Disciplines in 2004.

Findings by Mujtaba, Cavico and Weinstein (2004) revealed that there were no statistically significant differences in the performance of students in two courses ("Twenty First Century Management Practices" taught by Dr. Bahaudin Mujtaba, and "The Legal, Ethical, and Social Values of Business" taught by Dr. Frank Cavico) based on an objective final exam as the assessment instrument. The third course, however, ("Delivering Superior Customer Value" taught by Dr. Art Weinstein) showed a statistically signifi-

Adult Education in Academia, pages 239–261
Copyright © 2006 by Information Age Publishing
All rights of reproduction in any form reserved.

cant difference ($p < .05$) in the mean scores for the hybrid and on-ground students with the on-ground students having slightly better performance in the term project assignment that was used as the common evaluation tool. As stated previously, examining and documenting such comparisons of classes in different modalities are essential for measuring institutional performance and for continuous improvement. Research shows that demand for hybrid and online faculty members will increase dramatically in the next decade; so, best practices for those wishing to become hybrid and online educators are emphasized. Institutions wishing to remain or become industry leaders in online education that incorporates cyberspace technology must effectively integrate the available platforms into their teaching pedagogies to meet/exceed student and employer expectations.

ASSESSMENT IMPERATIVES IN BLENDED MODALITIES

Hybrid (blended) modalities of education and distance learning have existed for many decades. For example, Nova Southeastern University has offered blended forms of courses and programs through distance learning since the 1970s. In the late 1980s and early 1990s, doctoral students were using computer capabilities to communicate with faculty members; and then attended on-ground classes on monthly basis for two full days each month or for six consecutive days through "national clusters" in Fort Lauderdale, Florida. During the 48 face-to-face contact hours, faculty members could facilitate learning of the concepts through exercises or lectures and students could learn the material interactively with their peers. In the meantime, student groups could communicate with each other or with the faculty via email to prepare their assignments, conduct interviews and submit assignments for feedback and evaluation. Today, more sophisticated technologies such as bulletin boards, synchronized chat-rooms, voice cafes, video cameras, and assignment manager platforms are available to enhance distance modes of learning, while keeping the face-to-face aspect of education intact.

Adult education is making better use of blended modalities to enhance student learning. The H. Wayne Huizenga School of Business and Entrepreneurship at NSU started a cluster of MBA students in Manaus, Brazil, in 1998, using a "Hybrid" form of distance education. Students would start their courses using online modality and then the faculty members would travel to Brazil to conduct classes with students for 24 face-to-face contact hours which translates to about 60% face-to-face and 40% online. Furthermore, student groups informally met with their teammates to prepare projects and group presentations throughout the semester. The on-ground format allowed lectures, exercises, student presentations, and proctored examination. Such hybrid forms of distance education require experienced online and on-ground faculty members. Another version that the Huizenga School introduced in 2003 was the "Hybrid MBA Program," which allows students and faculty members to meet face-to-face for six hours at the beginning of the term and then classes are conducted online for about one month. Once again, faculty members and students meet face-to-face for six hours in the middle of the term. Then, classes are held online for another month, and students finally meet face-to-face for six more hours at the end of the semester.

The University of Phoenix implemented a similar program in 2001 called "Flexnet." Students enrolled in the Flexnet Program would meet for four hours face-to-face at the outset of each course and then again for four hours at the conclusion of the course. The weeks in between would be conducted using an online modality and requirements. The face-to-face contact hours are used for exercises, lectures, face-to-face teamwork, presentations, and examinations. Online formats provide a similar learning experience depending on the course and faculty preference. However, the on-ground sessions seem to fit best for presentations and proctored examinations since most faculty members feel more comfortable assessing students using traditional means. Hybrid education pedagogy is probably one of the most productive and efficient means of educating students while delivering quality learning in the allotted time period for adult learners. Yet, schools must document and demonstrate its learning equivalency with traditional programs on a continuous basis in order to make incremental or breakthrough improvements.

Scholars and philosophers have been questioning the quality of education since the beginning of time. Janet Moore (2002) said

> The quality framework, a tool for continuously improving online programs in higher education, provides ways of demonstrating distinctive institutional quality. As institutions continuously improve pedagogy, and as technology evolves, the framework itself is a work in progress, designed to facilitate the sharing of effective practices among institutions.

The process of learning and the quality of what we learn have been improving for thousands of years now, due to the inquisitive nature of educators who seek new and better ways for learning and teaching. For Plato, learning was a deductive process of stripping away sensory illusions to recall the good, the true, and the beautiful. On the other hand for Aristotle, learning was an inductive process of discovering one's purpose and developing it. Philip of Macedonia hired Aristotle to help his son Alexander to become great by learning the wisdom of the world in a qualitative manner from the best teacher money could get in those days. Parents wanted the best education for their children then; and now in the online world of education parents want the same level of quality in higher education for their offspring. As such, they are holding educational institutions responsible for the level of quality in their schools. It is expected that learners in online education receive the same education and competencies that are equivalent to education and competencies gained in any other format. Arguably, the end results of online education may be similar or even better than traditional formats. Recognize that online education has the power to change how courses are taught, learning is assessed, faculty and students are evaluated, and learning abilities are acquired and shaped in the long-term. Cyberspace technology enables schools to use interactive learning software to address various forms of pedagogy based on just-in-time learning that accompanies doing, by collaborative learning as a team, and through situational coaching based on the learner's level of readiness. Realize that the changes are continuous due to the amorphous form of education with advancing technology; schools are being asked to take a greater responsibility for their students' learning.

During the past two decades, the concepts of accountability and institutional effectiveness have been integrated into both the expectation and requirements of accrediting bodies. These regulators have called for accountability through assessment of multiple direct and indirect output measures that demonstrate documented learning. Such measures can include but are not necessarily limited to learning achievement in course competencies, skill building in each program, graduation rates, program completion years, scores on achievement tests, licensure examination passage rates, retention rates, employment placement rates, etc. Overall, assessment, documentation of consistently achieving learning outcomes, and continuous improvement is a necessity for educational institutions today if they are to remain successful, competitive and accredited. This chapter uses common evaluation methods to assess and compare student performance as a result of students attending class either in the hybrid format or on-ground to complete the required assignments. "*Hybrid*" format uses a blend of both online and on-ground teaching formats to best achieve course learning objectives. In contrast, the "*On-ground*" students received all of their instructions in the traditional face-to-face in-class format with the same faculty members during the same time period.

Distance and online education have been the reality of life for many institutions and adult learners in the past decade and it is becoming more widespread due to the rise of the internet in a time-pressured society. Changes in how education is delivered to students through blended and online education modalities have compounded the questions pertaining to institutional effectiveness. Moorhouse (2001) stated that much attention has been directed at the number of online and distance education offerings and delivery mechanisms during the past decade. Such attention has shown concerns about the equivalency of learning between internet-based education and courses offered through traditional, face-to-face means where faculty members and administrators can visit with students and respond to their needs on a regular basis each week and each day. Questions of equivalency have ranged from the resources provided to students in all modalities and the outcomes of student learning. As distance, blended, and online education both nationally and internationally increase in importance, continuous and documented evaluation will continue to be a critical component of process improvement. Also, many researchers agree that schools offering distance education programs should be accountable for achieving the same level of effectiveness as alternative approaches that are available for students. Such accountability requires that institutions understand their stakeholders and their needs on a proactive basis in order to deliver superior value to them in today's new and demanding economy. In today's market-based environment, institutions that do not continuously deliver value-added products and services will soon find their national and international competitors on their "doorsteps" pushing them out of the industry. A major element of delivering value for educational institutions is to assess the achievement of learning outcomes among their students and to use such results for continuous improvement.

The American Association of Collegiate Schools of Business (AACSB) in 1996 defined assessment as "the systematic collection, review, and use of information about academic programs in order to improve student learning, development, and success." Their guidelines and suggestions for assessment include the following:

1. Assessment should be guided by the school's mission.
2. The main purpose of assessment is to improve academic programs.
3. Assessment of student learning should be a collaborative process.
4. Assessment of results should not be used for faculty or staff evaluation.
5. Assessment activities should include multiple measures. Course learning outcomes can and should be assessed both inside and outside of the classroom through the staff, faculty and university administrators.
6. Students should be active participants in the assessment process.
7. Assessment measures should focus on the most important outcomes.
8. Assessment results should be used for decision-making to improve the learning and the institution.
9. The assessment process itself should be continuously evaluated and improved.

Key practice areas for learning effectiveness according to Janet Moore (2002) are assessment, course design, interaction, learning outcomes, learning resources, pedagogy, and student perceptions of learning. Effective administrators encourage and empower faculty members to integrate these key practices for student learning effectiveness and to measure the level of learning in their courses through various direct and indirect measurements for continuous personal and institutional improvement purposes. Aligned with twenty first century management principles, it is believed that the best way to improve institutional performance of the school is to improve the performance of every individual faculty in each course. Assessing learning outcomes for personal improvement and accountability purposes tends to be a characteristic of extraordinary faculty members as they attempt to continuously achieve extraordinary results. Various reports from the accrediting agencies have proposed assessment as a productive mechanism for responding to the concerns of students, parents, accrediting bodies, and government agencies. Assessment of higher education has been embraced at the state governmental levels as well as various educational foundations and organizations that are expressing concern and lobbying for responsiveness and continuous improvement.

In terms of responsiveness and accountability for institutional effectiveness, the focus is on the academic achievement of students and the improvement of such achievements over the years, using new technology and new methodologies. Assessment should be based on a consistent study using standardized key performance indicators (KPI) that are deeply entrenched within higher education. Standardized KPIs are becoming an integral part of how to manage higher education, with indicators serving as signals or guides for making comparisons in educational quality, effectiveness, and efficiency. Furthermore, another advantage of standardized KPIs is their usefulness as points of reference for comparing performance with peers over time, as well as achievement against desired objectives within the same institution.

MEASURING AND DOCUMENTING LEARNING EFFECTIVENESS

Assessing learning outcomes for personal improvement and accountability purposes tends to be an important characteristic of effective faculty members as they attempt to continuously achieve extraordinary results. Institutional accountability should become the focal point for each program offered by a school. Various reports from the accrediting agencies have proposed assessment as a productive mechanism for responding to the concerns of students, parents, accrediting bodies, and government agencies. Assessment of higher education has been embraced at the state governmental levels as well as various educational foundations and organizations that are expressing concern and lobbying for responsiveness and continuous improvement.

Because many organizations and other stakeholders in the community have been concerned about the quality of education and overall comprehension of students using distinctively different modalities, the Huizenga School has periodically been testing its program's achievements to ensure all programs demonstrate educational outcomes that are comparable to those traditional campus-based courses in Fort Lauderdale. Certainly, there are challenges when it comes to the assessment process because often times there are significant differences in the characteristics of different instructors as well as different timely and relevant cases, assignments, and examinations. Thus far, administrators and faculty members have successfully measured outcomes for students enrolled in different modalities and clusters. For example, the Office of University Research and Planning at NSU completed several studies designed to compare the performance of students in courses conducted in online and campus-based teaching modalities. In May 2000, the university examined comparative student performance in Internet-based courses and campus-based courses and found that there were differences in student performance for courses offered in two different modalities (Moorhouse, 2001). One significant finding was that undergraduate students in some campus-based sections outperformed those in the online sections. However, another significant finding was that graduate students in online format courses outperformed those in the traditional campus-based sections. Subsequent studies were initiated to study these findings more closely for selected academic programs, while examining student performance under different teaching modalities. As with any comprehensive study, it would need to be designed to identify differences in instructors, syllabi, texts, assignments, and examinations among online, offsite, and campus-based comparable courses in order to control for the possible effects of differences on student performance. The absence of effective control variables, when comparing two different teaching modalities, imposes limitations on inferences to be drawn from observable differences in student performance between non-traditional and traditionally-delivered course offerings.

Many studies have been undertaken that were designed to compare the outcomes of student learning under different teaching modalities at different sites. A California State University study compared college student achievement on midterm and final examinations in a statistics course taught using two different teaching modalities. In this study, one group was taught in a traditional face-to-face format and the other using the internet, course website for interaction, electronic mail, and electronic chat room in the online format. The researchers found that the latter group (online format) performed significantly better on both examinations (Moorhouse, 2001). So, distance education can be delivered just as effectively, if not more, as the regular face-to-face formats. There have been many other studies showing that distance education using web-based system have generated significantly greater knowledge transfer than face-to-face formats.

Another study at NSU conducted by Schulman and Sims (1999) assessed the comparative performance of online students and students receiving traditional in-class instruction in five different undergraduate courses conducted at Nova Southeastern University. The online and in-class sections of each course were taught by the same instructor. Students received a pretest and a posttest on subject matter content as part of the study. Results revealed that, while the online students scored significantly higher than the in-class students on the pretest, there was no significant difference in the posttest scores for the two groups. Many other studies have provided widespread evidence of similarities in the outcomes of student learning when traditional and distance delivery modalities are compared.

THE ON-GROUND AND HYBRID CLASSES

The classes under study for the sponsoring university were offered on the weekend format which offers more flexibility for working adult students. The on-ground classes met basically every other weekend for a total of five weekends on Friday nights for two hours in each course between 6:00-10:00 p.m. and on Saturdays for four hours in each course from 8:00 a.m. to 5:00 p.m. It should be noted that students may have met many other times at various locations to complete their group activities. The average time spent face-to-face or cyberspace in virtual teams through chat sessions or teleconferencing outside of class contact hours for group activities tend to average at minimum about ten hours for most courses at the masters program. Some groups may have met more often for team interaction, while others are able to use internet technology for asynchronous communication and teleconferencing to their advantage whenever possible in order to reduce real time discussions. The Hybrid students met three weekends face-to-face, at similar hours and times as the on-ground students, with one weekend each month for the three month term. In between each meeting, students were required to conduct all of their coursework just like online students, as required by the faculty. The online requirements for each online week included, but not limited, to posting individual answers on the bulletin (discussion) board to the weekly discussion questions, posting answers to exercises posted by the faculty on the discussion board, interacting among members for the group activities assigned, posting assignments on the Assignment Manager, and reading lectures provided by the faculty members. Also, two "one-hour" chat sessions were offered and students were encouraged to attend for real time discussion of course content and so they could have their questions answered by the faculty member facilitating the chat session and their colleagues who are in attendance. Students attending chat sessions were given participation points for their quality contributions.

The courses under study are requirements for those pursuing masters of business administration degrees. Students in both formats were very diverse, and their geographical locations ranged from Fort Lauderdale to Miami and other locations in Florida, as they were only required to travel to class on assigned weekends. One student, working as a business consultant, was traveling from Tampa since he wanted to complete the entrepreneurship specialization offered at the main campus. Almost all of the students reported that they were working students in various fields. The average age was not known, but many of the students reported ten or more years of work experience showing that these students were on the average older than the traditionally aged graduate students. Both groups showed interest in the topics as they all understood the importance of topics such as twenty first century management practices, ethics and delivering value which are critical for effectively serving stakeholders if an organization is to remain competitive in today's global environment of business.

Course Activities to Achieve the Learning Outcomes

Students in all three courses were required to read the assigned textbook readings, current event articles brought to the class by the faculty or students, and to conduct research for their individual and team projects. All courses required students to make individual and/or group presentations for selected assignments. This component was purposely designed as such so their colleagues could benefit from their thoughts and individual research. It is commonly understood that people learn best when they are personally involved in the learning process and when students are involved in the process as a community making it more of a social process. Experience has proven that personalizing instructions and assignments so students can relate to them in their current lives offers great learning opportunities for students and they tend to be effective pedagogical tools as it offers the faculty many chances to connect with students. The assignments were designed to offer students many interaction and collaboration opportunities with their colleagues and the faculty member thereby making the process much more active to suit individual learning styles and preferences.

The complete course description and learning outcomes for these courses can be reviewed in the appendix section of this document. The following table (Table 22) represents a summary of the activities required for "*The Twenty First Century Management Practices*" course. The other courses had similar activities as designed by the individual lead professor.

Cyberspace technology offers opportunities for androgogical orientation allowing flexibility and choice in assignments so they can be practical and problem oriented. Androgogical orientation is about finding out what stu-

Table 22.   Course Assignments for Submission

Assignments Topics	Points	Delivery Method	Due Date	Achieves Learning Objectives Number
"Topics for Discussion and Action"—End of chapter assignment (*team and individual*)	5%	Group discussion	Session 1	3, 4, 5, 6, 7, 8, and 9
"You are the Management Consultant" (*team and individual*)		Written and oral	Session 2	3, 4, 5, 6, 7, 8, and 9
Business Week Case in the News—from Textbook (*team and individual*)		Written	Session 3	3, 4, 5, 6, 7, 8, and 9
Market Based Management Application (*individual*)	10%	Written and oral	Session 4	1, 2, 4, 5, and 9
The Well Paid Receptionist Case Analysis—Using VDM Concept (*individual mid-term exam*)	10%	Written	Session 5	1, 2, 6, 7, 8, 9, and 10
Executive Book Summary Report (*individual*)	10%	Written and oral	Session 7	1, 2, 3, and 4
Management History and Environmental Forces Term Project (*team*)	35%	Written and oral	Session 9	1, 2, 3, 4, 5, 6, 7, 8, 9, and 10
Final Exam (*individual*)	10%	Written	Session 10	1, 2, 3, 4, 7, 9, and 10
Participation	20%	All sessions and all objectives		
Total:	100%			

dents need to know; when they need to know it and how to best help them learn what they need to know in the time allotted. Of-course, academic time limitation for assignment submission due dates tends to put boundaries on the possibilities. Nonetheless, diverse assignments tend to match the needs of diverse students based on their learning styles and preferences.

Overall, there were ten weeks during the term that the class was formally conducted face-to-face or in blended format which included some face-to-face and online classes each month. Also, assignments were totally clarified to students on the first session so they could complete their assignments on their time preference. As an example, hybrid students in the Twenty First Century Management Practices course were required to answer the assigned weekly discussion questions by Wednesday nights and they were required to submit a weekly summary by each Saturday night for online weeks. The discussion questions and weekly summary postings were to be posted on the class bulletin board for everyone's reading enjoyment, involvement and discussions. Furthermore, students were required to comment on at least two of their colleague's postings for each online week in order to receive full participation credit for the week. Some weekly summaries were exercises that needed to be submitted to the bulletin board so everyone in the class could read and comment on them. There were no required postings for participation on the first and last weeks of the class. However, hybrid students were encouraged to post a biography on the first few weeks of the class for introductions and relevant suggestions for improving the course on the last week.

Methodology and Results

The purpose of this study was to compare performance across different teaching modalities and to determine the significance of the results for objective exams and assignments when the groups received either face-to-face or blended instructions from the same faculty. Another intention for the study was to expand the body of knowledge regarding common evaluations on student performance; specifically, with these initial courses taken at the masters program. The three faculty members used the same evaluation medium in both sections of their courses to assess each group's performance to see if there is a statistically significant difference on the results when students completed the same activities using the same syllabus with the same instructor using different modalities.

The instrument used to measure student performance for this study was an objective examination consisting of a combination of standardized "multiple-choice", fill-in the blanks as well as true/false type of questions for the *Twenty First Century Management Practices* and the *Ethics* courses. The faculty in *Delivering Superior Customer Values* course used the Term Project to compare student performance between the two different formats. The administration of the tests, directions for assignments, and the evaluation of the student performance for each activity were exactly the same in both sections of these courses. There was no subjectivity or bias toward any specific group as the same faculty was evaluating students' performance in the same manner with exactly the same expectations from both groups.

For the Twenty First Century Management Practices course, there were a total of 100 points available for the objective final exam. The final exam made up only ten percent of the final course grade since there were more comprehensive assignments administered to develop their competencies. More specifically, the final examination included multiple-choice and true/false questions to reinforce the course objectives while assessing learning. It was assumed that the questions were equal in their level of difficulty. Also, students were allotted one hour and fifteen minutes to complete their exams and they were able to use their books and notes. Based on the preparation and reading requirements for the final exam as well as the diversity of questions related to the course topics, it was determined that the objective examination measured material related to learning outcomes 1, 2, 3, 4, 7, 9, and 10 from the syllabus. Students were encouraged to review the designated textbook readings for reinforcement of learning one more time prior to the final exam week. The faculty wanted to discourage rote memorization of the material; as such, the final exam was designed to be open book but time-bounded and dedicated only a small percentage of the final course grade to it. The faculty acknowledges that objective tests are not necessarily the best measures of learning with working adults and, as such, the final exam was one of many assessment methodologies available to measure learning. However, the objective form of examination was selected because of its convenience, consistency, validity, and the reliability it offers for future comparison purposes with different groups at different sites and modalities of education.

Similarly, the Ethics course used an objective examination for both groups using similar requirements and time allotment. Delivering Superior Customer Value course used the term project scores as a common measure of evaluation for this study since both groups had the same direction and opportunities to perform well.

The research question for this study was as follows: Is there a statistically significant difference in the performance of master of business administration hybrid and on-ground students in the common evaluation for courses when both modalities are facilitated by the same faculty using the same syllabus and activities?

- *Null Hypothesis:* Common evaluation scores for on-ground students will be similar to the common evaluation scores of students that completed the course in the hybrid format.
- *Alternate Hypothesis:* Common evaluation scores for on-ground students will NOT be similar to the common evaluation scores of students that completed the course in the hybrid format.

Research Findings

A descriptive summary of the scores for MBA students in the hybrid and on-ground sections are provided in Table 23. As an example, the scores for the hybrid students in the Twenty First Century Management Practices course ranged from a high of 98% to a low of 69% providing a range of 29 points. The scores for on-ground students ranged from a high of 99% to a low score of 75% providing a range of 24 points.

The "t-Test for Differences in Two Samples" was used to compare the scores for each group with the hybrid having the lowest number of students that completed the class. As such, the following paragraphs present a sum-

Table 23. Course Descriptive Statistics

Courses and Titles	Student Numbers		Grade Range		Mean Score		St. Deviation	
	Ground	Hybrid	Ground	Hybrid	Ground	Hybrid	Ground	Hybrid
GMP5012 Twenty First Century Mgmt. Practices	24	22	24	29	89.5	89.0	7.216	6.3199
GMP5015 Ethics	26	17	38	13	82	79	8.626	4.2422
GMP5017 Delivering Superior Customer Value	28	13	17	7	87.9	85	3.7245	2.5495

mary of the comparisons of student performance between the two different teaching modalities (on-ground and hybrid).

Using a 0.05 level of significance, the null hypothesis (*Common evaluation scores for on-ground students in "GMP5012—Twenty First Century Management Practices" will be similar to the common evaluation scores of MBA students that completed this course in the hybrid format.*) cannot be rejected because the t value falls within the critical values ($t = 0.24$, $p = 0.81$). Also, because the p-value is greater than alpha (α) = 0.05, there is not sufficient evidence to reject the null hypothesis. Based on these results, the on-ground student exam scores for this course appear to be similar to the hybrid student exam scores. As such, one can conclude that the on-ground and hybrid final exam scores are not significantly different. So, hybrid students performed similarly on the final examination to on-ground students that were tested in this study.

Using a 0.05 level of significance, the null hypothesis (*Common evaluation scores for on-ground students in "GMP5015—Ethics" will be similar to the common evaluation scores of students that completed this course in the hybrid format.*) cannot be rejected because the t value falls within the critical values ($t = 0.16$, $p = 0.88$). Also, because the p-value is greater than alpha (α) = 0.05, there is not sufficient evidence to reject the null hypothesis. Based on these results, the on-ground student exam scores for this course also appear to be similar to the hybrid student exam scores. As such, one can conclude that the on-ground and hybrid final exam scores are not significantly different. So, hybrid students performed similarly on the final examination to on-ground students that were tested in this study.

Using a 0.05 level of significance, the null hypothesis (Ho) is rejected because $t = 2.61$ which is larger than the critical value of $+2.0244$ ($t = 2.61$, $p = 0.013$). Also, because the p-value of 0.013 is less than alpha (α) = 0.05, there is sufficient evidence to reject the null hypothesis. Based on these results, the on-ground students' term project scores for "GMP5017—Delivering Superior Customer Value" scores appear to be significantly different than the hybrid students' term project scores. As such, one can conclude that the on-ground and hybrid term project scores are significantly different despite the fact that the average scores are only three points higher for the on-ground students. So, one can say that on-ground students performed better on the term project than hybrid students that were tested in this study.

STUDY IMPLICATIONS AND LIMITATIONS

There are many academic implications that can be drawn from the study. For example, one implication for the faculty is to continue facilitating similar activities and exercises for hybrid students, as they do seem to lead to a significant gain in learning the course objectives as measured through performance in the final examination with the GMP5012 and GMP5015 courses as well as the term project in GMP5017. In the meantime, the faculty could incorporate different activities and exercises with both groups of students in order to increase their average performance in future classes. It would be very interesting to see how these results compare to other groups of students in the same courses at different locations and teaching modalities using the same common evaluation instrument as a standard for sections taught by different faculty members. Furthermore, the administration of a common term project for the two groups of students in two different modalities seems to have produced statistically different results since hybrid group scores were almost three points lower than the on-ground students. Perhaps, the hybrid students were not as disciplined as the on-ground students to begin their projects early in the semester in order to finalize them with higher quality. On the other hand, it is possible that on-ground students had better performance because of the frequent face-to-face interaction with the faculty and their colleagues. It should be noted that on-ground students had 12 more face-to-face hours with the instructor. More studies will have to be conducted to determine the possible variables leading to the variance in student performance with regard to the term projects. A close study of the results with groups over several terms and at different sites may lead to a discovery of facilitation techniques and activities that are achieving extraordinary results. Such best practices and great facilitation techniques can be shared with others at the faculty development workshops. Studies show that the demand for online faculty members is expected to grow 36% or more in the next ten years. So, there will be a great demand for faculty development and training sessions in order to develop everyone's competencies on effectively using technology in their classes. University administrators can periodically make such development opportunities available for everyone.

As a result of the experiences of three different faculty members teaching classes in the hybrid and the on-ground modalities simultaneously, several suggestions were provided to the school administrators which included the Associate Dean for Academic Affairs, the Program Director, and the Program Manager responsible for the hybrid program. For example, it was suggested that hybrid courses should have similar limitations for enrollment as the online courses since weekly chat sessions and bulletin board interaction requirements and expectations are the same for both groups. It was also suggested that students registering for hybrid courses must complete an orientation for becoming familiarized with the online platform and technical challenges that accompany it. Such orientation requirements and enrollment limitations will provide better opportunities for quality interaction with all students without creating too much confusion for students who are new to online education while allowing the faculty to provide quality feedback to everyone in a timely manner. It was further suggested that the hybrid courses should begin at the same time period as the online courses even though the first face-to-face meeting session may come a few days/weeks later. Starting the class along with online students on the first day of the term in the online platform will allow students to get to know each other by posting their biographies, it will familiarize them with the course requirements prior to the first face-to-face session, and students can actually complete an assignment so they can receive feedback from the faculty faster than what has been the norm thus far. Furthermore, students will be able to solve their technical challenges in accessing online course material and the bulletin board during the first week rather waiting for the first face-to-face session to discuss these issues with the faculty. In most cases, the faculty members cannot assist students with technical challenges and, furthermore, the class time should be spent on content discussion for achievement of course learning outcomes. It is imperative that students be properly oriented with online expectations, computer literature and online prepared before entering the hybrid course. Another observation from the faculty perspective was that some students did experience confusion on their online and on-ground activities since their first introduction to the course, faculty member and their peers were on the initial face-to-face session while they were required to submit assignments online in the prospective weeks. Some complained that their hybrid course had turned into an online course due to the requirements of submitting assignments in the Assignment Manager section of the course newsgroup. They also did not like the weekly requirements of answering questions and interacting with their peers on the course newsgroup. Perhaps such dislikes can be eliminated with detailed orientation sessions to the hybrid program. Also, such confusion could be reduced if the face-to-face requirements were limited to the first and the last weeks of the course while all the remaining sessions in between would be conducted online with full online requirements such as discussion questions, submission of weekly assignments, analysis of case studies in teams, weekly interaction requirements, and other appropriate assignments as completed by traditional online students. Based on one of the author's experiences as a Campus College Chair for the Graduate Business and Management College in the Tampa Campus of an accredited for-profit university, which has over 50,000 online students nationally and internationally, the concept of meeting face-to-face on the first and last sessions seems to work best for most students. Over two hundred graduate students in the Tampa Campus during the years 2001 and 2002 were questioned about their preferences for hybrid format and the least confusing strategy was to have all of the sessions online except the first and the last sessions which should be face-to-face for lecture, presentations and testing purposes as appropriate. The hybrid format at the for-profit university has served its' population well because it integrated the best of on-ground and online modalities of education. As such, the hybrid program under study could benefit from such a standardized process to reduce the confusion for students and the bi-weekly chat sessions offered by most faculty members are a great means of keeping abreast of their progress throughout the semester. Successful implementation of the suggested changes will allow the faculty and students to focus on qualitative discussions starting on the first session of the face-to-face class. The administration agreed that many of the suggestions provided by the faculty members will be taken into consideration for implementation in future sessions of the hybrid program.

Like many other studies, this research also has limitations and assumptions that were taken into consideration. It was assumed that the evaluation method selected accurately measured material related to the designated learning outcomes from the syllabus. Another assumption has been that the final exam and term project scores are valid and reliable instruments to measure the stated course learning objectives as they were designed to test knowledge relevant to exit competencies required for the course and to serve as a reinforcement of the course material. In addition, assumptions were made that the instrument was valid and that there were no significant, systematic differences between the two section results (other than actual increased learning as a result of completing the activities and assignments during the term) to which study results may be attributed. The authors understand that objective tests are not necessarily the best measures of learning for adult students and as such the results drawn may be limited to only the groups under study. It is also understood that the final exam scores and term project scores were few of many assessment methodologies available, and they may not be effectively measuring the stated course learning outcomes due to their obvious limitations such as time limitations, student anxiety to do well, "cramming sessions" on the last few days, memorization patterns, writing skills, etc. In the case of final exam scores, the objective form of examination was selected for the two courses because of convenience, consistency, validity, and the reliability it offers over time with different groups. It is acknowledged that the chosen method of measurement and limited sample sizes are also limitations impacting inferences that may be drawn from results of the study. To reduce personal biases impacting the study, one of the authors discussed best practices in assessment with several experienced colleagues at the university as well as with professors attending workshops offered by AACSB and IACBE during 2003 before initiating the study. Nonetheless, the authors understand that the conclusions drawn from this study may be limited to improvement and future assessment opportunities for sections taught by the same faculty members. Furthermore, applicability of the results of this study is anticipated to be limited for on-ground and hybrid groups of students to documentation of comparable learning for some of the course objectives in the sections completed in the winter of 2004 using two different modalities.

SUMMARY

Adult education using blended pedagogies and cyberspace technology has achieved a special market by offering quality educational programs both nationally and internationally at times convenient to students. Through professional faculty members committed to student learning and their ability to combine academic theory with successful practical tools, as well as their ability to effectively adjust to the changing educational needs of working professionals, hybrid education offers great value to students and the community at large. In the study herein, it is concluded that students enrolled in the GMP5012 and GMP5015 courses offered on-ground and in the hybrid formats during the winter term of 2004 did show similar results as measured by the final exam scores. On the other hand, students enrolled in GMP5017 courses offered on-ground and in the hybrid formats during the winter of 2004 did show significantly different results as measured by scores on the term project for the course. On-ground students' performance, taking GMP5017, on the term project was significantly higher than the hybrid students. It is possible that the results of this study may be applicable to future offerings of the same course and/or to additional courses offered in the on-ground or hybrid formats; however, specific inferences drawn from data generated from this study should be limited only to similar situations.

The results of such studies can be compared among different modalities, groups and clusters to see which groups and clusters are more effectively achieving the stated learning outcomes. As such, benchmarking studies can be used to further enhance learning for all existing students that do not do as well as the best clusters. The best practices can be used for faculty development sessions to make sure all faculty members are able to achieve extraordinary results in their courses. Consequently, besides using the best practices for enhancing the curriculum and teaching effectiveness, such results can be documented for relevant agencies that need to see demonstrated and equivalent performance of learning for each program at the institution, regardless of teaching modality.

CHAPTER APPENDIX—
COURSE DESCRIPTION AND LEARNING OBJECTIVES

These courses prepared students to become competent coworkers and managers in today's diverse work place. Each course is designed to accomplish its stated learning outcomes that lead to the achievement of program goals upon successful completion.

GMP5012—Twenty-first Century Management Practices

The course began with an overview of the history of management and management thought (including such traditional models as Weber's theory of bureaucracy, Fayol's principles of management, and Mary Parker Follett's behavioral management theory), and an analysis of why such models and theories were adaptive in an earlier era, and why they are frequently not adaptive nor value creating in the new millennium. The course continued with an examination of Pohlman and Gardiner's philosophy of Value Driven Management, and an analysis of why this comprehensive and integrative way of looking at management is not a replacement, but a philosophy that compliments such other approaches to management as total quality management, restructuring and reengineering, participative management, empowerment, and open-book management. The course examined the value-creation process in some detail, and discussed management techniques and practices that seem to be effective in creating value for organizations in the 21st century. The concepts of values and value drivers were discussed, the notion of creating value over time (VOT) were analyzed in some detail, the assumptions of Value Driven Management were critiqued, the process for its effective implementation in organizations were also discussed. A final topic in the course were how the use of the principles of Value Driven Management can create value and happiness in our personal lives through more effective use of multifaceted decisional processes.

As is the case with all graduate level courses in The Huizenga School at NSU, the teaching philosophy guiding this course is that Nova Southeastern University MBA students, as adult learners and mature and experienced management professionals, work in a collaborative relationship with the course instructor. As colleagues in a learning organization, instructor and students jointly explore and anticipate future managerial environments; examine, explicate, and test management perspectives for their relevance in organizational decision-making.

As stated in the course syllabus, students were expected to meet the exist competencies at the end of the course based on the completion of the required readings and activities as determined by the Chairs and lead faculty members. Upon completion of this course, the student was expected to be able to:

1. Identify and use the management practices that are required to maximize value over time (VOT) in a new millennium, and to allow an organization to compete effectively in the global marketplace.
2. Apply the philosophy and premises of market-based management, and Value Driven Management, including an understanding of the role of values, the process of value creation, and the use of the process of Value Driven Management.
3. Appreciate the relevance of historic management theorists and practitioners to the 21st century practice of management.
4. Be able to speak about traditional organizations from the early part of the twentieth century and management practices that were utilized in such organizations.
5. Be able to use analytic-thinking skills in evaluating management methods and practices, current literature in the management field, and contemporary management models and theories.
6. Be able to apply basic management concepts using the case-study method.
7. Demonstrate both experientially and intellectually the uses and limitations of team-based management.
8. Appreciate the philosophy and methods of graduate education for adult learners, and the power of education in creating both personal and organizational value over time.
9. Make effective use of organizational and analytic decision-making skills in the context of Value Driven Management.
10. Think about values in concrete and specific ways.

The textbooks used for this included the following:

Jones, G. R., & George, J. M. (2003). *Contemporary Management.* Third edition.
Pohlman, R. A. & Gardiner, G. S. (2000). *Value-Driven Management: How to Create and Maximize Value Over Time for Organizational Success.*

Gable, W., and Ellig, J. (1993). *Introduction to Market-Based Management.* Fairfax, VA: Center for Market Processes. This textbook along with other online resources and case studies, upon registration, were made available in electronic format to students at the course website: http://www.huizenga.nova.edu/5012.

American Psychological Association. (2001). *Publication Manual of the American Psychological Association.* 5th ed. Washington, D.C.: American Psychological Association. *Note:* The APA manual is required for all graduate classes in the program.

To keep up with current trends in management and leadership, students were required to read a classic or recently published textbook related to course topics and write a summary of it while constructively evaluating the practical application of its content. Furthermore, students were encouraged to view relevant websites and newspaper or journal articles each week to see how firms are adjusting to, and capitalizing on, the diversity of their workforce and customers in the twenty first century.

GMP5015—The Legal, Ethical, and Social Values of Business

The course, known as the "Ethics" course, provided legal, ethical, and social components to business management education. Utilizing an interdisciplinary approach, the course explored the roles of government, the legal system, philosophical ethics, and society in governing business activity in a global context. There are three major "values" to the course: law, ethics, and social responsibility.

The legal "value" of the course examined constitutional law, statutory law, case law, and administrative rules that regulate business and that are relevant to the graduate business student's decision-making process; and examined their practical application in a modern, global, business environment. Some of the legal topics covered are the Bill of Rights as applied to business, trade regulation and anti-trust law, securities regulation law, employment law, such as the Civil Rights Act and labor law, and consumer protection and environmental law.

The ethics part of the course is presented as a natural part of the "value-driven theory of management," which is an essential aspect of the student's business management education at the school. The value theory of management encompasses a philosophical theory of value; and the issue of "value" always has been a prime concern of moral philosophy, which has treated value as morality, the "good," or rightfulness. Accordingly, the course examined important ethical theories, such as egoism, relativism, utilitarianism, and Kantian formalism, and the ethical principles stemming from such theories, to ascertain how various moral philosophers have defined the "value" of morality. The course then applied ethical principles to moral problems confronting business in order to render moral solutions.

The course also studied other ethical topics relevant to business, such as the moral responsibility of the corporation, employees' moral rights, codes and departments of ethics, and the issue of whistle-blowing. In the social responsibility section of the course, the students are asked to think beyond the law and beyond ethics and morality and to arrive at a definition of the "value" of "social responsibility" and what that meaning portends for business, particularly in a global context. The overall objectives of the course were to:

A. Educate the student as to the scope and variety of laws regulating business; inculcate the student with significant philosophical theories and fundamental ethical principles; and to expose the students to the concept of social responsibility.

B. Foster a consideration and integration of legal, moral, and social values relevant to the student's business decision-making process;

C. Provide students with an ethical framework and training to resolve moral issues as well as to ascertain whether the law itself is just;

D. Enhance the students' awareness of the many societal and cultural influences on business;

E. Foster the character development and social consciousness of the student by imparting a greater concern for the legal, moral, and social values of business decision-making; and

F. Create an atmosphere where students perceive the field of business management as an integral, dignified, socially useful, and value-enhancing part of a prosperous and just society.

As stated in the course syllabus, students are expected to meet exist competencies (learning outcomes) at the end of the course based on the completion of the required readings and activities as determined by the Chairs and lead faculty members. Upon completion of this course, the student is expected to be able to:

1. Possess a deeper knowledge of the value theory of management, law, ethics as a branch of philosophy, and the meaning of social responsibility;

2. Comprehend better the legal, moral, and social values in business decision-making;

3. Discuss the relationship, as well as the distinction, among law, ethics, and social responsibility;

4. Apply legal, ethical, and social principles and rules to solve business problems;

5. Be cognizant of the major moral issues confronting business today; and the qualities of moral companies and moral managers;
6. Recognize that various disciplines can be integrated to solve problems; and
7. Utilize case studies and deductive and inductive problem solving techniques more efficaciously.

The textbook used for this "Ethics" course was written by McAdams, Neslund, and Neslund (2004) titled *Law, Business, and Society*, 7th edition. Additional material was also made available to students via the course website and in the class by the faculty. To keep up with current event topics related to the class, students were encouraged to review at least one or two relevant newspaper or journal articles to see what ethical challenges are facing today's organizations and they are responding to these ethical dilemmas.

GMP5017—Delivering Superior Customer Value

The course stressed the service aspects of an organization, especially customer service, marketing and organizational responsiveness, and how to create superior customer value. Via an integrated marketing and operations perspective and the use of case analysis, students understood how to blend the delivery of service and quality, together with pricing strategies (as well as image, innovation, and intangibles) to maximize the value proposition. Strategies for optimizing and communicating customer value, measuring customer orientation, and relationship/retention marketing were also examined.

As stated in the course syllabus, students are expected to meet exist competencies (learning outcomes) at the end of the course based on the completion of the required readings and activities as determined by the Chairs and lead faculty members. Upon completion of this course, the student is expected to be able to:

1. Explain what is meant by customer orientation and responsiveness.
2. Discuss the concept of customer value and how it impacts business decision-making.
3. Discuss how the various components of customer value (quality, service, pricing, and image) interact to build customer satisfaction.
4. Use operations and logistics processes to improve the delivery, monitoring, and measurement of customer services.
5. Consider the impact of quality on the value of an organization's offering and how quality can be improved.
6. Demonstrate how pricing contributes to perceived customer value.

7. Examine how the relationship marketing paradigm creates long-term customer value.
8. Demonstrate a mature level of communication skills, especially the ability to present and defend positions; this is predicated on a sound value/values-based, customer-driven decision-making framework which responds to the business challenges of complex, competitive, and changing global markets.

The textbook used for the class was titled *"Designing & Delivering Superior Customer Value: Concepts, Cases & Applications"*, authored by Dr. Art Weinstein and Dr. Bill Johnson in 1999. Students thought the textbook was very timely and very relevant in terms of applicability for their places of employment. They seemed to enjoy the exercises, case studies and the application of the *"Customer Value Action Items"* to their current departments and customer base. Additional material was also distributed in class by the faculty. To keep up with current event topics related to the class, students were required and encouraged to review at least one or two relevant websites regularly along with newspaper or journal articles to see how firms are delivering value to their customers.

CHAPTER 12

A STUDY OF INSTRUCTIONAL METHODS[1]

The study presented in this chapter seeks to determine if there is any difference in learning outcomes when using traditional vs. accelerated learning instructional methods for productivity management education. A total of 139 individuals made up 4 groups to satisfy the requirements of the Solomon 4 group research design. A paper and pencil post-test was administered to control groups and experimental groups. The mean scores for the control groups were 13.97 and 12.25 respectively. The mean scores for the experimental groups were 22.69 and 23.12 respectively. The level of significance was 0.05. There were significant differences between the control groups and the experimental groups.

INTRODUCTION TO THE STUDY

Educators and trainers are increasingly being asked to provide learning opportunities that will have a positive impact on organizational productivity. Productivity management education and training have gained in stature as contributors to an organizations' success as well as a country's competitiveness. The impact of this education and training varies a great deal. Simply

---

[1] Reprinted with permission from the author (Dr. Robert Preziosi). Productivity and Quality Management Frontiers-V (1995). Institute of Industrial Engineers. pp. 808–815

Adult Education in Academia, pages 263–268

providing it is no guarantee it will be effective. There are a variety of factors that must be taken into account in providing effective productivity education. One of the most important is the instructional delivery methods that are used.

The purpose of this research is to increase the knowledge and understanding of instructional delivery methods used in a productivity management education classroom environment. University educators have relied on traditional methods when providing productivity education. Traditional methods are those that rely on lecture and are instructor focused. This research seeks to determine if accelerated learning methods can increase learning effectiveness. Accelerated learning methods are multi-sensory and are learner focused.

There is support among educators to increase the effectiveness of productivity management education. Research, though, has not focused on this. Management and Organization Behavior have received the bulk of the attention in this kind of research that focuses on the effectiveness of varied instructional methods. This study fills a void. It responds to a gap in the productivity management education literature.

LITERATURE REVIEW

This first important statement for the use of accelerated learning methods was set forth by Ostrander and Schroeder (1979). They reported the work of Georgi Lozanov. They were able to document that Lozanov had developed a teaching method which was the precursor to accelerated learning. The method improved both learning efficiency and learning effectiveness. Lozanov used Baroque music with a beat of 60 to 64 per minute that was played in the background during foreign language training. The use of such music resulted in a 97 percent retention rate.

Rose (1985) reported successful use of accelerated learning throughout the United States and Europe with both children and adult students. Among the principles that he developed for an effective learning program were:

1. A rich, stimulating, stress-free learning environment is best for learning.
2. Learning by example is better than learning by rote.
3. Learning is maximized when three senses are engaged; visual, auditory and kinesthetic.
4. Peripherals enhance learning. Peripherals are colorful and stimulating posters, etc. that enhance nonconscious learning.
5. Positive suggestion is a powerful technique for learning.

Meyers and Jones (1993) present practical and useful classroom strategies based upon academic research on the teaching/learning process. They discuss a variety of principles that can be traced to the foundations of accelerated learning. Those principles include; reducing or eliminating learning barriers, valuing the learner, providing for different learning styles, allowing for collaborative learning, and making learning fun. Their emphasis is on the instructor as facilitator of a wide variety of classroom instructional methods that actively engage the learners. Some specific methods they address include establishing an optimum learning environment, cooperative student activity, music, games, and creative applications for electronic teaching technology.

Hypothesis

This study examined the differences between traditional instructional methods and accelerated learning methods in productivity management education. This study builds on the available knowledge about the use of accelerated learning methods with adults. In assessing the literature discussion, it is expected that there would be differences in learning effectiveness between traditional instructional methods and accelerated learning methods. Therefore, this research will test the following single hypothesis: there will be meaningful differences in learning outcomes in productivity management education as measured by test scores between adult students taught using traditional methods and those taught using accelerated learning methods.

Methodology: Sample Design and Procedures

The Solomon 4—group research design was used. This design was used to remove the influence of pretesting. Thus, a kind of Hawthorne effect was eliminated as Leedy (1985) has set forth. This design as shown in Table 24.

Table 24.   Solomon 4–Group Research Design

Pre-test	Experimental Group I	Post-test
Pre-test	Control Group I	Post-test
	Experimental Group II	Post-test
	Control Group II	Post-test

The participants were 139 graduate management program students. They were taking their final course—Productivity Improvement—before being awarded masters degrees in business administration, health care administration, human resource management, international business administration, or public administration. A significant unique characteristic of the students was that they were gainfully employed in full-time professional or managerial positions in business and government. The average age was 31 years. The sample size for each of the four groups is shown in Table 25.

Table 25.   Sample Size for Experimental and Control Groups

Group	n = 139
Experimental I	n = 35
Control I	n = 37
Experimental II	n = 33
Control II	n = 34

Group membership was self-selected since students were permitted to register for any of the four groups (sections) of the course. Experimental Group I and Control Group I were given pre-tests to determine if there was any pre-existing differences in productivity between the management knowledge groups. The mean scores of 5.69 for the experimental group and 5.02 for the control group indicate no statistically meaningful difference between groups. Thus, self-selection did not contaminate treatment effects.

The control groups were taught using traditional instructional methods. Accelerated learning methods were used with the two experimental groups. Traditional instructional methods were defined as those which included; 1) lecture by the instructor, 2) one-to-one question and answer interactivity between the instructor and a single student, and 3) little, if any interaction between/among students during classroom learning activity. Accelerated learning methods are those characterized by; 1) the instructor performing the role of learning facilitator, 2) interaction between/among students during classroom learning activity, and 3) student use of somatic learning while engaged in classroom learning activity. Somatic learning is that which incorporates physical activity as part of the learning process. Outdoor/adventure learning is one example.

The productivity course was delivered in a one-week intensive format. An instructor developed test was administered as a post test to two control groups and two experimental groups for purposes of comparative analysis. The test was both factual and applied. The tests were scored by the instructor.

FINDINGS AND RESULTS

Table 26 shows the means and standard deviations of the post test scores for the four groups.

Table 26. Means and Standard Deviations for Test Scores

Group	Mean	Standard Deviation	n
Experimental I	22.69	7.43	35
Control I	13.97	7.62	37
Experimental II	22.14	6.78	33
Control II	12.25	4.78	34

This study examined the effects of using accelerated learning methods in productivity management education. The mean scores for both experimental groups, 22.69 and 22.14, indicate that more learning took place than for both control groups and mean scores of 13.97 and 12.25. Does use of accelerated learning methods with adult learners improve learning outcomes? This research indicated a yes answer.

The scores indicate that there are significant differences between the control groups and the experimental groups (alpha = .05). A one-way ANOVA analysis was utilized. The scores as shown in Table 27 support the findings of significant differences. The scores tell us that the variance between the experimental and the control groups is the result of experimental manipulation. There is between-groups variance. The F Probability score indicates that the resulting variance is not due to change to any extent whatsoever.

Table 27. One-way ANOVA Scores

D.F.	3.00
Sum of Squares	3029.28
Mean Squares	1009.76
F Ratio	22.29
F Probability	.0000

Thus, the hypothesis is supported. Use of accelerated learning methods with adult students in productivity education lead to significantly greater learning effectiveness than does use of the traditional methods.

Conclusion and Future Directions

Certainly educators and trainers in the productivity arena ought to be concerned about the effectiveness of the learning opportunities they are providing. The purpose of this research was to compare traditional instructional methods with accelerated learning methods to determine if effectiveness could be improved.

The study focused on paper and pencil test performance as a indicator of learning effectiveness. When accelerated learning techniques are used, the learning that takes place is significantly higher as demonstrated by the means reported in Table 26. These results are consistent with the literature on accelerated learning that reports better learning results with accelerated learning methods than with traditional methods.

The importance of these results cannot be understated. The whole purpose of productivity management education and training is to impact learners who will take their new learning into the workplace and have a positive impact on Productivity = output/input. This research exemplifies how educators and trainers can increase the productivity of their efforts. Using accelerated learning methods leads to an increase in output, while keeping input at the same level.

It is reasonable to believe that more research in this area is required before productivity management education and training methods are completely transformed. This research can help educators and trainers who wish to look at ways to improve the outcomes for their learners. Perhaps the transformation has already begun.

CHAPTER 13

PROGRESSING FORWARD

Educators are professionals working to advance people in various professions. Higher education is linked with professionals and members of various professions. Cavico and Mujtaba (2005) stated that "As society and business have become more complex and specialized, requiring distinctive knowledge and skills and advanced training and education, more people and groups attempt to identify themselves as professionals and as members of a profession." It is necessary to understand that "all members of a profession are professionals, but not all professionals are members of a profession" (Cavico and Mujtaba, 2005). As such, many professionals are not necessarily members of a profession. Professionals work on a full-time basis and possess the relevant work skills, expertise, and knowledge. Usually, professionals undergo specialized, systematic, and required training and learning. Cavico and Mujtaba mention that professionals are self-supervisory, tend to set their own tasks, often do not "punch" time clocks, and work as many hours as are required to do the job, often at inconvenient times. These professionals tend to possess status and rank with a specific organization in society. Does this describe a picture of the educator? Perhaps. However, educators need to go beyond this and understand the term profession. Members of the skilled trades, such as electricians and plumbers, commonly are regarded as professionals, so too are people who engage in "professional" activities, such as actors and athletes. These trade and professional activities, however, do not constitute professions. Members of a profession are professionals who meet certain "profession" characteristics

---

Adult Education in Academia, pages 269–280
Copyright © 2006 by Information Age Publishing
All rights of reproduction in any form reserved.

which command special prestige and respect. Members of a profession are usually admired and esteemed because they have advanced education and are usually updating their knowledge on a continuing basis.

Cavico and Mujtaba state that "The professions are autonomous; they are self-governing, self-regulating, and, in essence, are state-authorized monopolies" as their members control and regulate entry and they set the standards.

The professions are accorded influence and power because society requires such people to possess specialized knowledge that is clearly useful to the universe. A critical reason for granting autonomy to the professions is that the professions set higher moral standards for themselves than society sets for other people and groups, including professionals and managers. These higher moral standards, moreover, are embodied in the codes of ethics of the professions (Cavico and Mujtaba, 2005). Educators must continue to work as members of the profession and create innovative solutions for the twenty first century's global challenges. This is one best way for educators to continue making a difference in the lives of many current future leaders of the society.

THE TEACHER AND THE BOY

"The Teacher and the Boy" is a story about a teacher, the fifth grade class, and impact of making a difference (hopefully a positive one) in students' lives. The story was received through electronic communication in January of 2005, unknown author, and it is mentioned here because it is impactful and good for reflection.

> As she stood in front of her 5th grade class on the very first day of school, she told the children an untruth. Like most teachers, she looked at her students and said that she loved them all the same. However, that was impossible, because there in the front row, slumped in his seat, was a little boy named Teddy Stoddard. Mrs. Thompson had watched Teddy the year before and noticed that he did not play well with the other children, that his clothes were messy and that he constantly needed a bath. In addition, Teddy could be unpleasant.

> It got to the point where Mrs. Thompson would actually take delight in marking his papers with a broad red pen, making bold X's and then putting a big "F" at the top of his papers. At the school where Mrs. Thompson taught, she was required to review each child's past records and she put Teddy's off until last. However, when she reviewed his file, she was in for a surprise. Teddy's first grade teacher wrote, "Teddy is a bright child with a ready laugh. He does his work neatly and has good manners.... he is a joy to be around."

His second grade teacher wrote, "Teddy is an excellent student, well liked by his classmates, but he is troubled because his mother has a terminal illness and life at home must be a struggle."

His third grade teacher wrote, "His mother's death has been hard on him. He tries to do his best, but his father doesn't show much interest and his home life will soon affect him if some steps aren't taken."

Teddy's fourth grade teacher wrote, "Teddy is withdrawn and doesn't show much interest in school. He doesn't have many friends and he sometimes sleeps in class."

By now, Mrs. Thompson realized the problem and she was ashamed of herself. She felt even worse when her students brought her Christmas presents, wrapped in beautiful ribbons and bright paper, except for Teddy's. His present was clumsily wrapped in the heavy, brown paper that he got from a grocery bag. Mrs. Thompson took pains to open it in the middle of the other presents. Some of the children started to laugh when she found a rhinestone bracelet with some of the stones missing, and a bottle that was one-quarter full of perfume. But she stifled the children's laughter when she exclaimed how pretty the bracelet was, putting it on, and dabbing some of the perfume on her wrist. Teddy Stoddard stayed after school that day just long enough to say, "Mrs. Thompson, today you smelled just like my Mom used to." After the children left, she cried for at least an hour.

On that very day, she quit teaching reading, writing, and arithmetic. Instead, she began to teach children. Mrs. Thompson paid particular attention to Teddy. As she worked with him, his mind seemed to come alive.

The more she encouraged him, the faster he responded. By the end of the year, Teddy had become one of the smartest children in the class and, despite her lie that she would love all the children the same, Teddy became one of her "teacher's pets."

A year later, she found a note under her door, from Teddy, telling her that she was still the best teacher he ever had in his whole life.

Six years went by before she got another note from Teddy. He then wrote that he had finished high school, third in his class, and she was still the best teacher he ever had in life...

Four years after that, she got another letter, saying that while things had been tough at times, he'd stayed in school, had stuck with it, and would soon graduate from college with the highest of honors. He assured Mrs. Thompson that she was still the best and favorite teacher he had ever had in his whole life.

Then four more years passed and yet another letter came. This time he explained that after he got his bachelor's degree, he decided to go a little further. The letter explained that she was still the best and favorite teacher he ever had. But now his name was a little longer....

The letter was signed, Theodore F. Stoddard, MD.

The story does not end there... You see, there was yet another letter that spring. Teddy said he had met this girl and was going to be married.

He explained that his father had died a couple of years ago and he was wondering if Mrs. Thompson might agree to sit at the wedding in the place that was usually reserved for the mother of the groom.

Of course, Mrs. Thompson did... And guess what? She wore that bracelet, the one with several rhinestones missing. Moreover, she made sure she was wearing the perfume that Teddy remembered his mother wearing on their last Christmas together. They hugged each other, and Dr. Stoddard whispered in Mrs. Thompson's ear, "Thank you Mrs. Thompson for believing in me. Thank you so much for making me feel important and showing me that I could make a difference."

Mrs. Thompson, with tears in her eyes, whispered back. She said, "Teddy, you have it all wrong. You were the one who taught me that I could make a difference. I didn't know how to teach until I met you!" Teddy Stoddard is the doctor at Iowa Methodist in Des Moines that has the Stoddard Cancer Wing.

PROGRESSING FORWARD

In one of his articles titled "Getting Ahead," the President of Nova Southeastern University, Ray Ferrero Jr., said "Rapidly evolving technology, a competitive job market, and demanding employers are creating a new mandate for university students. More than ever, students, both undergraduate and graduate, must enter the educational atmosphere with clear goals and directives." His suggestions apply to faculty members as well since rapidly evolving technology, a competitive education industry, a demanding society, and the need for accountability are impacting all educators.

Like President Ferrero, we all have seen many rapid and evolutionary changes in the ways in which both students and faculty prepare to effectively meet the challenges of an increasingly competitive workforce. In order to succeed as educators, "it is vital that students begin their preparation and planning early on and maintain a steady course throughout their education" said President Ferrero. He continued to offer a few tips, based on his experiences as a top level administrator, to prospective students that can help them and faculty members utilize their education to the fullest and ultimately, get ahead in their chosen field. While his "tips" are geared toward students, they are equally applicable to faculty members as well.

Assess your skills. Your career path will be all the more enjoyable if you choose a profession that utilizes your natural talents and abilities, and any skills you have already mastered. Learners should always seek learning programs with a solid understanding of their skills and knowledge of what they intend to achieve.

Have a plan. Again, career consultants and professional advisors can help here. All learners can and should take time to map out their desired direction; it is never too early to develop a plan of action. Make sure the plans you choose give you the opportunities to enhance your education and implement your career plan.

Explore your options. Meet with your colleagues, family members, advisors, and counselors to make sure you are aware of all the career options that are available. For instance, there may be special programs that allow you to accelerate your learning and earning.

Take your education beyond the classroom. As important as it is to take the right classes to meet the needs of your career, there is no substitute for hands-on experience and community involvement. That kind of real world experience that can be shared with everyone can provide a competitive edge.

Never stop learning. Just because you've graduated and gotten the job of your dreams does not mean it's time to give up on your education. Education is a lifelong pursuit and the key to staying "on top" in your profession and as a member of your community. Schools offer endless opportunities for people with busy lives who are seeking the extra education they need to advance their thoughts and careers. Through flexible class schedules, online classes and distance education, learners can further their education (and obtain additional degrees if desired), while never leaving their home or workstations. Education is a privilege. Make the most of it and of yourself by taking the time to plan, research, and prepare for the road ahead. Choose learning programs of interest and quality offerings that provide you with the resources and abilities to meet your current and long range personal and professional goals.

PROFESSIONAL EDUCATORS AS VISIONARIES

As professionals, all educational leaders should "romanticize" for better days if they are to be visionaries and futuristic. Eva Gregory, coach and author, said "I see no point in looking back at what I didn't get done. I choose, instead, to acknowledge where I am and where I want to be; then determine what steps it will take to get me there." Wisdom comes from experiencing an event, an idea, a concept, or an endeavor; therefore, all failures are experiences which lead to knowledge. Professionals are good people and they are good because they have come to wisdom through experimentation and failure. Ralph Waldo Emerson, philosopher and author, said that "Bad times have a scientific value. These are occasions a good learner would not miss." There is very little wisdom in success. So, success should be judged accordingly as Robert Louis Stevenson, author, once said "Don't judge each day by the harvest you reap... but by the seeds you plant."

Effective leaders plan for learning and success through experimentation, structure, progress, and prioritization. Napoleon Hill, author, said "Reduce your plan to writing... The moment you complete this, you will have definitely given concrete form to the intangible desire." Professionals become leaders because they are able to commit to these tangible desires and convert them into action. Motivational speaker Anthony Robbins suggests that "Deciding to commit yourself to long-term results rather than short term fixes is as important as any decision you'll make in your lifetime." Ben Stein, actor and author says "The indispensable first step to getting the things you want out of life is this: decide what you want." This hard work of spending time to make the right decisions about a specific direction can be very worthwhile. Another author by the name of Ralph Marston said "The creativity and positive energy you put forth come back to you many times over. So, do the hurt and destruction. Which would you rather get back?" Once a decision has been made, then put your heart into its achievement. William James of Harvard University said "Most people never run far enough on their first wind to find out if they've got a second. Give your dreams all you've got and you'll be amazed at the energy that comes out of you." According to Professor James, "It is our attitude at the beginning of a difficult task which, more than anything else, will affect its successful outcome."

Instead of focusing on being more determined, some people are way too concerned about their competitors and the actions of others. Grace Lichtenstein, author, wrote that "Your opponent, in the end, is never really the player on the other side of the net, or the swimmer in the next lane, or the team on the other side of the field, or even the bar you must high-jump. Your opponent is yourself, your negative internal voices, your level of determination."

Charles Kettering, inventor and businessman said the following about imagination: "Our imagination is the only limit to what we can hope to have in the future." Julian Simon, economist, put it nicely when he said "The main fuel to speed the world's progress is our stock of knowledge, and the brake is our lack of imagination." Besides imagineering, one needs to envision the results and final outcomes. "Think and feel yourself there! To achieve any aim in life, you need to project the end-result. Think of the elation, the satisfaction, the joy! Carrying the ecstatic feeling will bring the desired goal into view" said Grace Speare, author. Commitments must be aligned with one's actions and beliefs in order for progress and success to follow. Dorothea Brande, author, said "All that is necessary to break the spell of inertia and frustration is this: act as if it were impossible to fail. That is the talisman, the formula, the command of right-about-face that turns us from failure toward success."

Ralph Waldo Emerson encouraged everyone to "Finish each day and be done with it. You have done what you could; some blunders and absurdities have crept in; forget them as soon as you can. Tomorrow is a new day; you shall begin it serenely and with too high a spirit to be encumbered with your old nonsense." Instead of being too focused on the past, all educators need to be forward-looking and anchored toward the future that we all desire for ourselves and our students. Productive individuals and effective leaders are forward-oriented and, at challenging times, use professionalism to create synergy with people of diverse backgrounds, ethnicities, and languages. *Professionalism* can be operationalized at all localities at the individual level by putting the needs of others in the community, organization, society and country above one's own through accountability, compassion, integrity, and mutual respect for all human beings and living creations in the society. All professionals are encouraged to review the following characteristics and share them with others for persistency and aspiration.

CHARACTERISTICS OF AN EFFECTIVE LEARNING ENVIRONMENT

The previous chapters have discussed many variables that can enhance or hinder learning. This section provides a clear and succinct summary of an effective learning environment. The following characteristics are created thanks to McEnerney and Webb, California State University Dominguez Hills, and to the Teaching in the Active Voice Institute, University of Prince Edward Island, Canada.

Effective Facilitation

- Focuses on teaching the audience, not just the subject.
- Has a title or topic statement.
- Contains a brief review of the main ideas covered in the previous class session and relates the present material to them. May also ask students to summarize the main ideas.
- Provides a preview of information prior to the explanation.
- Provides an outline in several formats (e.g, visible, audio, handout) so as to engage the different learning styles of students.
- Engages the attention and interest of the audience, often around a question.
- Organizes information logically for audience comprehension.
- Reinforces new or specialized vocabulary and important points in visible as well as audio formats; employs synonyms and descriptors; avoids jargon, slang, and undefined acronyms.

- Reinforces core information with audiovisual aids; repeats for reinforcement.
- Gives many concrete examples to illustrate information points.
- Uses analogies, metaphors, and/or stories frequently so that student can conceptualize concepts in more familiar contexts.
- Relates information to assigned readings and cites the location where students can find the information.
- Speaks clearly and loudly enough to be heard comfortably; uses a microphone or sign language interpreter as needed.
- Stops often within a lecture (e.g., the punctuated lecture) to check for comprehension.
- Clearly signals topic shifts and transitions by using verbal and non-verbal cues.
- Clearly signals digressions and indicates how a digression relates (or doesn't relate) to main points.
- Contains a visual and audio summary of main points at the end.
- Reserves time for student questions and comments.
- Respects audience needs by ending on time.
- Assesses student learning at multiple levels and intervals throughout the semester.
- Attends to fundamentals of public speaking and adjusts style to make language comprehensible
  - Speaks slowly and enunciates clearly so that all students can hear, understand, and write. Allows adequate pauses (count to twelve) to facilitate the decoding process so that listening becomes active and students can process information and generate questions.
  - Recognizes individual students and makes regular eye contact with them.
  - Modifies pace when audience behavior indicates changing needs.
  - Uses appropriate gestures and facial expressions to emphasize main points.
  - Doesn't let voice trail off at the end of a sentence or idea.
  - Uses transition phrases to link information.
  - Avoids nervous use filler words ("Okay...") and non-words ("Uh..., Um...").

Effective Questioning

- Asks clearly worded, focused questions that contain indicators for how to respond.
- Conveys to students a genuine interest in hearing what they have to say.

- Allows ample time (count to twelve) for a response before restating, modifying, or moving on.
- Makes eye contact with individuals and does not ask questions to the back wall, the blackboard, the video screen, or one individual repeatedly.
- Calls students by name when eliciting responses from specific individuals.
- Either restates the response or politely asks students to restart inaudible responses so the entire class can hear.
- Does not remain primarily in one place or engage in repetitive one-on-one questioning.
- Does not pester or hassle; aims at eliciting information flow and not at embarrassing individuals.
- Moves around the room so as to engage and retain group interest.
- Frequently asks a question before naming a respondent in order to encourage all students to listen and decide how they would answer.
- Does not allow a minority of more confident or impulsive students to dominate.
- Gives students who do not normally respond a chance to enter the conversation.
- Is egalitarian in order to capture a diversity of views.
- Uses a variety of strategies to allow different kinds of learners a chance to answer comfortably: students call out answers, a student is selected to answer, students raise their hands and volunteer to answer.
- Does not limit more challenging and stimulating questions to students perceived as having higher ability or knowledge.
- Asks students to justify and further explain responses.
- Encourages students to answer each others' questions.
- Allows time to consider different points of view and multiple responses.
- Does not overtly or covertly invalidate students' responses by unnecessarily changing their wording or meaning.
- Creates a safe and supportive atmosphere for student questions by answering them immediately and politely.
- Does not make students feel assailed, threatened, and passive by asking them too many questions.
- Invites questions as if they are a normal part of the teaching/learning process (e.g., "Now is a good time to hear your questions," instead of "Anybody come with any questions at this point?").
- Employs multiple formats and Classroom Assessment Techniques for questioning, such as the Unanswered Question and Muddiest Point.

- Uses "think–pair–share" in which students think of an answer, pair with another student, and discuss their answers before sharing with the entire group.
- Asks in a voice, tone, and manner that correspond to the accepted principles of public discourse.

Effective Group Work

- Creates or selects an activity that lends itself to group processes.
- Clearly explains the purpose and expected outcome of group activity.
- Gives clear expectations and accountability for the activity orally and in writing.
- Models the task in whole or in part.
- Breaks group activities into clear, manageable sequences or process.
- Assigns specific roles for each student, or allows group to assign specific roles.
- For each role, identifies specific behaviors necessary for completion of the task.
- Provides locations, times, and resources for group activities and for task completion.
- Allows an appropriate amount of time to complete the task satisfactorily.
- Assesses group progress early through Classroom Assessment Techniques or other methods and intervenes appropriately.
- Takes a facilitative rather than a dominating or disruptive stance while monitoring groups in process.
- Allows sufficient time after group work to integrate the activity as a unified class.

Effective Assessment

- Assesses what matters most. Assessment makes a difference when it illuminates questions people really care about.
- Focuses on processes as well as outcomes. Attention is given to main outcomes and also, equally, to the experiences that lead to those outcomes.
- Operates at key points in the educational process. Programs recognize those keys as having visible, clearly defined, explicitly stated purposes.
- Uses multiple measures over time. Assessment works best when it is ongoing, not episodic.

- Generates feedback for improving learning. Assessment of student learning begins with educational values.
- Provides feedback and development to those most affected. Improvement arises more easily when assessment operates in conditions where change is likely.
- Actively involves students and members of the teaching staff. Assessment fosters improvement when it engages the wider educational community.
- Is embedded in teaching and learning. Learning is understood as multidimensional, integrated, and revealed through performance over time.

An effective learning environment is effective because of continuous measurements, enhancements, improvements, and progress toward better outcomes which is quality education and graduates. Educators must remember that it is through a comprehensive assessment program that faculty members and their institutions acquire evidence to meet responsibilities to themselves, students, and the demanding public. So, make the assessment and creation of an effective learning environment simple but not simpler. Ralph Waldo Emerson said "The person who can make hard things easy is the educator."

The Tone of Voice

It's not so much what you say
As the manner in which you *say it*;
It's not so much the language you use
As the tone in which you *convey it.*

"Come here!" I sharply said,
And the child cowered and *wept.*
"Come here," I said—he looked and smiled
And straight to my lap he *crept.*

Words may be mild and fair
But the tone may pierce like a *dart*;
Words may be soft as the summer air
But the tone may break my *heart*;

For words may come from the mind
Grow by study and *art*—
But tone leaps from the inner self,
Revealing the state of the *heart.*

Whether you know it or not,
Whether you mean or *care*
Gentleness, kindness, love and hate,
Envy, anger are *there.*

Then, would you quarrels avoid
And peace and love *rejoice.*
Keep anger not only out of your words—
Keep it out of your *voice.*

(Unknown)

BIBLIOGRAPHY

AACSB, 1996. "*Achieving Quality and Continuous Improvement through Self-Evaluation and Peer Review.*" Standards for Accreditation: Guidelines for Self-Evaluation. St. Louis, Mo.

AACSB, (1999). *Standards for Accreditation: Business Administration and Accounting.* The Association for the Advancement of Collegiate Schools of Business International. Reprinted January 20, 1999.

American Association of Higher Education (AAHE), (December 1992). *Principles of Good Practice for Assessing Student Learning.* AAHE Assessment Forum.

ABC Prime Time, 2004. "*Caught Cheating in School.*" Aired on April 29, 2004. Hosted by Charlie Gibson.

Austin, Dan (2001). An Open-Door Policy. Foresight publication by Wayne Huizenga School of Business and Entrepreneurship. Nova Southeastern University. Summer Edition.

Bailey, Margaret, 2003. *Introduction to Typical Jamaican Family.* Retrieved 12/28/2003 from http://www.jamaicans.com/culture/intro/typical_family.htm.

Barnes, B. and Blackwell, C. (2004). *Taking Business Training Online: Lessons from Academe.* Journal of Applied Management and Entrepreneurship. Volume 9. Number 1. January Issue.

Barnum, P.; Liden, D. R. And DiTomaso, N., 1995. Double Jeopardy for Women and Minorities: Pay Differences with Age. *The Academy of Management Journal.* Vol. 38, # 3. June.

Bisoux, T. (2003). *Is There a Doctorate in the House.* BizEd, March/April issue.

Bloom, B. (1956). *Taxonomy of educational objectives: The classification of educational goals.* New York, N.Y. David McKay Co.

Bloom's Taxonomy of Learning, 2004. Retrieved on May 13, 2004 from: www.officeport.com/edu/blooms.htm,

Bolton, M. (1999). The role of coaching in student teams: A just-in-time approach to learning. *Journal of Management Education*, 23, 233–250.

Boyd, Drick (2004). *The Characteristics of Successful Online Students.* New Horizons in Adult Education. Volume 18, Number 2, Spring.

Adult Education in Academia, pages 281–288
Copyright © 2006 by Information Age Publishing
All rights of reproduction in any form reserved.

Brokaw, A. J.; Kennedy, W. A.; and Merz, T. E., (Spring 2004). *"Explaining Student Satisfaction."* Journal of the Academy of Business Education. Volume 5. ISSN: 1528-0721.

Business Week, 2004. *Is There a Doctor in the B-School? Universities are searching for ways to generate more business PhDs.* March 1st Issue.

Capra, F. (1996/7). *The web of life.* New York: Doubleday.

Carr, N.; Meyerson, D.; Rafarrete, R.; Saunders, J.; & Scharff, M. (2004). *A Systems Analysis of the U of P Doctor of Management Program.* Unpublished Manuscript. ORG701-Systems Thinking: The Web of Life.

Cavico, F. & Mujtaba, B., (October 2005). *Business Ethics: Transcending Requirements through Moral Leadership.* Pearson Custom Publications. U.S.A. ISBN: 0-536-85783-0. Address: 75 Arlington Street. Suite 300. Boston Mass, 02116. Phone: (800) 374-1200. Or: (800) 922-0579.

Checkland, P. B. (1999). *Systems Thinking, Systems: A 30 year retrospective* Practice, John Wiley and Sons, Chichester.

Checkland, P. & Scholes, J. (1999). *Soft systems methodology in action.* New York: Wiley.

Checkland, P. (1999). *Systems Thinking, Systems Practice: A 30-Year Retrospective.* New York, NY: John Wiley & Sons, Inc.

Chopra, D. (1993). *The seven spiritual laws of success.* San Rafael: Amber-Allen Publishing and New World Library.

Christ, F.L. & Ganey, R. L. (2003). *100 Things Every Online Student Ought to Know.* Cambridge Stratford Study Skills Institute, Williamsville, NY.

Colbeck, C. L., Campbell, S. E., & Bjorklund, S. A. (2000). Grouping in the dark: What college students learn from group projects. *The Journal of Higher Education,* 71, 60–83.

Collins. J.C. (2001). *Good to great: Why some companies make the leap…and others don't.* New York: Harper Collins.

Cordeniz, Judy, A. (2002). *Recruitment, retention, and management of Generation X: Focus on nursing professionals.* Journal of Healthcare Management. 47 (4): 237.

Covey, Stephen (1989). The Seven Habits of Highly Effective People.

Daly, H. (1996). *Beyond Growth. Boston.* Beacon Press.

Davidson, Marcia (2003). *Jamaican Culture: An Overview.* Retrieved on 12/28/03 from: http://www.jamaicans.com/culture/intro/index.htm

De Pree, M. (1992). *Leadership jazz.* New York: Currency Doubleday.

Debreceny, R. (1999) *Outcomes assessment: The accreditation process.* Available: http://www.lgc.peachnet.edu/sacs.html [November 19, 1999].

Desjardins, J. R., & Diedrich, E., (2003). *Learning what it really costs: Teaching business ethics with life-cycle case studies. The Journal of Business Ethics,* 48, 33.

Drucker, P. F. (1992). *Managing for the future: The 1990s and beyond.* New York: Truman Talley Books/Dutton.

Dupont, Kay (1997). Handling Diversity in the Workplace. AMI Publication. Forwarded by Dr. R. Roosevelt Thomas.

Eastmond, D. (1998). Adult learners and Internet-based distance education. *New Directions for Adult and Continuing Education,* 78, 33–41.

Educational Kit, (1999). *Think Ability.* President's Committee on Employment of People with Disabilities. See "A message from the chairman Tony Coelho."

Eisner, Susan P., (2004, September). *Teaching Generation Y College Students: Three Initiatives.* Journal of College Teaching and Learning, Volume 1, Number 9. pp. 69–84. ISSN: 1544-0389.

Fitz-enz, Jac (1995). *How to Measure Human Resources Management.* Second edition. McGraw-Hill, Inc.

Forum, 2004. *How Can Colleges Prove They're Doing Their Jobs?* Chronicles of Higher Education, September 3rd 2004.

Frey, H. William, (1999). Minority Majorities. *Written in American Demographics Books.* Page 6.

Gazzaniga, M. S. (1998). *The mind's past* (1st ed.). Los Angeles: University of California Press.

Greenberg, M. (2001). *What Administrators Should Know about Accreditation?* Chronicles of Higher Education: Career Network. October 26, 2001.

Gubernick, L. & Ebeling, A. (1997). I Got My Degree Through E-Mail. Forbes: Pages 84-92. June 16.

Hamilton, Jennifer (2004). *Grades, Goals and GMAT Scores Factors in MBA Success.* South Florida Business Journal: Guide to Education. July 16th 2004.

Harken, Gayla. (2000). Naked *Management: Bare Essentials for Motivating the X-Generation at work.* Psychiatric Rehabilitation Journal. 23 (4): 410.

Harris, Robert (October 2001). Anti-Plagiarism Strategies for Research Papers. Retrieved on 2/7/2002 from: http://www.virtualsalt.com/antiplag.htm

Henke, H. & Russum, J. (2000). Factors influencing attrition rates in a corporate distance education program. *Education at a distance, 14* (11), Article 03. Retrieved July 25, 2001 from http://www.usdla.org/ED_magazine/illuminactive/ NOV00_Issue/story03.htm

Hesselbein, F. Goldsmith, M. & Beckhard, R. (1996). *The leader of the future.* San Francisco: Jossey-Bass.

Hopkins, E. Willie (1997). *Ethical Dimensions of Diversity.* Sage Publications: Sage Series on Business Ethics.

Howard Community College (2001). Characteristics of Successful Online Students. Retrieved August 9, 2001 at http://www.howardcc.edu/online/requir_courseofferings.htm

Huizenga School, 2004. Retrieved in February 20, 2004 from: http://www.huizenga .nova.edu.

———, 2004. Website visited on September 2004 at: http://www.sbe.nova .edu/ and http://www.sbe.nova.edu/about/faculty.cfm

———, 2003. Retrieved in November 10, 2003 from: http://www.huizenga .nova. edu.

Jacques, R. (1996). *Manufacturing the employee: Management knowledge from the 19th to 21st centuries.* Thousand Oaks, CA: Sage.

Jain, Subhash C. (1997). *Marketing Planning & Strategy.* 5th Edition, Cincinnati, OH: Southwestern Publishing, pp. 348–349.

Jamaica, 2003. *Jamaica.* Retrieved from the following URL on 12/282003. http:// encarta.msn.com/encyclopedia_761561054/Jamaica.html.

Johnson, W., and Weinstein, A. (2004). *Superior Customer Value in New Economy.* Second Edition. CRC Press.

Kegan, R. (1982). *The evolving self* Cambridge, MA: Harvard University Press.

Knowles, M., Holton, E., & Swanson, R. (1998). *The definitive classic on adult education and training.* Houston, TX: Gulf.

Kolb, D.A. (1985). *Learning style inventory.* Boston, MA: McBer.

Kubasek, N.K., Brennan, B.A., & Brown, N.M. (2003). *Legal environment of business, The: A critical thinking approach,* 3/E. New Jersey; Prentice Hall.

Kupperschmidt, Betty, R. (2000). *Tips to help your recruit, manage, and keep generation X employees.* Nursing Management 31 (3): 58.

Lancaster, L., Stillman, D., & MacKay, H. (2002). *When generations collide.* New York: HarperCollins

IACBE, 2002. *Faculty Characteristic.* International Assembly for Collegiate Business Education's Faculty Manual. Pages 19-23.

Levine, D. I. (1995). *Reinventing the workplace: How business and employees can both win.* Washington, DC: The Brookings Institution.

Lang, J., & Dittrich, J. (1982). Information, skill building, and the development of competence: An educational framework for teaching business policy. *Academy of Management Review,* 7, 269-279.

Leedy, P. (1985) *Practical Research.* New York, Macmillian.

Lieb, Stephen (1991). Principles of Adult Learning. *VISION.* Fall of 1991. Retrieved on December 20, 2002 from: http://www.hcc.hawaii.edu/intranet/committees/FacDevCom/guidebk/teachtip/adults-2.htm

MacFarland, Thomas W., (November, 2003). *Students in Jamaica Evaluate Resources and Services of Nova Southeastern University Library, Research, and Information Technology Center.* Summer Term 2003. Report 03-18. Research and Planning.

Marquand, Barbara (2004). *Ask Questions before Heading to Graduate School.* South Florida Business Journal: Guide to Education. July 16, 2004.

Marwick, J. D. (1998, July 20). *Academic outcomes assessment, a tool for student learning.* Urbana-Champaign, IL: University of Illinois. (ERIC Document Reproduction Service No Ed 422 991).

McEnerney and Webb, (2003). *Some Characteristics of an Effective Learning Environment.* California State University Dominguez Hills and to the Teaching in the Active Voice Institute, University of Prince Edward Island, Canada. Received on 11, 14th 2003.

McGlynn, A. P. (2001). "Successful beginnings for college teaching." Madison, WI: Atwood Publishing, Inc.

Mitchell, C. (2003). *A short course in International Business Ethics: Combining Ethics and Profits in Global Business.* World Trade Press: Professional Books for International Trade. Pages 110–122.

Moore, J. (2002). *Elements of Quality: The Sloan-C Framework. The Sloan Consortium.* Pillar Reference Manual.

Moorhouse, D. (2001). *Effect of Instructional Delivery Method on Student Achievement in a Master's of Business Administration Course at the Wayne Huizenga School of Business and Entrepreneurship.* Research and Planning Report. Retrieved from NSU's website on March 20, 2004. URL: http://www.nova.edu/cwis/urp/index.html

———, and Mujtaba, B. (2004). *Effect of Instructional Modality on Student Achievement in GMP5017, a Master's of Business Administration Course Offered by the H. Wayne Huizenga School of Business and Entrepreneurship.* Nova Southeastern University.

Research and Planning Report. Retrieved from NSU's website on March 05th 2004. URL: http://www.nova.edu/cwis/urp/index.html

Morgan, C. L., & Morgan, L. V. (1935, September). Effects of immediate awareness of success and failure upon objective examination scores. *Journal of Experimental Education, 4*(1), 63–66.

Mujtaba, G. B. and Kennedy, W. K., (March 2005). *Facilitating through Collaborative Reflections to Accommodate Diverse Learning Styles for Long-Term Retention.* Association for Business Simulation and Experiential Learning (ABSEL) Proceedings.

_____, and Kennedy, J. W., (February 2005). *Mentoring and Socialization Programs in the Twenty First Century Environment.* Fifth Annual International Business Research Conference, University of North Florida, Jacksonville, 2-11-05.

_____, and Kennedy, J. W. (2005). *Affective Teaching and Facilitation: Increase Learning, Enforce Ethical Standards, and Reduce Dishonesty in the College Classroom.* Proceedings of College Teaching and Learning Conference, January 2005.

_____, and Abratt, R. (2005). Quality Assurance and Assessment of Doctoral Programs: The Comprehensive Exams. Applied Business Research Conference Proceedings. January 3-7.

_____,; Cavico, F. J.; and Weinstein, A. (2004). *An Assessment of MBA Student Performance Based on Teaching Modality: The On-Ground versus the Hybrid Format.* Proceedings of the Academy of Business Disciplines, Proceedings of Sixth Annual Conference. November 11-13.

_____, & Mujtaba, L. (March 2004). "*Diversity Awareness and Management in Adult Education.*" Journal of College Teaching and Learning. Volume 1, Number 3. Pages 65-75.

_____, & Mujtaba, L. (2004). "*Creating a Healthy Learning Environment for Student Success in the Classroom.*" The Internet TESL Journal. Vol. X, No. 2, February 2004. The article can be retrieved via the following URL link: http://iteslj. org/ or: http://iteslj.org/Articles/Mujtaba-Environment.html.

_____, (2004). "*Faculty Training and Development Practices in Distance Education to Achieve High Performance through Extraordinary Teaching.*" Journal of College Teaching and Learning. Volume 1, Number 6. June Issue. Western Academic Press. ISSN: 1544-0389. CIBER Research Institute.

_____,; Preziosi, R.; & Mujtaba, L. (April 2004). "*Adult Learning, Assessment, And the Extraordinary Teacher.*" Journal of College Teaching and Learning. Volume 1, Number 4. Pages 29-37. ISSN: 1544-0389. Western Academic Press.

_____, (2003). "*Faculty Training and Development Practices in Distance Education to Achieve High Performance through Extraordinary Teaching.*" Journal of College Teaching and Learning. June Issue. Volume 1, Number 6. Western Academic Press. ISSN: 1544-0389. CIBER Research Institute.

_____, (2003). Ethical Implications of Employee Monitoring: What Leaders Need to Consider! *Journal of Applied Management and Entrepreneurship.* Volume 8, Number 3. July/August Issue of 2003.

Munchnick, M. (1996). *Naked Management: Bare Essentials for Motivating the X-generation at work.* Delray Beach, Florida: St Lucie Press.

Myers, C. and Jones, J.B. (1993). *Promoting Active Learning.* San Francisco, Jossey-Bass.

Neely, L., Niemi, J. & Ehrhard, B. (1998). *Classes going the distance so people don't have to: Instructional opportunities for adult learners.* T.H.E. Journal, 26(4), 72.

Nelson, C.A. (1999). *International Business: A Manager's Guide to Strategy in the Age of Globalism.* International Thomson Business Press. Pages: 72-74.

Nova Southeastern University, 2004. Website visited on October 2004 at: http://www.nova.edu/

Nova Southeastern University, 2003. Retrieved in November 10, 2003 from their website links: NSU's Website: http://www.nova.edu

NSU e-Bulletin, 2004. NSU Leads the Nation in the Number of Doctorate Degrees Awarded to Minorities. August 8. Retrieved on August 8th 2004 from: http://www.nova.edu/cwis/ia/pubaffairs/news/july-sept2004/doctorates.html

NSU (2003). *Get the Star Treatment.* Retrieved from NSU's website on July 23rd 2003 from: www.nova.edu

O'Neill, Edward. (2002). *Shaping America's health care professions: How the health sector will respond to "generation X".* Western Journal of Medicine. 176 (2): 139.

Ostrander, S. and Schroeder, L. (1994). *Super learning 2000,* New York, Delacorte Press.

Pohlman, R. & Gardiner, G. (2000). *Value Driven Management: How to Create and Maximize Value Over Time for Organizational Success.* New York: AMACOM.

Publix, (1999). *Learning How to Learn.* Workshop provided by Publix Trainers. Lakeland, Florida.

Randolph, P. (2001). *Dean's Message.* Foresight publication by Wayne Huizenga School of Business and Entrepreneurship. Nova Southeastern University. Summer Edition.

Preziosi, R. (2001). *Making a Lasting Impression: Preziosi honored as Professor of the Decade. Foresight publication by Wayne Huizenga School of Business and Entrepreneurship.* Nova Southeastern University. Summer Edition.

——— and Preziosi, K. (2001). *"How to be a World Class Facilitator of Learning."* The 2001 Manual: Training. Jossey-Bass / Pfeifer: San Francisco. Pages 229-238.

———; Barnes, B.; Rivers, E.; and Gooden, D., (2000). *"The Impact of Ground-based vs. Electronic-based Instructions Modality and Learning Style Preference on Learning Achievement among Selected HRM Topics in an MBA Program."* Proceedings of the Institute for Behavioral and Applied Management. November 2000, San Diego, CA.

——— 1993. *Ideas and Practices for Adult Learning and Teaching.* Made available to faculty members at the School of Business and Entrepreneurship-Nova Southeastern University.

——— (1994). *Tens ways to create a motivating learning environment.* APICS Proceedings. Falls Church, VA: American Production and Inventory Control Society.

——— (1999). Icebreakers. *Info-line.* Alexandria, VA: American Society for Training and Development.

Profiles in Diversity Journal. A publication for sharing diversity information. Volume 1, number 2. Summer 1999.

Reichheld, F.F. (1996). *The Loyalty Effect,* Mass: Harvard Business School Press.

Richards, C. & Ridley, D. (1997). *Factors affecting college students' persistence in online computer-managed instruction. College Student Journal, 31,* 490-495.

Roblyer, M. (1999). *Is choice important in distance learning? A study of student motives for taking Internet-based courses at the high school and community college levels. Journal of Research on Computing in Education, 32* (1), 157-71.

Rodriguez, R.O., Green, M. T., Ree, M.J. (2003). *Leading Generation X: Do the old rules apply?* Journal of Leadership & Organizational Studies. 9 (4): 67.

Ron and Susan Zemke, (1984). Thirty Things We Know for Sure About Adult Learning. *Innovation Abstracts* Vol VI, No 8, March 9, 1984.

Rose, C. (1985). *Accelerated Learning.* New York, Dell Publishing.

Rossman, M. (2000). *Andragogy and distance education: Together in the new millennium. New Horizons in Adult Education, 14*(1), 3-9. Retrieved on October 20th 2004 from http://www.nova.edu/~aed/horizons/vol14n1.htm

SACS (2003). *Principles of Accreditation.* Decatur, Georgia: Commission on Colleges. Southern Association of Colleges and Schools

———— (2001). *Principles of Accreditation: Foundations for quality Enhancement: A Proposal.* The Southern Association of Colleges and Schools.

———— (1994). *Criteria for Accreditation.* Decatur, Georgia: Commission on Colleges. Southern Association of Colleges and Schools.

Salghur, S. & Mujtaba, B. (January 2005). *What Online Students Should Know: Essential Cyberspace Skills for Chatting, Emailing and Learning.* College Teaching and Learning Conference Proceedings. Best paper winner.

Salopek, J. (1999, February). Stop playing games. *Training & Development, pp.* 26-30.

Salter, Chuck (2001). *Attention, Class! 16 Ways to Be a Smarter Teacher.* Fast Company. Retrieved on 3/5/04 from: http://www.fastcompany.com/magazine/53/teaching.html

Scholtes, P.R., (1998). *The leader's handbook.* New York: McGraw Hill.

Schulman, A.H. and Sims, R.I. (1999). *Learning in an online format versus an in-class format: An experimental study. T.H.E. (Technical Horizons in Education) Journal, 26,* 54-56..

Senge P. (1994). *The Fifth Discipline Fieldbook: Strategies and tools for building and learning.* New York, NY: Doubleday.

———— (1992). *Learning Organizations and Human Resources.* American Society for Training and Development (ASTD) National Conference. New Orleans.

———— (1990). *The Fifth Discipline: The Art and Practice of the Learning Organization.* New York, NY: Currency/DoubleDay.

Shaohua, C, M., & Gnyawali, D, R. (2003). Developing synergistic knowledge in student groups. *The Journal of Higher Education, 74,* 689-711.

Sheehy, G. (1995). *New passages: Mapping your life across time.* New York: Random House.

Simons, George and Zuckerman, Amy J. (1994). *Working Together: Succeeding in a Multicultural Organization.* Revised edition. Crisp Publications.

Sim's, R. R. (2004). *Business Ethics Teaching: Using Conversational Learning to build an effective classroom learning environment. The Journal of Business Ethics, 49,* 201.

Spence, L. d. (2001, November). The Case Against Teaching. Change 33 (6), 10 (10). Retrieved October 25th 2004 from EBSCO Database.

Spitzer, D. (1995, December). 20 ways to motivate trainees. *Training, 32,* 54-57. Retrieved February 15, 2004 from ProQuest database.

Stone Soup Legend, 2003. The Stone Soup Legend. Retrieved November 10th 2003 from the following URL: http://www.kousi.gr.jp/kousi/syoukai/hp-siryou/stone-soup.html

Stuart, P. (1992). *New Direction in Training Individuals.* Personnel Journal, 71, 86. Retrieved on February 12, 2004 from ProQuest database.

Sugar, S. (1998). *Games that teach.* San Francisco, CA: Jossey-Bass/Pfeiffer.

The Communicator: Council of Graduate Schools (January/February, 2004). *Addressing attrition in Ph.D. Programs.* Volume XXXVII, Number 1.

The Guest, (2004). Follow up videos is titled *"The Difficult Guest."* Phone: (800) 575-4001 or (561) 575-4001. Retrieved on 9/5/03 from: http://www.customerserviceuniversity.com/theguest.html

The US Education Information Center (2004). *Doctoral programs in business.* Visited on October 23rd 2004 on URL: http://www.useic.ru/ and their website on: http://www.useic.ru/study/apply/business.htm.

The View, 2004. *Interview with Jason Ritter.* Show on American Broadcasting Corporation (ABC) aired on October 15th 2004 at 11:00-12:00 AM, EST.

Training across cultures (1995). *Employee counseling [sic] Today,* 7, 17. Retrieved February 12, 2004 from ProQuest database.

Tulgan, B. (1996). *Correcting the "slacker myth" - managing generation X in the workplace.* Manage, 48, 14-16.

Von Bertalanffy, L. (1969). *General system theory: foundations, development, applications.* New York: Gordon and Breach Science Publishers.

Waters, J. (1988). *Integrity Management: Learning and Implementing Ethical Principles in the Workplace',* in S. Srivastva and Associates (ed.), *Executive Integrity.* San Francisco: Jossey Bass, 123-138.

Wilson, P. Bradford, (October 1998). *The Phenomenon of Grade Inflation in Higher Education.* Presented at a meeting of Virginia Association of Scholars, Radford University, on October 24, 1998.

Wren, D. A. (1994). *The evolution of management thought.* New York, NY; John Wiley & Sons, Inc.

PART III

APPENDICES

APPENDIX A

SAMPLE EMAIL TO PROSPECTIVE FACULTY MEMBERS

Hello,

I have received your résumé in regard to your interest in teaching at Nova Southeastern University (NSU). I'll keep your résumé on file for future scheduled Assessment and Orientation sessions and teaching opportunities. There are no immediate needs but possibilities do exist in the future.

When needed, we do hire adjunct faculty members who have appropriate degrees for the subject areas where we need faculty. When we need an instructor for one or more of our courses/clusters, then we might be able to interview and possibly hire you (provided that you successfully go through one of the scheduled assessment and orientation sessions at that time) in the business department. Often, we will have an assessment and an orientation session scheduled to hire adjunct faculty members based on our prospective needs. We will repeat this process (assessment and orientation sessions) three to four times each year, if needed, to fill our needs. So, I'll keep your résumé on file for consideration in one of our upcoming assessments. If you are considered for our future needs, then someone from our office will contact you. For your information, here is a process we typically use at the business department for hiring of adjunct faculty members:

- Résumés are reviewed to see if their academic achievements and practical experiences meet our needs for subject areas that need more instructors.

Adult Education in Academia, pages 291–292
Copyright © 2006 by Information Age Publishing
291

- *Interview (Face-to-Face):*   Qualified candidates are then screened and interviewed by phone to discuss possibilities for a face-to-face interview and/or Assessment. Face-to-face interviews are conducted and those who match our needs (and the needs of accreditation criteria) will be invited for the Assessment which is inclusive of presentations and other exercises to assess each applicant's ability to facilitate discussion/teach content and his/her style of teaching with adult learners. In the case of prospective Adjunct Faculty members, living outside of Fort Lauderdale of Florida, who cannot attend one of our scheduled Assessment and Orientations, other options will be discussed at that time.
- *Assessment:*   Assessment sessions are often inclusive of a presentation on a topic (about 10–15 minutes) in the applicant's area of academic expertise to see his/her teaching/lecture style. Those who successfully complete the assessment process will be invited for the hiring and orientation session. While the initial assessment is over after this session, it really continues till the successful completion of the faculty member's first course. Instructors who do not have a successful teaching experience in their first course may either receive more mentoring or coaching or may not be scheduled for future courses (if the situation cannot be improved).
- *Hiring and Orientation:*   Hiring and orientation are scheduled on a separate day for qualified applicants who have gone through the screening process. After the successful completion of the above steps and the required paperwork, new faculty members can be scheduled for courses in the coming semesters (year) with an assigned Lead Faculty serving as a mentor/coach for the first course. The mentor may recommend future course assignment possibilities and/or more training for the newly hired faculty to the Director based on the effectiveness of the first course (mentorship assignment).
- *Mentorship:*   It starts with the approval of course syllabus/teaching content: Once a course and mentor has been assigned, the new faculty member would need to submit electronic copies of his/her syllabus for the scheduled course (along with possible exams, quizzes, and teaching plans) to the Lead Faculty (mentor) for approval at least three weeks prior to the first session. Once this material has been approved (or revised as needed) by the mentor/coach (Lead Faculty), then it should be submitted to the director for archiving purposes (records are kept for auditing needs). At this time, you can call on your mentor/coach for directions and guidance as well as on the academic director. Good luck and we wish you a successful experience in all of your courses.

Thanks for your interest and we hope to see you at one of our prospective assessment and orientation sessions! Take good care and, once again, thanks for your interest at NSU. Thanks.

Bahaudin

APPENDIX B

SAMPLE INTERVIEW QUESTIONS (BY PHONE OR FACE-TO-FACE)

1. What most appeals to you about teaching at the Nova Southeastern University and why?
2. Do you feel that you will have adequate time outside your full-time work to prepare for class, travel to class, teach once/twice each week, be available occasionally for faculty meetings (once to twice each year), and/or be available to students outside of class (by phone, e-mail, online, or in person)?
3. Do you have a current ISP (Internet Service Provider)? If not, can you get one immediately. This is required for all faculty members.
4. Are you familiar with (or able to personally learn and become familiarized with them) the basics of commonly used software such as Microsoft Word, PowerPoint, Excel, Project, etc. in case they are used for a course?
5. What are some subject areas that you have at least 18 credit hours at the graduate level (Masters and Doctorate level courses) to meet accreditation requirements in the State of Florida?
6. How would you handle a situation in which one of your students was more knowledgeable or experienced than you in a specific area? Let

Adult Education in Academia, pages 293–294

293

us say, s/he has been a CEO for over ten years and has taught corporate courses in the subject area.

7. How much credibility do you give to student evaluations and feedback on your teaching?
8. How would you respond to students' complaint that you should be "teaching" more (i.e., lecturing during class time) and that you require them to do too much of the work for this course?
9. How would you promote active learning and participation in class?
10. What are some of the things you are doing to stay current in your field of expertise?
11. What has been your teaching experience with traditional students and adult learners who may also have plenty of work experience?
12. What criteria do you consider when grading assignments such as papers/presentations?

APPENDIX C

EVALUATION FORM FOR INTERVIEW—ADJUNCT FACULTY CANDIDATE

Candidate's Name: _____

Date: _____

Rating Scale: 4 = Very Good, 3 = Good, 2 = Marginal, 1 = Unsatisfactory

Standards	Interview Phone/Face-to-face	Assessment Presentation/Essay
1. Résumé/Application is all clear and set-up		
2. Candidate can teach several courses either online, Main Campus and/or in clusters.		
3. Computer Competency and Email Account (ISP)—Required for all faculty members.		
4. Teaching Skills/Behaviors		
5. Technical/Professional Knowledge (Special Job Factors)		
6. Oral Communication (Presentation Style)		
7. Lecture Style and Adult Learning Style Facilitation		
8. Writing Skills (Essay Writing & Grading)		
9. Grading Style, Experience & Familiarity		
10. Other (Specify)		
Total Score		

Adult Education in Academia, pages 295–296
Copyright © 2006 by Information Age Publishing

Candidate's strengths:

Candidate's limitations and areas for needed training:

General comments:

Recommended Action:
❏ Invite to Assessment/Orientation   ❏ Needs Training   ❏ Do Not Hire

Signature _____ **Date**: _____

EVALUATION FORM—
FACULTY CANDIDATE
ASSESSMENT FORM

Candidate's Name: _____

Date: _____

Rating Scale: 4 = Very Good, 3 = Good, 2 = Marginal, 1 = Unsatisfactory, NA = Not Applicable

Please rate the following elements as per your observation of the candidate	4	3	2	1	NA
1. Job Stability					
2. Ability to Get Along With Others					
3. Job Knowledge and Skills					
4. Education					
5. Experience					
6. Communication Skills					
7. Mental Alertness					
8. Maturity					
9. Energy Level					
10. Inter-Personal Skills (Poise and Bearing)					
11. Oral Communication/Presentation Style					
12. Lecturing Skills/Style					
13. Facilitation/Flexibility for Adult Learning Style					
14. Other (Specify)					
15. Other (Specify)					
Total Score					

Adult Education in Academia, pages 297–298
Copyright © 2006 by Information Age Publishing
297

Candidate's strengths:

Candidate's limitations and weaknesses:

Recommended Action:
❏ Invite to Orientation   ❏ Needs Training   ❏ Do Not Hire

Signature _____ **Date:** _____

ADJUNCT FACULTY— INVITATION TO ASSESSMENT/ ORIENTATION LETTER

Dear _____,

Thank you for your continued interest in teaching with us. You have been selected to participate in our Faculty Assessment process so you can gain more information about the university as well as our needs and expectations while we become familiarized with you to see if there is a match between your style of teaching and the university's needs. We are looking forward to (possibly) having you on board with us at Huizenga School of Nova Southeastern University after the successful completion of Faculty Assessment and Orientation sessions along with the needed paperwork. This letter provides some information for the Assessment and Orientation sessions. Please bring official copies (not student copies as they cannot be used to process employment package) of all your undergraduate and graduate transcripts to the Assessment Session or forward originals to the Program Coordinator, _____, before the Assessment and Orientation date.

The Faculty Assessment and Orientation Dates

- *Location of Assessment*: Main Campus at Parker Building on _____ at 6:00–10:00PM. Please come to Parker Building—Second floor at room _____.

Adult Education in Academia, pages 299–300

- ***Orientations:*** Will be held at the Main Campus—Parker Building on Saturday starting at 8:00 AM–5:00 PM on _____ for approximately nine hours. Please come to Parker Building—Second floor at room _____.

Your invitation packet includes Times of Assessment, Directions to the Campus, Transcript Request form, and information on Presentation for the Assessment Session. Please read these documents and forward/bring the needed documents to us or bring them to the Assessment.

Bring/prepare the Following for Orientation:

1. Make copies (and bring) of your Social Security card and driver's license.
2. Make a copy of your CPA, RN, or BAR license, etc. as appropriate and necessary for your field.
3. Order the *official* transcripts of all your academic degrees.
4. Bring your updated résumé/curriculum vitae which states this year's date on it with your latest address, phone number, email address, etc.

APPENDIX F

EMAIL FOR FACULTY ORIENTATION DATES AND LOCATIONS

-----Original Message-----
From: Mujtaba, Bahaudin
Sent: Thursday, February 13, 2003 5:48 PM
To: Lunan, Anika; Full-time Faculty, Adjunct Faculty
Cc: Gooden, Ella; Juliett Reid (E-mail); 'Sumulong-Soodjinda, Liza'; 'Janet Lunde Koppi'; Preston Jones (E-mail); 'Corene Violanti'; Smiley, Paulette; 'Dr. Peter T. Di Paolo'
Subject: NSU-Undergrad Faculty Meeting/Gathering!

Dear Undergraduate Business Faculty,

We hope all is well. We have arranged a series of Faculty Orientation and Update meetings for all Undergrad Business Faculty (full-time and adjuncts) so we can meet as a group for about 6–8 hours discussing our undergraduate business program, any updates about the integration with Huizenga School, as well as to discuss some teaching guidelines and best practices! So, it will be a combination of updates and best practices for dealing with adult learners. Depending on time, we will try to view/discuss one or two relevant videos that relate to teaching effectively.

If you are living in Florida, Bahamas, or Jamaica, please arrange your schedule so you can attend one of the scheduled sessions in your area. For

Adult Education in Academia, pages 301–303
301

those of you living outside of Florida in the USA, we will try to make other arrangements. You can choose the choice of "Other" when you respond to or RSVP Nicky. We will try to have a similar schedule in 2004 as well. The following are the scheduled meeting dates and times. Please try to attend one of the scheduled sessions at a location nearest you so we can meet face-to-face and network while discussing the updates. The Bahamas and Jamaica sessions are for local faculty in those locations (living or teaching there on the scheduled weekends). For address and exact location (if needed) directions, please contact the local person/coordinator at the site.

1. *Nassau:* Will be held at **Nassau, Bahamas**—Hilton Hotel/Exuma Room on 2/22/03 on Saturday starting at 9:00 AM–5:00 PM or 6:00–10:00PM. British Colonial Hilton Hotel—**The telephone # for Hilton is: (242) 302-9060.** Locally, you can contact Juliett Reid, coordinator for NSU's Bahamas operations, for more information. Phone: (242) 364-6766 or (242) 364-6772. Cell: (242) 427-7609. Email: jahrd@yahoo.com or jvreid@nova.edu .

2. *Kingston:* Will be held at **Kingston of Jamaica**—CourtLiegh Hotel on 3/01/03 on Saturday starting at 9:00 AM–5:00 PM. Locally, you can contact Ella Gooden, coordinator for NSU's Jamaica operations, for more information. Ella Gooden at phone: (876) 978-3311 or mail: egooden@cwjamaica.com

3. *Tampa:* Will be held at NSU site in **Tampa** on 3/15/03 on Saturday starting at 9:00 AM–5:00 PM. *Address is:* 9503 Princess Palm Ave. Tampa, FL 33619. Locally, you can contact Liza Soodjinda for more information. Phone: (813)740-2774. Email: Sumulong-Soodjinda, Liza [sumulong@horatio.sbe.nova.edu].

4. *Orlando:* Will be held at NSU site in **Orlando** on 3/22/03 on Saturday starting at 9:00 AM–5:00 PM. *Address is:* NSU 501 N. Wymore Road Winter Park, FL 32789.Locally, you can contact Dr. Peter DiPaolo for more information. Phone: 407-647-4193 Alt: 407-804-520. Email: pdipaolo@nova.edu.

5. *Fort Lauderdale:* Will be held at the **Main Campus** (Fort Lauderdale, Davie Campus) on 3/29/03 **and on 4/5/03** on Saturday starting at 9:00 AM–5:00 PM. Location will be "Auditorium" at Mailman Building on the Second floor next to the Administration building. Locally, you can contact Paulette Smiley for more information. Phone: (954) 262-917. Email: psmiley@nova.edu. Direction to our Main Campus is available online on our website: http://www.nova.edu. Take I-595 west to Davie Road Exit; proceed south one traffic light and turn right onto Nova Drive. Proceed west one traffic light and turn left (south) onto College Avenue. Proceed south on College Avenue to

NSU's main entrance, turn right, and follow the signs to the Mail-man-Hollywood Building.

Attending one of the above sessions can count as part of one's "faculty development units" that we will be focusing on in future sessions/years. Some of the above meetings will include new adjunct faculty that complete their assessment session the week/day before since we are recruiting qualified faculty (in specific subject areas) at different locations outside of South Florida. We will expand on the new process a little more in the meeting. Enclosed, you will find a file titled "*Location and Address Info for Undergrad Contact at NSU*" that you can open, save and print for your future records. This file has information on the location and contact information for all of our current undergraduate sites.

Please RSVP by contacting Nicky (Anika) Lunan (ext. 8114) or through email (lunana@nova.edu) to let her know which session you will be attending. Jacksonville faculty can hopefully attend either the Orlando or Tampa meeting as per your availability. If you cannot attend any of the above dates, please let Nicky know to mark you down for the "Other" option. Thank you and I look forward to seeing you at one of the above sessions.

Best regards!
Bahaudin.

Dr. Bahaudin Mujtaba, Director
Undergraduate Business Programs
H. Wayne Huizenga School of Business and Entrepreneurship
Nova Southeastern University

APPENDIX G

SAMPLE WRITTEN PAPER GUIDELINES AND EVALUATION ELEMENTS

Content—50%

	All key elements of the assignment are covered in a substantial way
	Content is comprehensive, accurate and/or persuasive and convincing
	Points are stated clearly and supported by specific details, example or analysis
	Theories are linked to practical experience
	Research is adequate and timely
	Writing is clear and well-organized
	Addresses the "so what" aspect of the topic
	Explores beyond the obvious
	Illustrates clear understanding of the topic and application to business situation
	Work is original

Adult Education in Academia, pages 305–306
Copyright © 2006 by Information Age Publishing

Organization and Structure—20%

	Structure of the paper is clear and easy to follow
	Organization of the paper emphasized theme
	Transitions are logical; maintains flow throughout the paper
	Ideas flow in a logical sequence
	Introduction provides sufficient background and previews major points
	Conclusion is logical, flows from the body of the paper and reviews major points

Format—10%

	Citations, and references are used appropriately
	Paper follows APA format
	Paper is laid out effectively and is reader-friendly
	Headings aid the readability and are not overused or underused
	Paper is neat and meets the page requirement

Grammar/Punctuation/Spelling—10%

	Rules of grammar, usage and punctuation are followed
	Spelling is correct

Readability and Style—10%

	Sentences are complete, clear and concise
	Sentences are well-constructed and make sense
	Written in a business style
	Transitions are present and maintain the flow of thought
	Words are precise and not ambiguous
	Tone is appropriate

APPENDIX H

SAMPLE ORAL PRESENTATION GRADING CHECKLIST

Content—50%

	Content of presentation clearly follows written paper on which it is based
	Topic is relevant and addresses specifics of the assignment
	Content presented is comprehensive, accurate and believable
	Key points are noted and presented logically
	The "so what" of the topic is clearly addressed
	Presentation illustrates depth of understanding and goes beyond the surface
	Presentation addresses why this is important

Organization and Structure—20%

	Presentation is well-organized, clear and effectively structured
	Group presentations are integrated rather than disjointed individual presentations
	All members of the group participate fully in group presentations
	Business language is used effectively
	Presentation is organized as a presentation and not just reading of the paper
	Creativity is incorporated into the organization of the presentation
	Introduction and conclusion are used effectively

Style and Presentation—10%

	Non-verbal gestures are appropriate to the presentation and flow of ideas
	Confidence and knowledge of the content are evident
	Audience is engaged
	Time is used effectively
	Presentation is not rushed
	Speaker adheres to the time limits

Visual Aids—10%

	Visual aids are clear and effective
	Visual aids are well-used and used appropriately
	Visual aids contribute to a focused and integrated presentation

Questions and Comments—10%

	Audience feedback is solicited
	Audience questions are effectively addressed and correctly answered
	Presentation easily generated audience questions

MENTORSHIP INFORMATION EMAILED TO PROSPECTIVE MENTORS

Hello,

This is more information and follow-up on the Mentorship Process for Adjunct Faculty because during the next few months/year you might be assigned as a mentor for some of the new adjuncts. As discussed in the Faculty Meeting in December of 2002, the new Adjunct Faculty Assessment and Orientation process requires that each incoming adjunct faculty have an assigned mentor for his/her first course at NSU. The incoming faculty members from the pilot Assessment and Orientation session which took place last month will be beginning their mentorship part soon and you will receive copies of emails that tells them who their assigned mentor is and what they need to submit to their mentors.

As an assigned mentor, when the new adjunct faculty members communicate with you, please give them as much assistance as they ask for and/or need. Also, give them suggestions and support to build their self-confidence so they can enforce high academic standards and enforce NSU's rules! Please review their syllabus, course activities, etc. for the accuracy of rules and policies at NSU/Huizenga School and to make sure they are using the stated exit competencies from the standard syllabus. They can add assignments, exams, quizzes, and other relevant activities to the course syllabus as per their preference for assessing students' learning. However, they

Adult Education in Academia, pages 309–312
Copyright © 2006 by Information Age Publishing
309

should not eliminate any major activities from the standard syllabus without your permission as their mentor. They are required to submit their course syllabus to you at least three weeks before their course begins for your suggestions and review. Once they have integrated your suggestions (if there are any), then they will need to submit an electronic copy to the Program Office (myself, Paulette Smiley, or Beverly White) for archiving/auditing purposes.

As a mentor, you are not necessarily required to visit the new faculty member's class or meet with them face-to-face. However, I do encourage face-to-face visitation since you can ask them to come and visit with you during your office hours or even to observe one of your classes. They can even serve as a guest speaker in your class, depending on their availability. If they are teaching on Main Campus, please stop by and observe one of their sessions (preferably first or second session) for a brief period to see them in action and to support them with NSU's policies or anything specific to our operations. Whether you visit them or not is totally up to you and based upon your availability. We have purposely left the process very flexible, at least for the time being, because of budget issues, distance, time conflicts, and because this is still its pilot stage. Therefore, if you can visit their class, great! Otherwise, make sure they are going into their first session with a complete syllabus and a good plan of action for the course!

Enclosed is the content of the email that will be sent to them once they are assigned a mentor (the assigned mentor will be copied on it) as well as a Mentor Checklist/Evaluation form for you to use once they contact you. It is their responsibility to contact you for your advice and suggestions. All you have to do is ask them to call you once their course/class ends and grades are submitted to see how the course went. At that time, you can tell them that you will make your recommendation to the Director/Dean as you see appropriate. You can either congratulate them for a job well done, if you think they have done well, or thank them and make a recommendation to the Director. We will need to see the student evaluations to determine if there is a need for more training with this new faculty. Next year, we can revise and adjust the process as appropriate based on your experience and recommendations. Thanks for your cooperation with this new format in its pilot stage.

Thanks!
Bahaudin.

MENTOR ASSIGNMENT LETTER/EMAIL TO NEW ADJUNCTS

Hello,

Congratulations on successfully completing the Faculty Assessment and Orientation phases. You are well on your way to joyfully teaching your first course. As you know, we want you to have successful experiences in all of your teaching assignments with us at Nova Southeastern University. Therefore, you have an assigned mentor (often a Lead Faculty for the course) to help you have an excellent teaching experience beginning with your first course. As a matter of fact, the last essential part of being certified as a faculty member is to complete a Mentorship under the direction of an assigned mentor/lead faculty.

Assigned mentors can assist new faculty members in their preparation for their first course. Mentors may also observe class(es) to make sure that the new faculty member:

- Teaches to the course objectives,
- Encourages student involvement,
- Uses a variety of teaching methods,
- Uses appropriate classroom management techniques,
- Creates a healthy learning atmosphere and facilitates learning,
- Uses and enforces the required procedures and standards,
- Evaluates student progress and performance,
- Uses effective interpersonal skills,
- Prepares organized and productive sessions,
- Uses text and current relevant journal articles appropriately,
- Uses and enforces APA format requirements for writing, and
- Manages group activities effectively.

Upon observation of the new faculty member and/or discussions with him/her, mentors are required to recommend that the New Faculty Member:

- Is ready to proceed and successfully teach more courses;
- Should repeat training or portions of it before more assignments are provided; OR
- Should be deactivated and not receive any future course assignments.

As you can see, mentors are a very critical part of enforcing the standards and the University's curriculum. So, please communicate with your mentor at least three weeks before your course begins via email and/or telephone to establish an initial connection. Let your mentor know the dates of your assigned course; send him/her your syllabus for approval and suggestions; and, let him/her know of your plans and/or concerns on teaching/facilitation of the assigned course. Once you have finalized your syllabus, please send a copy to the department (Program Coordinator) for the University's documentation file, the week before your course begins. You are welcome to ask for assistance from your assigned mentor before your course, during your course, and upon its conclusion for online grade entry guidelines and submission.

Your assigned mentor is:

Name: Professor/Dr. _____.
Email Address:
Office Phone: (954) 262-8100 or (800) 672-7223

Your mentor (or his/her designee) may observe your classes one or more times, if needed or when time permits. Good luck and let me know if I can be of any further assistance.

Best regards,

APPENDIX J

COURSE PROFILES AND TEACHING REQUIREMENTS (SAMPLE OF COURSES)

Course Code and Title:	ACCT 2100—Managerial Accounting
Course Description:	Integrates the accounting process with the planning, coordinating, and control functions of the business organization. Topics include strategic planning, tactical and operational decision-making, budgeting, responsibility accounting, and performance measurement. It is recommended that students have computer competency and have taken ECON 2020 before enrolling in this course.
Teaching Qualifications and Requirements:	• Master degree in the subject area with 18 graduate credit hours in the field is required. Undergraduate specialization may substitute for three graduate credit hours (one class). • Doctorate degree along with five years of experience preferred. CPA Preferred. • Teaching experience at the college level preferred.

Adult Education in Academia, pages 313–320
Copyright © 2006 by Information Age Publishing
All rights of reproduction in any form reserved.

Course Code and Title:	**ACCT 2200—Financial Accounting I**
Course Description:	Provides an introduction to financial accounting and its decision-making elements. Areas covered are the conceptual frameworks of accounting, financial statements and their components, and financial statements and their components, and advanced manufacturing environments.
Teaching Qualifications and Requirements:	• Master degree in the subject area with 18 graduate credit hours in the field is required. Undergraduate specialization may substitute for three graduate credit hours (one class). • Doctorate degree in the field along with five years of experience preferred. CPA Preferred. • Teaching experience at the college level preferred.

Course Code and Title:	**ACCT 3030—Cost Management**
Course Description:	Students learn cost measurement techniques in the manufacturing and service sectors. Using a strategic approach, the course examines the design and operation of cost accounting systems in both traditional and advanced manufacturing environments.
Teaching Qualifications and Requirements:	• Master degree in the subject area with 18 graduate credit hours in the field is required. Undergraduate specialization may substitute for three graduate credit hours (one class). • Current CPA and/or CMA (Cost Management Accountant) certification required. • Doctorate degree in the field along with five years of experience preferred. • Teaching experience at the college level preferred.

Course Code and Title:	**ACCT 3050—Financial Accounting II**
Course Description:	A continuation of Financial Accounting I (ACCT 2200). The concepts underlying valuation of assets and liabilities are covered
Teaching Qualifications and Requirements:	• Master degree in the subject area with 18 graduate credit hours in the field is required. Undergraduate specialization may substitute for three graduate credit hours (one class). • Current CPA and/or CMA (Cost Management Accountant) certification required. • Doctorate degree in the field along with five years of experience preferred. • Teaching experience at the college level preferred.

Course Code and Title:	**ACCT 3060—Financial Accounting III**
Course Description:	A continuation of Financial Accounting II. Topics include conceptual foundations of equity, earning per share, the income statement, leases, and deferred taxes.
Teaching Qualifications and Requirements:	• Master degree in the subject area with 18 graduate credit hours in the field is required. Undergraduate specialization may substitute for three graduate credit hours (one class). • Current CPA and/or CMA (Cost Management Accountant) certification required. • Doctorate degree in the field along with five years of experience preferred. • Teaching experience at the college level preferred.

Course Code and Title:	**ACCT 3110—Federal Taxation I**
Course Description:	Examines the fundamentals of individual income taxation. A background of accounting courses is not essential for this course. The course may be of special interest to nonbusiness majors. Topics include exemptions, exclusions, and deductions available to the individual. These concepts will aid the student in the preparation of an individual tax return.
Teaching Qualifications and Requirements:	• Master degree in the subject area with 18 graduate credit hours in the field is required. Undergraduate specialization may substitute for three graduate credit hours (one class). • Current CPA and/or CMA (Cost Management Accountant) certification required. • Doctorate degree along with five years of experience preferred. • Teaching experience at the college level preferred.

Course Code and Title:	**ACCT 3120—Federal Taxation II**
Course Description:	Provides an overview of the Internal Revenue Code as it applies to partnerships, corporations, estates, and trusts.
Teaching Qualifications and Requirements:	• Master degree in the subject area with 18 graduate credit hours in the field is required. Undergraduate specialization may substitute for three graduate credit hours (one class). • Current CPA and/or CMA (Cost Management Accountant) certification required. • Doctorate degree with five years of experience preferred. • Teaching experience at the college level preferred.

Course Code and Title:	**ACCT 4010—Financial Accounting IV**
Course Description:	A continuation of the study of financial accounting. Topics include pensions, correction of accounting errors, cash flow statements, fundamental consolidation concepts, international currency accounting, and fund accounting for governments and nonprofit organizations.
Teaching Qualifications and Requirements:	• Master degree in the subject area with 18 graduate credit hours in the field is required. Undergraduate specialization may substitute for three graduate credit hours (one class). • Current CPA and/or CMA (Cost Management Accountant) certification required. • Doctorate degree in the field along with five years of experience preferred. • Teaching experience at the college level preferred.

Course Code and Title:	**ACCT 4050—Acct. Info. Systems**
Course Description:	Examines the design, construction, and operation of accounting information systems. Information theory, database construction, computer hardware and software selection, and internal control are also covered.
Teaching Qualifications and Requirements:	• Master degree in the subject area with 18 graduate credit hours in the field is required. Undergraduate specialization may substitute for three graduate credit hours (one class). • Doctorate degree in the field and certification along with five years of experience preferred. • Teaching experience at the college level preferred.

Course Code and Title:	**ACCT 4210—Auditing**
Course Description:	Provides an overview of basic auditing concepts, auditing standards, and audit programs. Special emphasis is given to preparing the student for the auditing section of the CPA examination.
Teaching Qualifications and Requirements:	• Master degree in the subject area with 18 graduate credit hours in the field is required. Undergraduate specialization may substitute for three graduate credit hours (one class). • Current CPA and/or CMA (Cost Management Accountant) certification required. • Doctorate degree in the field and certification along with five years of experience preferred. • Teaching experience at the college level preferred.

Course Code and Title:	**BUSS 2150—Business Law I**
Course Description:	Applies the fundamentals of business law, contract law, property law, and negotiable instruments to business organizations. Credit cannot be obtained for both BUSS 2150 and LEGS 3400.
Teaching Qualifications and Requirements:	• JD/Law Degree is required. • Doctorate degree in the field and current BAR certification along with five years of experience preferred. • Teaching experience at the college level preferred.

Course Code and Title:	**BUSS 3050—Organization Theory**
Course Description:	Emphasizes the structure of modern organizations and systems. The special problems of complex organizations, project and/or program management, matrix management, venture management, and contingency management.
Teaching Qualifications and Requirements:	• Masters or Doctorate degree in business, organizational behavior, or other related areas • Senior or mid-level manager with 5 years of managerial experience with progressively increased responsibility in private sector • Previous teaching experience is desirable

Course Code and Title:	**BUSS 3150—Business Law II**
Course Description:	A continuation of Business Law I. Applies law, bailments, and the Uniform Commercial Code to business organizations.
Teaching Qualifications and Requirements:	• JD/Law Degree is required. • Doctorate degree in the field and BAR certification along with five years of experience preferred. • Teaching experience at the college level preferred.

Course Code and Title:	**BUSS 3550—Intro to Int'l Business**
Course Description:	Surveys the legal and cultural environment of international business; international financial system; management of international operations; personnel and labor relations; international marketing; international economics, trade, and finance; multinational enterprise; and international accounting. Prerequisites: ECON 2010 and 2020.
Teaching Qualifications and Requirements:	• Master degree in International Business and/or close to 18 graduate credit hours in the field is required. Undergraduate specialization may substitute for three graduate credit hours (one class). • Doctorate degree in the field along with five years of recent international experience preferred. • Teaching experience at the college level preferred.

Course Code and Title:	**BUSS 4100—Business Ethics**
Course Description:	Examines the nature of morality and theories of normative ethics. Identifies a variety of ethical issues and moral challenges involving consumers, the environment, the professions, and the role of the corporation in our society.
Teaching Qualifications and Requirements:	• Master degree in the philosophy or business related field with some graduate credit hours in ethics is required. Experience with ethical issues is preferred. • Doctorate degree along with five years of teaching and/or training research/experience in ethics preferred. • Teaching experience at the college level preferred.

Course Code and Title:	**BUSS 4300—Export/Import Trade**
Course Description:	Managing the export/import department; government regulations affecting imports; financing, insuring, transporting, and marketing of exported or imported raw materials and finished products; methods of purchasing foreign products and selling domestic goods abroad; joint marketing; licensing; distributor relations. Prerequisite: BUSS 3550.
Teaching Qualifications and Requirements:	• Master degree in International Business and/or 18 graduate credit hours in the field is required. Undergraduate specialization may substitute for three graduate credit hours (one class). • Doctorate degree in the field and certification along with five years of recent international experience preferred. • Teaching experience at the college level preferred.

Course Code and Title:	**BUSS 4610—Business Research Methods**
Course Description:	Examines research designs commonly used in business decision making. Topics include survey, observation, data analysis, sampling, and quasi-experiments as they relate to problems in an organizational setting. Students submit a research proposal as part of the course requirements.
Teaching Qualifications and Requirements:	• Master degree (business related field) with 18 graduate credit hours in research is required. • Doctorate degree along with five years of experience preferred. • Teaching experience at the college level preferred.

Course Code and Title:	BUSS 4880—Business Strategy and Policy
Course Description:	This course is designed to illustrate development, implementation, and reformulation of business strategy. The course stresses the need for awareness of, and accommodation to, change in a company's internal and external environments. Generic types of business strategies and techniques for analyzing strategies are also included.
Teaching Qualifications and Requirements:	• Masters or Doctorate degree in business, management science, organizational behavior or related areas. • Work experience as a senior level manager with five years of responsibility for strategic decision-making with a mid-to-large sized private organization or business.

Course Code and Title:	ECON 2010—Principles of Macroeconomics
Course Description:	A study of basic economic concepts as this applies to the aggregate economy. Topics include concepts of national income and its determination, economic fluctuations, monetary and fiscal policies, and economic growth. Students who have completed ECON 3150 may not enroll for this course.
Teaching Qualifications and Requirements:	• Master's Degree in Economics or MBA with 18 graduate hours in economics. Undergraduate specialty in economics can count toward three graduate hours. • Doctorate in Economics or other doctorate in Business with 18 hours in Economics courses preferred. • Teaching and work experience in economics preferred.

Course Code and Title:	ECON 2020—Principles of Microeconomics
Course Description:	Examines the processes of price determination output and resources allocation in perfect and imperfect competition. Topics include labor economics, international trade and finance, and alternative economic systems.
Teaching Qualifications and Requirements:	• Master's Degree in Economics or MBA with 18 graduate hours in economics. Undergraduate specialty in economics can count toward three graduate hours. • Doctorate in Economics or other doctorate in Business with 18 hours in Economics courses preferred. • Teaching and work experience in economics preferred.

Note: This process of documenting "Teaching Qualifications and Requirements" was completed for all undergraduate courses in order to assist Faculty Coordinators in selecting the right candidates and the newly hired faculty members in determining which courses they qualify to teach. These "teaching qualification and requirements" are used by newly hired faculty members to complete their Course Approval Request (CAR) forms. It is important to mention that if the teaching requirements of a course changes, then this form can also be updated immediately as well to reflect the latest qualifications.

APPENDIX K

COURSE APPROVAL
REQUESTS (CAR)

Name: Bahaudin Mujtaba

Date: December 20, 2002

Degrees Completed:

(Exact title as they appear on official transcript)

Year: **Institutions/University:**

(Completion)

Degree	Year	Institution
Bachelor of Science in Business Administration	1991	University of Central Florida
Master of Business Administration	1993	Nova University
Doctor of Business Administration— HRM & International Mgmt Specialties	1996 & 1997	Nova Southeastern University

I am available to teach classes in (circle/bold all that apply):

1—Days   2—Evenings   3—Weekends   4—Online
(Main Campus)   (trained, certified)

Adult Education in Academia, pages 321–323
321

NSU Course Name/Title	Degrees Completed (Exact title as they appear on transcript along with specializations/major)	Experience and/or Certifications (details should appear in résumé)	Dean's Office Use
GMP5012— Twenty-first Century Mgmt Practices	• CSA6151—Advance Readings, 4 cr. • CSA6010—Administrative Theory and Practices, 4 cr. • CSA6020—Org Behavior/ Personnel Mgmt, 4 cr. • CSA6050—Operations Management, 4 cr. • CSA606—Business and Public Policy Seminar, 4 cr. • CSA5325—Employee Relations/Services, 4 cr. • GMP5030—HR Management, 3 cr. • CSA6315—Strategic Programming in HR Mgmt, 4 cr. • CSA6330—Performance & Reward Systems, 4 cr.	• Have worked, lived and taught in six different countries. • Speak three languages.	
GMP5015— Legal, Ethical, and Social Values of Business	• GMP5012—Management Ethics, 3 cr. • CSA6151—Advanced Readings in Ethics, 4 cr. • CSA6090-4—Dissertation on Ethics, 8 cr. • CSA6020—Org Behavior/ Personnel Mgmt, 4 cr. • CSA6470—International Legal Framework, 4 cr. • CSA6410—International Management, 4 cr.	• Ten publications on ethics. • Corporate training on ethics. • Ethics conference certification.	
GMP5017— Delivering Superior Customer Value	• CSA6010—Administrative Theory and Practices, 4 cr. • CSA6050—Operations Management, 4 cr. • CSA606—Business and Public Policy Seminar, 4 cr. • CSA5325—Employee Relations/Services, 4 cr. • CSA6330—Performance and Reward Systems, 4 cr.	• TQM Trainer and certification.	

NSU Course Name/Title	Degrees Completed (Exact title as they appear on transcript along with specializations/major)	Experience and/or Certifications (details should appear in résumé)	Dean's Office Use
GMP5020— Managing Organizational Behavior	• CSA6020—Org Behavior/ Personnel Mgmt, 4 cr. • GMP5020—Managing Organizational Behavior, 3 cr. • CSA5325—Employee Relations/Services, 4 cr. • GMP5030—HR Management, 3 cr. • CSA6315—Strategic Programming in HR Mgmt, 4 cr. • CSA6330—Performance and Reward Systems, 4 cr. • CSA6151—Advance Readings, 4 cr. • CSA6010—Administrative Theory and Practices, 4 cr.	• Manager and certified management development specialist for ten years. • Certified "Situational Leadership" trainer.	
GMP5030, 5300, 5320, 5340, 5360, 5365, 5375, 5380, and 5386	• GMP5030—HR Management, 3 cr. • CSA6315—Strategic Programming in HR Mgmt, 4 cr. • CSA5325—Employee Relations/Services, 4 cr. • CSA6330—Performance & Reward Systems, 4 cr. • CSA6020—Org Behavior/ Personnel Mgmt, 4 cr. • CSA6151 – Advance Readings, 4 cr. • CSA6010—Administrative Theory and Practices, 4 cr.	• HR Training specialist for over six years.	
GMP5821, and GMP5824— International Human Resource Mgmt	• CSA6110—International Business and Finance, 4 cr. • CSA6470—International Legal Framework, 4 cr. • CSA6410—International Management, 4 cr. • GMP5030—HR Management, 3 cr. • CSA6315—Strategic Programming in HR Mgmt, 4 cr. • CSA6330—Performance and Reward Systems, 4 cr. • CSA5325—Employee Relations/Services, 4 cr.	• Cross Cultural experience and publications. • Lived and worked in over five different countries. • HR Specialist, 1995–2000.	

Associate Dean/Program Chair Signature: _____

Date: _____

MENTORING EVALUATION FORM FOR MENTORS

Please complete this form once the mentoring process has ended. Provide new faculty member with a copy following this report and appropriate feedback (if needed and appropriate).

New Faculty:_____ Mentor: _____

Course: _____ Start Date: _____

   1. Describe your impression of the new faculty.

Adult Education in Academia, pages 325–326
Copyright © 2006 by Information Age Publishing
All rights of reproduction in any form reserved.

2. What are some things that the new faculty member should start doing in future courses?

3. What is your overall recommendation about the faculty? Should the new faculty be assigned more courses? Should s/he be provided more mentoring/training? Or, should s/he be thanked for his/her services and de-activated from the faculty list?

Use additional paper as necessary

Signature of Mentor _____ Date: _____

APPENDIX M

MENTORING CHECKLIST FOR MENTORS

Initial Contact

❏ Contact (phone) new faculty member about three week before
course begins to confirm mentor assignment with them and to see if
they have any questions.
❏ Set-up initial meeting with faculty member 2–3 weeks before course
start date, if at all possible.

Pre-Observation Meeting

❏ Review with new faculty course syllabus to ensure that appropriate
criteria have been met (grading requirements, availability through
phone or email, clearly written directions for assignments, concisely
stated grading evaluations, etc.)
❏ Review importance of setting clear expectations for students.
❏ Discuss grading and performance evaluation.
❏ Discuss importance of being available to students outside of class.
❏ Share effective classroom management strategies.

Adult Education in Academia, pages 327–328
Copyright © 2006 by Information Age Publishing
327

Classroom Observations

❑ Observe the new faculty teaching a session (if possible).

❑ If you have concerns at any point in the mentoring process, please contact the Director immediately.

❑ Guide new faculty through their evaluation of the first written assignment.

❑ Schedule with new faculty another class observations, if needed.

Debrief

❑ May meet with new faculty member to debrief experience once you are certain s/he can successfully teach the class!

❑ Complete the *"Mentoring Evaluation Form"* and submit to the Program Office for records. Provide a copy of the evaluation and appropriate feedback to new faculty, if appropriate!

ASSESSMENT AND ORIENTATION FEEDBACK AND RECOGNITION EMAIL

-----Original Message-----
From: Mujtaba, Bahaudin
Sent: Friday, January 31, 2003 2:02 PM
To: Work, Gerry; Dean, Jim; Olson, Olson; 'Ordean Olson'; Manyak, Terrell; 'Neil Chapman'; 'Stephanie Brown'
Cc: 'Randy Pohlman (E-mail)'; Rosenblum, Don; Goonen, Norma; 'Preston Jones (E-mail)'; Smiley, Paulette; Steve Harvey (E-mail); Gooden, Ella; Juliett Reid (E-mail); Abraham, Rebecca; Alexakis, George; DiPaolo, Peter; Harrington, Charles; Harris, Judith; Johnson, Micki; Lucille Genduso; Platt, Alan; Seyoum, Belay; Sims, Randi; Work, Gerry
Subject: FACULTY ASSESSMENT & ORIENTATION PILOT @ NSU

Hello everyone,

The pilot of our Faculty Assessment (on 1/25/03) and Orientation (on 1/26/03) sessions at the Main Campus were a great success and now we have 27 new adjunct faculty members as a result of everyone's hard work. I want to extend my appreciation and thanks to Dr. Preston Jones, Dr. Ordean Olson, Dr. Gerry Works, Dr. Terrell Manyak, and Professor Jim Dean for taking the time to come on a Friday night to assist in the Assessment Process. The assessment began at 6:00 PM and ended at 9:40 PM. Dr. Jones welcomed everyone to

---

Adult Education in Academia, pages 329–330
Copyright © 2006 by Information Age Publishing
329

the assessment and then full-time faculty members introduced themselves and welcomed candidates to the session at NSU. We had 27 candidates that successfully went through the Assessment process on Friday night and attended the Orientation from 8–5 on Saturday. We treated them to lunch at our cafeteria on Saturday and they became familiarized with our beautiful library since the Orientation was held there. They were very impressed with the level of professionalism shown in the two days and very much enjoyed meeting our full-time faculty members on Friday night and two of our current adjunct faculty on Saturday at the Orientation. Also, special thanks go to our current adjunct faculty members (Dr. Stephanie Brown and Professor Neil Chapman) for participating in the Orientation and assisting with the interaction of exercises on Saturday. The newly hired adjunct faculty members greatly appreciated the networking opportunity with our full-time and adjunct faculty members since it provided them the opportunity to ask questions about NSU's culture. During the coming semesters, the newly hired adjuncts will be assigned a course as well as a "mentor" (Lead Faculty) to assist them be successful in the classroom. Thanks in advance for helping with the mentorship process!

I also want to extend special thanks to Paulette Smiley for successfully coordinating the Assessment and Orientation sessions. She had all 27 new adjuncts complete their HR paperwork in the first 30 minutes of Saturday morning and had collected all of their required hiring material before 10:00 AM. Many of the official transcripts are already here and the rest should be here in two weeks. Due to hard work and coordination from Paulette and our team of full-time faculty and adjunct faculty members, the sessions were a great success and now we have 27 qualified adjuncts to assist us in the coming semesters and years. The next tentative date for another Assessment and Orientation in Fort Lauderdale is set for March 28 and 29 of this year. I'll keep you updated on the progress as the date becomes closer.

At the mean time, we will have an Assessment and Orientation session in Jamaica and one in Nassau in the next two months to bring on more local faculty in those locations. Ella (Jamaica) and Juliett (Bahamas) are assisting in the recruitment and coordination processes. Later in the year, we will have a similar process to certify faculty members who would like to teach online classes. Eventually, special online training certification for on-ground faculty members that want to teach online will be created and implemented by the end of 2003. The objectives will be to bring about more standardization across the teaching modalities and to assist new online faculty members be successful.

Remember, this University and the experiences of our students will be a little better or not as good because of you! You can and do make a huge difference! **THANK YOU FOR YOUR COOPERATION, SUPPORT AND PARTICIPATION!**

Bahaudin.
Undergraduate Business Programs

INDEX

A

AACSB 8, 13, 64, 65, 144, 146, 243, 255, 281

Adam Smith 21, 174

Adelphia 19

Adult education 240, 255

Adult learning 3

Afghanistan 107, 202, 209, 237

American Association of Collegiate Schools of Business 13, 243

American Broadcasting Corporation 168, 209, 288

Androgogical 247

anti-plagiarism 178

Assessing learning outcomes 244

Assessment xii, xiii, xiv, 3, 4, 8, 12, 13, 14, 35, 42, 63, 68, 70, 71, 72, 73, 76, 77, 78, 89, 91, 92, 93, 94, 95, 108, 111, 113, 121, 133, 143, 144, 149, 150, 151, 152, 153, 154, 159, 165, 193, 194, 233, 237, 239, 240, 242, 243, 244, 245, 250, 254, 255, 277, 278, 279, 281, 282, 284, 285, 291, 292, 295, 296, 297, 299, 300, 303, 309, 311, 329, 330

Assignment Manager 246, 253

ASTD 11, 287

A Class Divided 188

B

baby boomers 199, 204, 206, 208

Bahamas 61, 64, 68, 112, 154, 220, 225, 226, 227, 232, 234, 237, 301, 302, 330

Bahamian 225, 236

Barnes 38, 41, 281, 286

Bass 81, 283, 286, 288

behavioral learning theory 20, 32

Benjamin Bloom 167

Bhopal tragedy 215

Bishop 149

Bisoux 147, 281

BizEd 147, 281

Bjorklund 174, 282

Blackwell 38, 41, 281

Blanchard 34, 106

Blavo 18

blended 37, 50, 56, 59, 149, 164, 240, 242, 248, 249, 255

Bloom 19, 22, 23, 24, 167, 173, 174, 195, 281

Bloom's Taxonomy 19, 22, 23, 24, 167, 174, 195, 281

Bolton 174, 281

Brainstorming 203

Brande 274

Brazil 50, 61, 154, 226, 237, 240

Brennan 22, 23, 284

Adult Education in Academia, pages 331–336
Copyright © 2006 by Information Age Publishing

331

ABOUT THE AUTHORS

Bahaudin Mujtaba

Dr. Bahaudin Mujtaba is an Assistant Professor of Management and International
Management. In the years 2003–2005, he
was the Director of Institutional Relations,
Planning, and Accreditation for Nova
Southeastern University at the H. Wayne
Huizenga School of Business and Entrepreneurship in Fort Lauder, Florida. As a director, he was responsible for the planning
of accreditation reviews for all Huizenga
School's academic programs in all locations throughout United States of America

and abroad. In administrator and faculty capacities since 1996 in academia,
Bahaudin has prepared for and worked with the requirements of Southern
Association of Colleges and Schools (SACS), International Assembly for
Collegiate Business Education (IACBE), Association to Advance Collegiate
Schools of Business (AACSB), North Central Association (NCA)/High-
er Learning Commission (HLC), and the University Council of Jamaica
(UCJ). Bahaudin was appointed as the Director of Business Department for
Undergraduate Studies at the Farquhar Center of NSU in the year 2002. As
an academic Director, he was responsible for the operation of Undergradu-
ate Business Programs. He has been serving as an Assistant Professor of
Human Resources and International Management at the Huizenga School
since 2002. Bahaudin had originally joined Nova Southeastern University
in 1996 as an Adjunct Professor of Management and Human Resources
Management at the Graduate Business Programs for the School of Business

Adult Education in Academia, pages 337–340
Copyright © 2006 by Information Age Publishing

and Entrepreneurship. Bahaudin has been a speaker for 'The Caribbean Area Network for Quality Assurance in Tertiary Education" (CANQATE) in Jamaica, IACBE (USA), and the Association for Tertiary Institutions in the Bahamas (ATIB) in the Nassau, Bahamas.

Bahaudin has worked as an Internal Consultant/Trainer/Teacher at the Education and Training Development Department of Human Resources with Publix Super Markets Inc. for six years. He also worked with Publix in retail management for ten years. As a consultant, he coaches, trains, educates, and develops managers. In his capacity as a consultant and trainer, Bahaudin has worked with various firms in the areas of management, cross-cultural communication, customer value/service, and diversity training. Normally, he helps firms begin a management-training program or class, trains the trainers to carry the program on their own, and then leaves them alone unless they need further assistance. Bahaudin is a certified Cultural Diversity trainer through the National Multi-Cultural Institute (NMCI) which is based out of Washington DC. He has been involved in diversity education and awareness since the late 1980s.

Academically, Bahaudin has been teaching regular MBA classes, MIBA, MBA/HR and eMBA (online classes) nationally and internationally. Bahaudin has authored and co-authored many different books in the areas of leadership, adult education and workforce development in Afghanistan. His current research and writing interests are in the areas of customer value/service, international management, and diversity management. He has been listed in the various publications of *Who's Who in America*, *Who's Who in American Education*, *Who's Who in Management*, and *Who's Who in the World*.

Bahaudin worked as a manager, an Internal Consultant, Trainer, and Teacher at the Education and Training Development Department of Human Resources with Publix Super Markets Inc. for sixteen years. He worked with Publix in retail management for ten years. As a consultant, he coaches, trains, educates, and develops managers. In his capacity as a consultant and trainer, Bahaudin has worked with various firms in the areas of management, cross-cultural communication, customer value/service, and diversity training. Bahaudin is a co-author of several textbooks including the following:

Mujtaba, B. G. (2006). *Privatization and Market-Based Leadership in Developing Economies: Capacity Building in Afghanistan*. Llumina Press.
Mujtaba, B. G. (2006). *Cross-Cultural Change Management*. Llumina Press.
Mujtaba, B. G. and Cavico, F. J., (2006). *Age Discrimination in Employment: Cross Cultural Comparison and Management Strategies*. BookSurge. ISBN: 1-4196-1587-4.
Mujtaba, Bahaudin (2006). *The Art of Mentoring Diverse Professionals: Employee development and retention practices for entrepreneurs and multinational corporations*. ISBN: 1-59427-052-X. Aglob Publishing Inc. Hollandale, Florida USA. Available on amazon.com

Mujtaba, Bahaudin (2006). *AFGHANISTAN: Realities of War and Rebuilding.* ISBN: 1-59427-0481. Aglob Publishing Inc. Hollandale, Florida USA. Available on: amazon.com

Mujtaba, Bahaudin (2005). *The Ethics of Management and Situational Leadership in Afghanistan.* Aglob Publishing Inc. ISBN: 1-59427-047-3. Hollandale, Florida USA. Website: www.aglobpublishing.com. Phone: (954)465-1476. Available on: amazon.com

Cavico, F. & Mujtaba, B., (2005). Business Ethics: Transcending Requirements through Moral Leadership. Pearson Custom Publications. U.S.A. ISBN: 0-536-85783-0. Web address: http://www.pearsoncustom.com/best/0536857830.html#. Physical Address: 75 Arlington Street. Suite 300. Boston Mass, 02116. Phone: (800) 374-1200. Or: (800) 922-0579.

He was born in Logar and raised in Kabul of Afghanistan. Bahaudin has been a guest speaker at conferences in the United States of America, Jamaica, Bahamas, and *by* the Society of Afghan Engineers (SAE) at their annual international conferences.

Author Contact Information:

Dr. Bahaudin Mujtaba
Office Phone: (954) 262-5045, or (800) 338-4723 ext. 5045.
Email: Mujtaba@nova.edu or, Bahaudin66@nova.edu
Faculty website: www.huizenga.nova.edu/about/facultybios/mujtaba.cfm

Robert Preziosi

Dr. Robert C. Preziosi is a professor of management education at the Huizenga Graduate School of Business and Entrepreneurship at Nova Southeastern University in Fort Lauderdale, Florida. He is currently the Chair for Nova's Master of Science program in Human Resource Management and the originator of the curriculum and design for Nova's Doctorate program in Human Resource Management. In December of 2000, he was named *"Professor of the Decade"*. In 1997, he received the school's first "Excellence in Teaching Award." He has been Vice President of Management Development and Training for a Fortune 50 company. In 1984, he was given the Outstanding Contribution to HRD Award by the American

Society for Training and Development. In 1990, he received the "Torch Award," the highest leadership award that the Society can give. He was named HRD Professional of the Year for 1991. He has recently been named to the first edition of International Who's Who in Quality. In June 1996, he received his second Torch Award from the Society-the first time ASTD has given a second Torch Award to one individual.

Dr. Preziosi has worked as a human resources director, line manager, business school dean, and leadership training administrator. He has been published in various national publications, including *Training and Development, National Productivity Review, The Teaching Professor,* and *Quality Review.* He is the editor of the *Pfeiffer Annual on HRM.* He has been a consultant to consultants, educator of educators, and a trainer of trainers. He has been called a motivating management educator, and has worked with students, executives and trainers from all over the world. He is the Director of The Huizenga' School's Leadership Impact Lab and The Faculty Chair for the MBA in Leadership.

He has a B.A. degree in Social Science and M.Ed. degree in Educational Psychology. He received his Doctorate degree in Management. He has a special certification in Participative Leadership and Consulting Skills, and has completed study at Harvard University's Institute for the Management of Lifelong Education. He is listed in *Who's Who in the World,* and *Who's Who in American Education.* Three times he's been recognized in *Who's Who Among America's Teachers.* Dr. Preziosi has been a national seminar leader for American Management Association and Dun & Bradstreet. He has presented to regional and national and international conferences on various aspects of leadership, values, and adult learning. He has recorded a video entitled, "The High Performing Adult Educator," and a six-part audio program entitled, "Executive Success Strategies," as well as produced a six-part audio series on "Maximizing Adult Learning."

Dr. Preziosi was invited to write his autobiography for the 2006 publication, *Quintessential Adult Educators of the Twenty-first Century.*

Printed in the United Kingdom
by Lightning Source UK Ltd.
112163UKS00001B/169-171